D0065158

Financial Statements—
Present and Future Scope

Ahmed Riahi-Belkaoui

Q

QUORUM BOOKS
Westport, Connecticut • London

Library of Congress Cataloging-in-Publication Data

Riahi-Belkaoui, Ahmed, 1943–
    Financial statements : present and future scope / Ahmed Riahi-Belkaoui.
        p.   cm.
    Includes bibliographical references and index.
    ISBN 1–56720–392–2 (alk. paper)
    1. Financial statements.   2. Corporation reports.   I. Title.
    HG4028.B2R5   2001
    657'.3—dc21   00–062527

British Library Cataloguing in Publication Data is available.

Library of Congress Catalog Card Number: 00–062527
ISBN: 1–56720–392–2

First published in 2001

Quorum Books, 88 Post Road West, Westport, CT 06881
An imprint of Greenwood Publishing Group, Inc.
www.quorumbooks.com

Printed in the United States of America

The paper used in this book complies with the
Permanent Paper Standard issued by the National
Information Standards Organization (Z39.48–1984).

10 9 8 7 6 5 4 3 2 1

To Dimitra

Contents

List of Exhibits

Preface

Financial statements as prepared in conformity with generally accepted accounting principles focus mainly on the reporting of the financial structure (Balance Sheet), performance (Income Statement), and conduct (Statement of Changes in Cash Flows) of a firm for a given period of time. As such they fail to provide the additional disclosures deemed necessary to reach a high level of disclosure adequacy, namely vital information about (a) the measurement and disclosure of the impact of inflation, as measured by both the changes in general price level and specific price levels, (b) the measurement and disclosure of the total wealth generated by the total production team rather than merely the return to stockholders, (c) the disclosure of the necessary information on employees and about employees that can be useful to employee decision making, (d) the measurement and disclosure of the social costs and benefits resulting from the environmental effects of organizational behavior, and (e) the measurement and disclosure of the value of the human assets.

It is therefore the object of this book to first explicate the theories, methods, strengths, and weaknesses underlying conventional accounting statements (Chapter 1 on the balance sheet; Chapter 2 on the income statement; Chapter 3 on the statement of changes in cash flows) before exploring the nature, composition, behavioral and market impact, and/or experiments with the needed additional disclosures as covered largely in the literature and in some cases in practice (Chapter 4 on the inflation report; Chapter 5 on the value added report; Chapter 6 on the employee report; Chapter 7 on the social performance report; and Chapter 8 on the human asset report). The book will be of value to professional accountants, academic researchers, and accounting and finance students interested in the expansion of financial disclosures.

Many people helped in the development of this book. I received considerable assistance from the University of Illinois at Chicago research assistants, especially Ewa Tomaszewska, Yukie Miura, and Vivian Au. I also thank Eric Valentine, Lynn Zelem, and the entire production team at Quorum Books for their continuous and intelligent support.

Chapter 1

The Balance Sheet

INTRODUCTION

While the profit statement measures the performance of a firm over a period of time, the balance sheet measures the financial position at a point in time.

Each of the approaches to the financial statements, namely

1. the revenue-expense approach,

2. the asset-liability approach, and

3. the nonarticulated approach,

has influenced the present state of the balance sheet. In addition various transactions, known as off-balance sheet transactions, are not yet recognized in the balance sheet. A good example of the off-balance sheet transactions relates to new financial instruments; the general classification scheme used in balance sheet presentation goes as follows:

Current assets

- Investments

- Property, plant, and equipment

- Intangible assets
- Other assets

Liabilities
- Current liabilities
- Long-term liabilities
- Other liabilities

Stockholders' equity
- Capital stock
- Additional paid-in capital
- Retained Earnings

This chapter reviews the definitions, the principles of recognition, and the measurement rules for these components of the balance sheet.

MEASURING THE ELEMENTS OF THE BALANCE SHEET

The balance sheet measures the financial position or the revenue structure (i.e., major classes and amount of assets) and the claims against the resources or financial structure (i.e., major classes and amount of liabilities and equity). It is best expressed by the following equation:

Assets = Liabilities + Stockholders' Equity.

The measurement of each of the three elements of the balance sheet is an important task for any standard setting bodies. Five alternatives have been identified for measuring these elements. The list includes

1. historical cost/historical proceeds,
2. current cost/current proceeds,
3. current exit value,
4. net realized value, and
5. present value.

These alternative valuation techniques are used in certain circumstances for selected elements of the balance sheet. As will be seen in the remainder of this chapter, the end result is that the balance sheet is the combined application of various valuation techniques, raising doubt about (1) the additivity of the resulting measures and (2) the overall significance of the whole document as a measure of the wealth of the firm.

ASSETS

Definition

The importance of the definition of assets lies in the fact that it identifies the economic events to be recognized, measured, and reported in the balance sheet. Most definitions focus on some of the characteristics that are common to all assets. These characteristics include the following:

1. identification of a future benefit characteristic (including similar notions such as "service potential" of value to the reporting entity and "economic resources");
2. identification of a cost sacrifice, acquisition at a cost or unexpired cost as being relevant;
3. delineation in terms of accounting process;
4. specification of the connection with a specific entity;
5. specification of the time dimension (exclusion of "future assets") other than by reference to cost;
6. inclusion of measurability characteristic in definition other than by references to cost;
7. inclusion of measurability characteristic.[1]

Assets are probable future economic benefits, or are controlled by a particular entity as a result of past transaction or events. An asset has three essential characteristics:

1. It embodies a potential, alone or in combination with other assets, to contribute directly or indirectly to future net cash inflows;
2. A particular enterprise can obtain the benefit and control others' access to an asset.
3. The transaction or other event giving rise to the enterprise's right to or control of the benefit has already occurred.[2]

The focus in the Financial Accounting Standards Board (FASB) definition is

1. the presence of probable future economic benefits that characterize the asset as providing an economic revenue;
2. the fact that these benefits accrue to the particular entity to be considered an asset of the entity; and
3. the specification of a past time-dimension.

Missing from the FASB definition is the condition of exchangeability or severability. The condition has been advocated as critical for the definition of assets and the exclusion of goodwill as an asset. According to Kenneth MacNeal,

A good that lacks exchangeability must lack economic value because its purchase or sale must forever remain impossible and thus no market price for it can ever exist.[3]

Raymond Chambers also argued for severability in his definition of asset and for excluding goodwill as an asset. His reasons are as follows:

[T]he definition arose from the necessity of considering the capacity of an entity to adapt itself to changes in its state and its environment. Adaptive behavior implies that the goodwill subsisting in any collection of assets and liabilities is so susceptible to variation as to have no enduring quality.[4]

The FASB, however, rejected the idea of severability as being important for the definition of an asset. Basically, the benefits of assets are not restricted to their exchangeability. As Maurice Moonitz correctly states, "[E]xchange does not make values, it merely reveals them."[5] Severability reduces value to the dimension of market prices and denotes a conservative approach that restricts the types of assets to be included in the balance sheet.

Recognition and Measurement of Assets

When it comes to recognition and measurement of assets, options abound, differing for each component of the balance sheet. In the case of recognition, various attempts have been made to identify criteria or tests of recognition. Robert Sterling has suggested the following mix of tests to provide necessary and sufficient conditions for the recognition of a thing as an asset.[6]

1. First, *the detection of existence test* requires the detection of events that may be candidates for recognition.

2. Second, *the economic resources and obligations test* requires that the kinds of things that are to be recognized are economic resources that are characterized by being

   a. scarce,

   b. desirable,

   c. commanding a price.

3. Third, *the entity association test* requires that the entity controls the resource.

4. Fourth, *the non-zero magnitude test* requires that the thing must have a non-zero magnitude.

5. Fifth, *the temporal association test* requires that the thing satisfies all tests at the balance sheet date.

6. Sixth, *the verification test* requires that there must be assurance of the representational faithfulness of

   a. the existence of the thing,

   b. that it is an economic resource and obligation,

   c. that it is under the control of or obligates the entity under consideration,

   d. that the magnitude of the yet-to-be-selected attribute has been reasonably measured or estimated, and

   e. that all of those tests are satisfied at the date of the statement of financial position.[7]

The official FASB pronouncement of the general principles of recognition was included in the Statement of Financial Accounting Concepts No. 5, *Recognition and Measurement in Financial Statements of Business Enterprises*.[8] The statement provides the following four "fundamental" recognition criteria:

Definition—The item meets the definition of an element of financial statements.

Measurability—It has a relevant attribute measurable with sufficient reliability.

Relevance—The information about it is capable of making a difference in user decisions.

Reliability—The information is representationally faithful, verifiable, and neutral.[9]

Both Sterling's and the FASB's tests are too elaborate and vague to be practical. That is why various pervasive principles are stated for the initial recognition and measurement of both assets and liabilities. A first example, provided by Malcolm Miller and Atiqul Islam, is as follows:

It is proposed in this monograph that an item satisfying the definition of an asset be recognized in the financial statements when, and only when

   (a) it is probable that the future economic benefits embodied in the asset will eventuate; and

   (b) it possesses a relevant attribute that can be quantified in units of money with sufficient reliability.[10]

A more practical example, provided by the Accounting Principle Board (APB), is as follows:

Assets and liabilities generally are initially recorded on the basis of events in which the enterprise acquires the resources from other entities. The assets and liabilities are measured by the exchange prices at which the transfers take place.[11]

The APB principle points to recognition when control effectively occurs and to measurement at the market value (exchange price) of the consideration exchanged or sacrificed. Miller and Islam's definition ties measurement to the specification of an attribute that can be quantified in units of money. As will be seen later, various attributes are generally measured in the balance sheet in violation of the additive principle of measurement theory. The attributes considered in the balance sheet include original acquisition cost (historical cost), net book value, and various forms of current costs which contribute to the lack of additivity of the balance sheet.

Current Assets

The Committee on Accounting Procedure defined current assets as cash and other assets or resources commonly identified as those which are reasonably expected to be realized in cash or sold or consumed during the normal operating cycle of the business or one year, whichever is longer.[12] By "operating cycle" is meant the average time intervening between the acquisition of materials or services and the final cash realization. These current assets are classified in the balance sheet in order of their decreasing liquidity. They include cash, marketable securities, receivables, inventories, and prepaid expenses. The recognition and measurement of each of these components of current assets differ.

Receivables, consisting of claims against customers and other parties arising from the operations of the business enterprise, are valued at historical cost, adjusted by the estimate of uncollectible amounts. The attribute to be measured is an approximation of the net realization value.[13]

Inventory is valued at cost at acquisition, which has been generally defined as the price paid or consideration given to acquire it. When inventory is manufactured, Accounting Research Bulletin No. 43 holds that inventory costs include acquisition and direct and indirect production costs, whereas "general and administrative expenses should be included as period changes, except for the portion of such expenses that may be clearly related to production and thus constitute a part of inventory. Selling expenses constitute no part of inventory costs."[14] Both the costs of purchase and the costs of production added to the beginning inventory constitute the cost of goods available for sale. Thus total cost needs to be allocated to the cost of goods sold and the ending inventory by means of a cost flow assumption. Major alternative flow assumptions include specific identification, first-in, first-out (FIFO), average cost, and last-in, first-out (LIFO). The choice of a flow method is intended to provide a proper determination of income through the process of matching appropriate costs and revenues. The choice, as with any allocation technique, is arbitrary and incorrigible. However, the valuation at this historical cost, as determined by the cost flow assumption, is modified by the lower of cost or market rule, requiring that the inventory be written down to its market value when its utility is due.[15] Accounting Research Bulletin No. 43 states

A *departure* from the cost basis of pricing the inventory is required when the utility of the goods is no longer as great as its cost. Where there is evidence that the utility of goods, in their disposal in the ordinary course of business, will be less than cost, whether due to physical deterioration, obsolescence, changes in price levels or other causes, the difference should be recognized as a loss of the current period. This is generally accomplished by stating such goods at a lower level commonly designated as *market*.[16]

Market value is defined as the current replacement cost, and not the selling price, where (a) the upper constraint is that the market values should not exceed the net realizable value, and (b) the lower constraint is that the market value should not be below the net realizable value, reduced by an allowance for a normal profit margin.

Prepaid expenses include such items as office and factory supplies, prepaid rent, unexpired insurance, prepaid interest, and prepaid taxes. They represent resources committed for the current operating cycle. They are valued at their unexpired historical cost.

Temporary rather than long-term investments are classified as current assets, as they are expected to be converted into cash within the current operating cycle or a year, whichever is longer. The valuation of temporary securities can be made using

1. the historical cost method,

2. the market value method, or

3. the lower cost or market method.

The position taken in FASB Statement No. 12, *Accounting for Certain Marketable Securities*, favors the lower of cost or market method for equity securities where the difference between aggregate cost and market value is disclosed by means of a valuation allowance account offset against the original cost of the temporary investment account.[17]

Investments

Investments that are not readily salable and do not meet the expectation that they will be converted into cash within one year or by the end of the operating cycle are classified as long-term investments. The percentage of common stock ownership determines the valuation procedure to be used. Basically the lower of cost or market is used for ownership of less than 20 percent of the outstanding voting stock of the investee. Ownership of more than 20 percent requires the use of the equity method.[18,19] Ownership of more than 50 percent requires a consolidation with the investor's own accounts.

Investments in bonds or notes are valued at their acquisition cost, adjusted for the amortization of any purchase premium or discount.

Property, Plant, and Equipment

Property, plant, and equipment, also called fixed assets or plant assets, constitute tangible noncurrent assets. Some of these assets are subject to depreciation or depletion. The acquisition of property, plant, and equipment may occur either

1. singly or by a lump-sum purchase,

2. with deferred payments,

3. through the issuance of securities,

4. in exchange for another asset,

5. by self-construction,

6. by donation, or

7. through a lease.

The acquisition of the asset singly is valued at the invoice price less any applicable cash or trade discounts, plus freight, assembly, installation, and testing costs. In addition the costs incidental to the transaction and necessary for making the asset useful are accounted for. In the case of land, these costs include

1. the costs of closing the transaction and obtaining title, commissions, options, legal fees, title search, insurance, and past due taxes;

2. the land survey costs;

3. the costs of preparing the land for its particular use.

The acquisition of different assets for a single lump-sum purchase price is followed by an allocation of the acquisition price proportionally to the relative market values of the individual assets.

The acquisition of the asset on a deferred payment basis is valued at its fair value or the fair value of the liability at the date of the transaction. In those cases where both valuation bases are not easily determined, the acquisition is valued at the present value of the deferred payments at the stated interest rate, if it is not materially different from the market rate, or at the market rate.

The acquisition of the asset by issuance of securities is valued at the fair value of the asset or the stock, whichever is more verifiable.

The acquisition of the asset by exchange of other assets, known as a non-monetary exchange, is valued at the fair value of the asset(s) surrendered, and a gain or loss is recognized on the exchange for dissimilar assets.[20]

The acquisition of the asset through self-construction or manufacturing leads to two problems: (1) the determination of production costs and (2) the treatment of interest costs. With regard to the determination of production costs, the two debated methods, absorption costing and variable costing, agree that all variable manufacturing costs are product costs and hence inventoriable. The controversy lies in the treatment of fixed manufacturing overhead, with (a) the absorption costing method treating it as inventoriable product cost and (b) the variable costing method treating it as a period cost. The absorption costing alternative is the most employed in practice. With regard to the treatment of interest costs, FASB Statement No. 34 requires the capitalization of interest in certain situations, namely for the assets that are either constructed for a firm's own use or constructed as discrete projects for sale or lease to others, but not for routine inventory production.[21] The amount of interest to be capitalized is "intended to be that portion of the interest cost incurred during the assets' acquisition periods that theoretically could have been avoided."[22]

Assets acquired through donation are valued at their fair market value and conditions imposed on the firm through the donation should be disclosed in the footnotes.

The valuation of assets acquired through a lease depends on the type of lease. In the case of the lessee, an operating lease is accounted for by the expending procedure of the operating method; a capital lease is accounted for by the capitalization procedure of the capital lease method. Basically, FASB Statement No. 13 asserts that a lease that transfers substantially all the ownership privileges of an asset—the risks and benefits of property ownership—represents in substance a purchase by the lessee and a sale by the lessor.[23] Accordingly, in such a case an asset—lease equipment under capital leases—and a liability—obligation under capital leases—are created and valued at the lower of following two options:

1. The sum of the present value at the beginning of the lease term of the minimum lease payments during the lease term, excluding that portion of the payments representing executory costs such as insurance, maintenance, and taxes paid by lessor, together with any profit thereon.
2. The fair value of the leased property at the inception of the lease.[24]

In the case of the lessor, an operating lease is valued by the revenue procedure of the operating method, while a sales-type lease and a direct financing lease are valued by the capitalization procedure of, respectively, the sales financing method and the financing method.

In the case of oil and gas properties, the debate centers on whether to use the successful-efforts method, which requires the capitalization of costs associated with successful wells and the expensing of costs associated with unsuccessful or dry wells, or the full-costing method, which requires the capitalization associated with all costs, whether or not the wells were successful. FASB Statement No. 19, issued in 1978, required the use of the successful-efforts method.[25] It was suspended after the Securities and Exchange Commission (SEC) objected, however, and required the use of Reserve Recognition Accounting (RRA). Subsequently the SEC rescinded the RRA and allowed the use of either the successful-efforts method or the full-costing method.

Intangible Assets

Intangible assets lack a physical substance, but result from legal or contractual rights. A distinction is generally made between (a) *identifiable intangible assets* such as patents, franchises, organization costs, computer software costs, leases and leasehold improvements, deferred charges, and trademarks and (b) *unidentifiable intangible assets* such as goodwill. The valuation of intangibles as required by APB Opinion No. 17 requires

1. externally acquired identifiable intangibles to be capitalized;
2. externally acquired unidentifiable intangibles to be expensed;
3. internally developed identifiable intangibles to be capitalized, with the exception of research and development; and
4. internally developed unidentifiable intangibles to be expensed.[26]

The opinion also required the amortization of intangibles, stating,

The value of intangible assets at any one date disappears and . . . the recorded costs of intangible assets should be amortized by systematic charges to income over the periods estimated to be benefitted.[27]

The exception made for the capitalization of internally developed identifiable intangibles was for research and development. FASB Statement No. 2 requires that all research and development costs be expensed as incurred, given the uncertainty surrounding the realization of benefits from probable future patents or products having economic value.

LIABILITIES

Definition

An early and exhaustive definition of liabilities that includes deferred credits is contained in Accounting Terminology Bulletin No. 1 as follows:

Something represented by a credit balance that is or would be properly carried forward upon a closing of books of account according to the rules or principles of accounting, provided such credit balance is not in effect a negative balance applicable to an asset. Thus the word is used broadly to comprise not only items which constitute liabilities in the popular sense of debts or obligations (including provision for those that are unascertained), but also credit balances to be accounted for which do not involve a debtor and creditor relation. For example, capital stock and related or similar elements of proprietorship are balance sheet liabilities in that they represent balances to be accounted for, though these are not liabilities in the ordinary sense of debt owed to legal creditors.[28]

The reference to deferred credits was dropped, however, by FASB Statement No. 6, as follows:

Liabilities are probable future sacrifices of economic benefits arising from present obligations of a particular entity to transfer assets or provide services to other entities in the future as a result of past transactions or events.[29]

Three essential characteristics of a liability appear:

1. It embodies a present duty or responsibility to one or more other entities that entails settlement by probable future transfer or use of the assets at a specified determinable date, on occurrence of a specific event, or on demand.

2. The duty or responsibility obligates a particular entity, leaving it little or no discretion to avoid the future sacrifice.

3. The transaction or other event obligating the entity has already happened.[30]

Types of liabilities include *contractual, constructive, equitable,* and *contingent* liabilities and *deferred credits.* Contractual liabilities are based on written or oral agreements to pay cash to provide goods and services to specified or determinable entities.

Constructive obligations are created, inferred, or construed from the facts in a particular situation rather than contracted by agreement with another entity or imposed by government, such as in the case of vacation pay or year-end bonuses.[31] Equitable obligations arise from ethical or moral constraints rather than from rules of common statute law, such as in the case of the obligation to complete and deliver a product to a customer that has no other source of supply.[32] Finally, contingent liabilities have been expanded in Statement of Financial Accounting Concept No. 5 to include

an existing condition, situation, or set of circumstances involving uncertainty as to possible gain (hereafter a "gain contingency") or loss (hereafter a "loss contingent to an enterprise that will ultimately be resolved when one or more future events occur or fail to occur"). Resolution of the uncertainty may confirm the acquisition of an asset, the reduction of a liability or the loss or impairment of an asset or the incurrence of a liability.[33]

Owing to conservatism, examples of loss contingencies to be recognized included noncollectibility, product defects, premium offers, risk of loss or damage of enterprise property by fire, explosion, or other hazards, threat of expropriation of assets, pending or threatened litigation, actual or possible claims and assessments, guarantees of indebtedness of others, and agreement to repurchase receivables that have been sold.[34]

Finally, deferred credits are of two types: type 1 includes prepaid revenues that create a contractual duty to provide goods or services; type 2 results from a deferral and income statement recognition of an item to future periods, such as in the cases of investment credits[35] and deferred gains on sale-leaseback transactions.[36] Type 2 deferred credits do not constitute a liability. This is reflected in the following FASB position:

Deposits and prepayments received for goods or services to be provided—"unearned revenues," such as subscriptions or rent collected in advance—likewise qualify as liabilities under the definition because an entity is required to provide goods or services to those who have paid in advance. They are mentioned separately from other liabilities only because they have commonly been described in the accounting literature and financial statements as "deferred credits" or reserved.[37]

Recognition and Measurement of Liabilities

The general principle for the measurement of liabilities is the use of the amount established in the exchange. In general, for current liabilities the amount is the face value of the obligation to be settled in the future. In long-term liabilities the general rule is to recognize the true value of money. The discounting calculation used goes as follows:

$$PV = F (1 + r)^{-t}$$

where

F is a future cash flow occurring t periods from the valuation date
PV is the present value on the valuation date after discounting F at the interest rate r.

Theoretically, an item should be discounted if the item satisfies the following criteria:

1. The item represents a claim to or an obligation to pay, an amount the firm can estimate with reasonable precision.
2. The firm will collect or pay the amount more than one year after the balance sheet date.
3. (a) The claim or obligation arises from other than an executory contract, or (b) the firm has revalued the balance sheet item because of new information.[38]

There are, however, cases meeting the above conditions for which discounting is not allowed in Generally Accepted Accounting Principles (GAAP). Examples include

1. deferred income taxes,
2. convertible bond debt,
3. liabilities for amounts received for goods or services the firm will provide in the future,
4. contractual payments made or rents collected under troubled debt restructuring.[39]

For some of these cases the excuse used is the immateriality of the present value from the nondiscounted future value. Another, more plausible reason is stated as follows:

I believe that the current state of accounting for the time value of money is due to exceptional lobbying power on the part of banks and other financial institutions and the apparent discomfort of many accountants with compound interest arithmetic. The savings and loan crisis seems to be reducing the clout of the banking industry while the accounting profession is becoming more comfortable with compound interest.[40]

EQUITY

FASB Statement of Concepts No. 6 defines equity as "the residual interest in the assets of an entity that remains after deducting its liabilities."[41] A proprietary theory of the firm characterizes the FASB decision in the sense that equity is the ownership interest, ranking after liabilities as a claim to or interest in the assets of the firm. Another characteristic of the equity is that it may change as a result of activities from owner and nonowner sources. Both characteristics of equity are stated as follows:

1. Equity is the same as net assets, the difference between the enterprise's assets and its liabilities.
2. Equity is enhanced or burdened by increases and decreases in net assets from non-owner sources as well as investments by owners and distribution to owners.[42]

The basic framework of stockholders' equity is shown in Exhibit 1.1. It shows the legal distinction given in the corporate form of ownership among contributed capital, earned capital or retained earnings, and unrealized capital adjustments.

1. The contributed capital includes both legal capital and other contributed capital. The legal capital as measured by the par value of stocks represents the amount of the net assets that cannot be distributed to stockholders. The excess of par value received for shares is classified as additional paid-in capital. Other sources of contributed capital include, for example:
   a. conversion of convertible debt,
   b. issuance of detachable stock warrants with debt,
   c. common stock from the reissuance of treasury stock,
   d. common stock from the reissuance of employee stock options.
2. Unrealized capital includes, for example:
   a. donated capital,
   b. unrealized losses on long-term investments in equity securities,
   c. any excess of additional pension liability over unrecognized prior service cost as a negative compound,

Exhibit 1.1
Owners' Equity

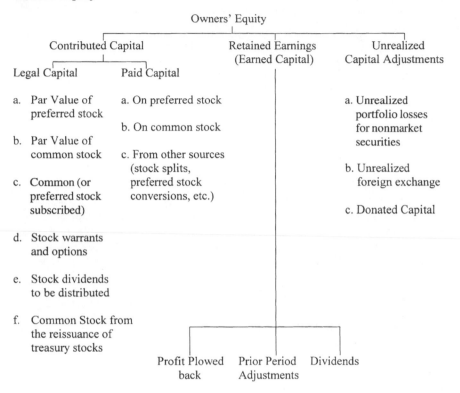

d. unrealized foreign exchange gains or losses from the translation of foreign net assets into dollars.

3. Retained earnings represent the cumulative net profit of a firm that has not been distributed as dividends. It changes through income-related transactions, dividend distributions, and prior period adjustments.

This threefold segregation in shareholders' equity rests in state legal capital requirements for the protection of creditors. A minimum capital equal to the par value of common stock is used to buffer the claims of creditors against bankruptcy.[43] Five judicial theories are generally used for stockholders' liability for stocks issued at less than par value:

1. A *trust fund theory*, where stockholders hold the contributed capital in trust for creditors, retaining a residual interest upon liquidation;

2. A *fraud theory*, where capital contributions are required to avoid a fraud upon other investors such as creditors;

3. A *statutory obligation theory*, where stockholders are held liable on the basis of state statutory requirements for the maintenance of minimum capital;

4. A *contract by subscription theory*, where the stockholders' liability is based on their subscription contract;

5. A *balance sheet misrepresentation theory*, which is a classic tort misrepresentation that shares were fully paid when, in fact, they were not.[44,45]

It is, however, a fact that the recent wave of restructuring has diluted the importance of legal capital in those cases where the distributions to stockholders exceeded the net book value of the firm's assets. Witness the following comment:

In this century, restrictions on corporate distributions based on legal capital have had little impact because the practice of using nominal accounts for par or stated values of capital stock has evolved, thereby giving corporate directors much latitude in declaring distributions to stockholders. In addition, although corporate boards of directors were statutorily bound to preserve paid-in capital in excess of par, they often were given the ability under state law to make transfers from paid-in capital in excess of par value to retained earnings by resolution. The recent wave of corporate restructuring has resulted in distributions in which the impairment of capital, at least as measured by GAAP, is clear-cut. Given the large number of restructuring transactions that have occurred, and the fact that many of these have been possible only because of the new flexibility of corporate laws, the relevance of the traditional accounting disclosures about a corporation's compliance in the state law and the corporation's capacity for making distributions to stockholders merit reconsideration.[46]

What has happened has been a gradual reliance, in these restructurings, on fair valuation of the assets, contributing to the erosion of the outmoded concepts of stated capital and par value. This was reinforced by the Committee on Corporate Laws in its report on the 1980 revisions to the Model Business Corporation Act, which specifically authorizes departures for historical cost accounting and sanctions the utilization of appraisal methods for the purpose of determining the funds available for distributions.[47] What this position implies is that the notion of par, or stated, value will no longer have the importance it once had as a legal capital.

FINANCIAL INSTRUMENTS AND OFF-BALANCE SHEET TRANSACTIONS

The new, complex reality of today's markets, with increased interest rate volatility, frequency of tax and regulatory changes, deregulation of the financial services industry and increased investment banking competition, demands a lot of financial innovation. It is the objective of financial engineering to provide such innovations. As defined by John Finnerty: "financial engineering involves the design, the development, and the implementation of the innovative financial instruments and processes, and the formation of creative solutions to problems in finance."[48]

The following factors have been identified as being primarily responsible for these new financial instruments:

1. tax advantages,
2. reduced transaction costs,
3. reduced agency costs,
4. risk reallocation,
5. increased liquidity,
6. regulatory or legislative factors,
7. level and volatility of interest rates,
8. level and volatility of prices,
9. academic work,
10. accounting benefits,
11. technological developments, and other factors.[49]

These innovations can be classified as debt innovations, preferred stock innovations, convertible debt or preferred stock innovations, and common equity innovations. Those instruments do not necessarily fit the conventional definitions of debt, equity, and hedging instruments. They are hybrids of the conventional instruments. The challenge to the accounting profession is how to create special or different accounting for these instruments. To deal with these issues the FASB issued in November 1987 an exposure draft, *Disclosures about Financial Instruments*, that would have required for all financial instruments disclosures about credit risks, contractual futures, cash receipts and payments, interest rates, and current market values. Because of the response of the constituents, the FASB decided to focus first on off-balance sheet risk and concentration of credit risk. In July of 1989 it issued a revised exposure draft, *Disclosures of Information about Financial Instruments with Off-Balance Sheet Risk and Financial Instruments with Concentration of Credit Risk*.

The project's intention is to provide an answer to such questions as

• Should financial assets by considered *sold* if there is recourse or other continuing involvement with them? Should financial liabilities be considered *settled* when assets are dedicated to settle them? Under what other circumstances should related assets and liabilities be derecognized, not recognized, or offset?

• What should be the accounting treatment for financial instruments and transactions that seek to transfer market and credit risk—for example, futures contracts, interest rate swaps, options, forward commitments, nonrecourse arrangements, and financial guarantees—and for the underlying assets or liabilities to which the risk-transferring items are related?

• How should financial instruments be measured, for example at market value, amortized original cost, or at the lower of cost or market?[50]

Effective with the 1989 calendar year reporting, firms have had to include extent nature and terms of financial instruments with off-balance sheet credit risk. Information about collateral and concentrations of credit risk has had to be disclosed in financial statements for fiscal years ending after June 15, 1990.

Basically the statement requires all entries to disclose information about the following, for financial instruments with off-balance sheet risk:

• The face, contract, or notational principal amount and the amount recognized in the statement of financial position.
• The nature and terms of the instruments and a discussion of the credit, market liquidity risk and related accounting policies.
• The accounting loss the entity would incur if any counterparty to the financial instrument failed to perform.
• The entity's policy for requiring collateral or other security on financial instruments it accepts, and a description of collateral on instruments presently held.[51]

The accounting loss from a financial instrument includes four risks, as follows:

1. A *credit risk*, or the possibility of loss, from the failure of another party to perform according to the terms of a contract,
2. A *market risk*, or the possibility that future changes in market prices may make a financial instrument less valuable or more onerous,
3. A *liquidity risk*, or the possibility that an entity may be obligated to pay cash that it may not have available;
4. A *risk of theft or physical loss*.

Which financial instruments have off-balance sheet risk, which refers to the risk of accounting loss (credit, market, or liquidity risk) that exceeds the amount recognized, if any, in the statement of financial position, remains to be determined. In the 1989 exposure draft, FASB also provided a definition of a financial instrument that distinguished between instruments that entail one party's right to receive and another party's obligation to deliver, and those that entail rights and obligations to exchange. It defined a financial instrument as cash, evidence of an ownership interest in an equity, or contract, that is both

1. a (recognized or unrecognized) contractual *right* of one entity to (a) receive cash or another financial instrument from another entity or (b) exchange other financial instruments on potentially favorable terms with another entity; or
2. a (recognized or unrecognized) contractual *obligation* of another entity to (a) deliver cash or another financial instrument from another entity or (b) exchange other financial instruments on potentially favorable terms with another entity.

This definition results in six tentatively identified instruments:

1. unconditional receivable (payable),
2. conditional receivable (payable),
3. forward contract,
4. option,
5. guarantee or conditional exchange,
6. equity instrument.

These instruments need to be broken down to determine their economic substance and thoroughly develop consistent accounting standards:

The approach is based on the premise that all financial instruments are made up of a few different "building blocks," fundamental financial instruments, and that determining how to recognize and measure those fundamental instruments is the key to reaching consistent solutions for the accounting issues raised by other, more complex instruments and by various relationships between instruments.[52]

CONCLUSIONS

It is apparent that a lot remains to be done. The valuation bases for liabilities, assets, and equities are at best eclectic and sometimes lack conceptual validation. In addition, the financial instruments, created by the financial engineering drive, need more than the piecemeal approach adopted by the FASB. All their problems need to be corrected to make the balance sheet a more relevant source of information.

NOTES

1. Malcolm C. Miller and A. Atiqul Islam, *The Definition and Recognition of Assets* (Gaufield, Victoria: Australian Accounting Research Foundation, 1988), pp. 34–36.
2. Financial Accounting Standards Board (FASB), Concepts Statement No. 3, *Elements of Financial Statements of Business Enterprise* (Stamford, CT: FASB, Dec. 1980), para. 19.
3. Kenneth MacNeal, *Truth in Accounting* (Philadelphia: University of Pennsylvania, 1939), p. 90.
4. Raymond Chambers, *Accounting, Evaluation and Economic Behavior* (Englewood Cliffs, NJ: Prentice-Hall, 1966), pp. 209–10.
5. Maurice Moonitz, Accounting Research Study No. 1, *The Basic Postulates of Accounting* (New York: American Institute of Certified Public Accountants [AICPA], 1961), p. 18.
6. Robert R. Sterling, *An Essay on Recognition* (Sydney, Aus.: Accounting Research Center, The University of Sydney, 1985), pp. 69–71.
7. Ibid., p. 69.

8. FASB, Statement No. 5, *Recognition and Measurement in Financial Statements of Business Enterprises* (Stamford, CT: FASB, 1984).

9. Ibid., para. 63.

10. Malcolm C. Miller and A. Atiqul Islam, *The Definition and Recognition of Assets*, p. 59.

11. Accounting Principles Board, APB Statement No. 4, *Basic Concepts and Accounting Principles Underlying Financial Statements of Business Enterprises* (New York: AICPA, 1970), para. 145.

12. Accounting Research Bulletin No. 43, *Restatement and Revision of Accounting Research Bulletins* (New York: AICPA, 1953), Ch. 3A.

13. Ibid., Ch. 4, para. 4.

14. Ibid.

15. Ibid.

16. Ibid., Ch. 4, para. 7.

17. FASB, Statement of Financial Accounting Standard No. 12, *Accounting for Certain Marketable Securities* (Stamford, CT: FASB, 1975).

18. Accounting Principles Board, APB Opinion No. 18, *The Equity Method of Accounting for Investments in Common Stock* (New York: AICPA, 1971).

19. FASB Interpretation No. 35, however, presents various facts and circumstances that preclude an investor from using the equity method to account for its investment of 20 percent or more in the investee.

20. American Institute of Certified Public Accountants, APB Opinion No. 25, *Accounting for Nonmonetary Transactions* (New York: AICPA, 1973), para. 18.

21. FASB, Statement of Financial Accounting Standard No. 34, *Capitalization of Interest Cost* (Stamford, CT: FASB, 1979), para. 10.

22. Ibid., para. 12.

23. FASB, Statement No. 13 as Amended and Interpreted through May 1980, *Accounting for Leases* (Stamford, CT: FASB, 1980).

24. Ibid., para. 10.

25. FASB, Statement of Financial Accounting Standards No. 19, *Financial Accounting and Reporting by Oil and Gas Producing Companies* (Stamford, CT: FASB, 1978).

26. Accounting Principles Board, APB Opinion No. 17, *Accounting for Intangible Assets* (New York: AICPA, 1970).

27. Ibid., para. 27.

28. Committee on Terminology, Accounting Terminology Bulletin No. 1, *Review and Resume* (New York: AICPA, 1953), para. 27.

29. FASB, Statement of Financial Accounting Concepts No. 6, *Elements of Financial Reporting of Business Enterprises* (Stamford, CT: FASB, Dec. 1985), para. 28.

30. Ibid., para. 36.

31. Ibid., para. 40.

32. Ibid.

33. FASB, Statement of Financial Accounting Standards No. 5, *Accounting for Contingencies* (Stamford, CT: FASB, 1975), para. 1.

34. Ibid., para. 40.

35. Accounting Principles Board, APB Opinion No. 2, *Accounting for the Investment Credit* (New York: AICPA, 1962).

36. FASB, Statement of Financial Accounting Standards No. 13, *Accounting for Leases* (Stamford, CT: FASB, 1976).

37. FASB, *Elements of Financial Reporting of Business Enterprises*, para. 197.

38. Roman L. Weil, "Role of Time Value of Money in Financial Reporting," *Accounting Horizons*, Dec. 1990, p. 50.

39. Ibid., p. 48.

40. Ibid., p. 61.

41. FASB, Statement of Concepts No. 6, *Elements of Financial Statements of Business Enterprises* (Stamford, CT: FASB, 1985), para. 49.

42. Ibid., para. 60.

43. M. A. Miller, *Miller Comprehensive GAAP Guide 1990* (New York: Harcourt Brace Jovanovich, 1989), p. 38.01.

44. B. Manning, *A Concise Textbook on Legal Capital*, 2d ed. (Mineola, N.Y.: Foundation Press, 1981), 16.

45. Michael I. Roberts, William D. Samson, and Michael T. Dugan, "The Stockholders' Equity Section: Form Without Substance," *Accounting Horizons*, Dec. 1990, pp. 37–38.

46. Ibid., pp. 38–39.

47. "The Report of the Committee on Corporate Laws," *The Business Lawyer*, July 1979, pp. 1867–89.

48. John D. Finnerty, "Financial Engineering in Corporate Finance: An Overview," *Financial Management*, Winter 1988, p. 19.

49. Ibid.

50. Clifford C. Woods III, "An Overview of the FASB's Financial Instruments Project," *Journal of Accountancy*, Nov. 1989, p. 44.

51. H. G. Bullen, R. C. Wilkins, and C. C. Woods III, "The Fundamental Financial Instrument Approach," *Journal of Accountancy*, Nov. 1989, p. 72.

52. Ibid., p. 71.

REFERENCES

Measurement of Assets and Liabilities in General

American Accounting Association. "Report of the Committee on Accounting Valuation Bases." *Accounting Review* 47 supp. (1972): 535–73.

Henderson, M. Scott. "Nature of Liabilities." *The Australian Accountant*, July 1974, 329–34.

Kulkami, Deepak. "The Valuation of Liabilities." *Accounting and Business Research*, Summer 1980, 291–97.

Ma, Ronald, and Malcolm C. Miller. "Conceptualizing the Liability." *Accounting and Business Research*, Autumn 1978, 258–65.

Miller, Malcolm C., and A. Atiqui Islam. *The Definition and Recognition of Assets*. Gaufield, Victoria: Australian Accounting Research Foundation, 1988, 34–36.

Moonitz, Maurice. "The Changing Concept of Liabilities." *Journal of Accounting*, May 1960, 41–46.

Sprouse, Robert T. "Balance Sheet-Embodiment of the Most Fundamental Elements of Accounting Theory." In *Foundations of Accounting Theory*, edited by Willard E. Stone, 90–104. Gainesville, FL: University of Florida Press, 1968.

Staubus, George. "Measurement of Assets and Liabilities." *Accounting and Business Research*, Autumn 1973, 243–62.

Sterling, Robert R., ed. *Asset Valuation and Income Determination*. Lawrence, KS: Scholars Book Company, 1971.

Walker, Robert G. "Asset Classification and Asset Valuation." *Accounting and Business Research*, Autumn 1974, 286–96.

Warrell, C. "The Enterprise Value Concept of Asset Valuations." *Accounting and Business Research*, Summer 1974, 220–26.

Weil, Roman L. "Role of Time Value of Money in Financial Reporting." *Accounting Horizons*, Dec. 1990, 47–67.

Measurement of Specific Assets and Liabilities

Anthony, Robert N. *Accounting for the Cost of Interest*. New York: Lexington Books, 1975.

Barden, Horace G. Accounting Research Study No. 13, *The Accounting Basis of Inventories*. New York: AICPA, 1973.

Beidelman, Carl R. Accounting Research Study No. 7, *Valuation of Used Capital Assets*. Sarasota, FL: American Accounting Association, 1973.

Chasteen, Lanny G. "Economic Circumstances and Inventory Method Selection." *Abacus*, June 1973, 22–27.

Clancy, Donald K. "What is a Convertible Debenture? A Review of the Literature in the USA." *Abacus*, Dec. 1978, 171–79.

O'Connor, Melvin C., and James C. Harnre. "Alternative Methods of Accounting for Long-Term Nonsubsidiary Intercorporate Investments in Common Stock." *The Accounting Review*, Apr. 1972, 308–19.

Sterling, Robert R. *An Essay on Recognition*. Sydney, Aus.: Accounting Research Center, The University of Sydney, 1985.

Measurement of Owners' Equity

American Accounting Association. "The Entity Concept Report of the 1964 Concepts and Standards Research Committee." *The Accounting Review*, Apr. 1965, 358–69.

Birnberg, Jacob G. "An Information-Oriented Approach to the Presentation of Common Shareholders' Equity." *The Accounting Review*, Oct. 1964, 963–71.

Manning, B. *A Concise Textbook on Legal Capital*. 2d ed. Mineola, N.Y.: Foundation Press, 1981.

Melcher, Beatrice. Accounting Research Study No. 15, *Stockholders' Equity*. New York: AICPA, 1973.

Roberts, Michael, William D. Samson, and Michael T. Dugan. "The Shareholders' Equity Section: Form Without Substance." *Accounting Horizons*, Dec. 1990, 37–38.

Scott, Richard A. "Owners' Equity, the Anachronistic Element." *The Accounting Review*, Oct. 1979, 750–63.

Smith, Ralph E., and Leroy F. Imdieke. "Accounting for Stock Issued to Employees." *Journal of Accountancy*, Nov. 1974, 68–75.

Chapter 2

The Income Statement

INTRODUCTION

The income statement reports the results of a firm's operations for the accounting period. Other labels used include *statement of income; statement of earnings*; or *statement of operations*. Two concepts of income exist:

1. the capital maintenance concept,
2. the transactional approach.

According to the *capital maintenance concept*, income is earned after capital (physical or financial) is maintained. A more useful approach to the determination of income is the transactional approach. The *transactional approach* relies on accrual accounting where the financial impacts of transactions and events on a firm are recorded for the period in which they occur, rather than when cash is received or paid. This chapter examines the theoretical and practical issues underlying the determination and preparations of the income statement under accrual accounting.

VIEWS OF ARTICULATION AND EARNINGS

Articulation

The relation between balance sheet, income statement, and statement of cash flow is based on a principle of articulation, in the sense that they are all part of the same measurement process.

The Financial Accounting Standards Board (FASB) conceptual framework views articulation as an important feature of financial statements. Consider the following statements from Statement of Financial Accounting Concepts No. 5:

The financial statements of an entity are a fundamentally related set that articulate with each other and derive from the same underlying data. . . . [1] A fully articulated set of several financial statements that provide those various kinds of information about an entity's financial position and changes in its financial position is necessary to satisfy the broad purposes of financial reporting.[2]

Financial statements interrelate (articulate) because they reflect different aspects of the same transactions or other events affecting an entity.[3]

Robert Sterling suggests the following articulation test:

Articulation requires that the sum of the separate effects of all events during a fiscal period equal the change in magnitude of the pertinent economic resources and obligations from the beginning to the end of the period. If the sum of the separate effects recognized does not equal the change in magnitude, it is conclusive evidence that there were additional events that occurred during the period that have not yet been recognized. The difference between the sum of the separate effects recognized and the change in magnitude is the combined effects of the additional previously unrecognized events. The difference must be recognized prior to the issuance of financial statements.[4]

Sterling again argues that articulation is a matter of the additivity of the selected attribute and provides the following example:

The quantity of cash, for example, is additive and therefore a cash flow statement *must* articulate with a cash position statement if *both* statements are faithful representations. If the cash flow statement shows a net cash increase of X dollars while the cash position shows a difference between the beginning and ending amount that is different from X dollars, then at least one of the statements is not a faithful representation. Articulation is not a convention to be decided by the FASB but rather a factual question about the behavior of the phenomena. The cash flow statement must articulate with the cash position statement for the straight-forward reason that the phenomena articulate.[5]

Within the articulation principle, there are two alternative views of earnings:

1. the revenue-expense approach;
2. the asset-liability approach.

Views of Earnings

The asset-liability view (also called the balance sheet or capital maintenance view) holds that revenues and expenses result from changes in assets and liabilities. Revenues are increases in assets and decreases in liabilities; expenses are decreases in assets and increases in liabilities. The focus under the asset-liability view is in the measurement and reporting of assets and liabilities. The income statement is reduced to reporting and measuring the changes in net assets.

The revenue-expense view, also called the income statement or matching view, holds that revenues and expenses result from the need for a proper matching. The view focuses primarily on the measurement of the earnings of the firm, rather than the increase or decrease in net capital. As a result the balance sheet contains not only assets and liabilities, but also deferred charges and credits that are residuals to be carried to future periods in order to ensure proper matching and avoid distortion of earnings.

REVENUES AND GAINS

Nature of Revenues and Gains

The literature distinguishes between two approaches to the nature of revenues:

1. an *inflow concept*,
2. an *outflow concept*.

The inflow concept of revenue defines revenue as an inflow of assets or an increase in assets arising from the operational activities of the firm. It represents an asset-liability approach. It is also consistent with the following Accounting Principles Board (APB) and FASB definition of revenue:

Revenue—gross increases in assets and gross decreases in liabilities measured in conformity with generally accepted accounting principles that result from those types of profit-directed activities. . . . [6]

Revenues are the inflows or other enhancements of assets of an entity or settlements of its liabilities (or a combination of both) during a period from delivering or producing goods, rendering services, or other activities that constitute the entity's ongoing major or central operations.[7]

The outflow concept of revenue defines revenue as an outflow of goods and services, a result of selling products, rendering services, and disposing of services. It represents a revenue-expense approach. Witness the following depiction of revenue:

Revenue results from the sale of goods and rendering of services and is measured by the charge made of customers, clients, or tenants for goods furnished to them.[8]

In both concepts, revenue does not include gains in their definitions. They are nonrecurring income to be displayed separately in the financial statements under the current operating income concept and under the all-inclusive income concept. They have been defined as follows:

Gains are increases in net assets from peripheral or incidental transactions of an entity and from all other transactions and other events and circumstances affecting the entity during the period except those that result from revenues or investments by owners.[9]

Revenue Recognition

Robert Sprouse and Maurice Moonitz state that

[R]evenues should be identified with the period during which the major economic activities necessary to the creation and disposition of goods and services have been accomplished, provided objective measurements of the results of those activities are available. The two conditions, i.e. accomplishments of major economic activity and objectivity of measurement, are fulfilled at different stages of activity in different cases, sometimes as late as time of delivery of product or the performance of a service, in other cases, at an earlier point in time.[10]

What the definition implies is that the accomplishment of the major economic activities can take place at different times and periods, which makes it an awkward method. One alternative to the reporting of revenue at the time of accomplishment of the major economic activities is the *critical event approach*. Under the critical event approach, the revenue from the sale of a product or service is recognized in full at a critical event date when the most critical decision is made or where the most difficult task is performed. The events or points in time for recognizing revenue are as follows:

1. during production,
2. at the completion of production,
3. at the time of sale,
4. when cash is collected,
5. until a future event occurs.

Revenue Recognition during Production

The accretion approach suggests the recognition of revenue during production. The best example is furnished by accounting for long-term contracts. Because the construction can take place for a long period and the firm needs to show income every year, the question of revenue recognition is crucial. Two approaches exist:

1. the percentage-of-completion method,
2. the completed contract method.

The *completed contract method* recognizes profit only when the contract is completed. The *percentage-of-completion* method recognizes the profit each period during the life of the contract in proportion to the accomplishment, in terms of either *input measures* or *output measures*. The input measures include either (a) the *cost-to-cost method*, where the percentage of completion is measured by a comparison of the costs incurred to date with the expected contractual total costs or (b) the *efforts-expended method*, where the percentage of completion is measured by a comparison of the work performed to date, as measured by labor hours, labor dollars, machine hours, or material quantities, to the expected amount on the contract. The output measures rely on key indicators of accomplishment of the contract that reflect the results achieved to date, such as units produced, units delivered, value added, or units of works accomplished.

Revenue Recognition at Completion of Production

Revenue is recognized at the completion of production for certain agricultural and mining operations. For those operations, not only is the production process a crucial part of the firm's operations, but also (a) the products have an immediate marketability at quoted prices, given the existence of a determinable selling price, and (b) there is an interchangeability of units, or (c) the producer is unable to determine costs. This method of revenue recognition is, however, rare.

Revenue Recognition at Time of Sale

Revenue is recognized most often at the time of sale, when legal title is transferred and the amount of revenue can be estimated with reasonable certainty. This approach is best expressed in Chapter 1 of Accounting Research Bulletin (ARB) 43:

Profit (revenue) is deemed to be realized when a sale in the ordinary course of a business is effected, unless the circumstances are such that collection of the sales price is not reasonably assumed.[11]

Revenue Recognition Where Cash Is Collected

The measurement of revenue subsequent to sale represents a revenue-allocation approach. It takes place when

1. the accurate measurement of the asset received in exchange in the transaction is impossible to measure; or
2. there is a likelihood of additional material expenses related to the transaction and that cannot be estimated with a reasonable degree of accuracy; or
3. there is no reliable basis for estimating the collectibility.

Two methods are generally used for deferring revenue recognition:

1. the installment method,
2. the cost-recovery method.

Under the *installment method*, revenue is recognized at the time of cash collection, and a portion of gross profit is recognized in proportion to the cash received. The *cost-recovery method* is similar to the installment method, except that no gross profit is recognized until the cost of the product sold as been recovered.

Revenue Recognition Delayed until a Future Event Occurs

When there is insignificant transfer of risk and benefits of ownership, revenue is deferred until an event occurs that corrects the situation and transfers sufficient risks and benefits to the purchasers. Generally, the "deposit" method is used to defer the recognition of revenue, until exact determination is made of the event that transfers the sufficient risks and benefits to the purchasers.

EXPENSES AND LOSSES

Nature of Expenses and Losses

In introducing expenses and losses, a distinction has to be made of costs as well. They are conceptually related. The term *cost* has different meanings to accountants, economists, engineers, and others facing managerial problems. Consider the following definitions from the cost accounting literature:

The term cost would seem to refer to some type of measured sacrifice evolving from an operational sequence of events and centering upon a particular activity or product.[12]

Cost is a foregoing, measured in monetary terms, incurred or potentially to be incurred to achieve a specific objective.[13]

The amount, measured in money, of cash expended or other property transferred, capital stock issued, services performed, or a liability incurred, in consideration of goods and services received or to be received. Costs can be classified as unexpired or expired costs. Unexpired costs (assets) are those which are applicable to the production of future revenues. . . . Expired costs are those which are not applicable to the production of future revenues, and for that reason are treated as deductions from current revenues, or charged against retained earnings.[14]

The following from case analyses of costs may help avoid the confusion between cost, expense, loss, and asset:

Case 1: The acquisition of resources with potential benefits results in the creation of assets or unexpired costs.

Case 2: The use of the assets in the manufacturing process results in the cost of a product that is inventoried. The eventual selling of the product transforms this product cost into an expense to be matched with sales. This is consistent with the following definitions of expense:

> Expense in the broadest sense includes all expired costs which are deductible from revenue ... [15]
>
> Expense—gross decreases in assets or gross increases in liabilities recognized and measured in conformity with generally accepted accounting principles that result from those type of profit directed activities of an enterprise.[16]

Both definitions represent the traditional revenue-expense orientation.

Case 3: The use of assets in the selling and administrative processes results in an expense to be recognized for the period. This is consistent with the following definition of expense:

> Expenses are outflows or other using up of assets or incurrences of liabilities (or a combination of both) during a period from delivering or producing goods, rendering services, or carrying out other activities that constitute the entity's major or central operations.[17]

The FASB definition represents a strong asset-liability approach.

Case 4: The decrease of the assets from peripheral or incidental transactions and events that are beyond the control of the firm result in a loss. This is consistent with the FASB definition of a loss:

> Losses are decreases in equity (net assets) from peripheral or incidental transactions of an entity and from all other transactions and other events and circumstances affecting the entity except those that result from expenses or distributions to owners.[18]

What appears from the above definitions is that cost corresponds to a sacrifice resulting from the use of assets. A basic distinction should be made between unexpired cost (asset) and expired cost (cost), as well as between cost and expense. According to the third definition, cost results from the use of assets towards the creation of revenues. "Cost" also must be distinguished from the term "expense." The American Institute of Certified Public Accountants (AICPA) Accounting Study No. 3 defines expense as follows:

> The decrease in net assets as a result of the use of economic services in the creation of revenues or the imposition of taxes by government units.
>
> Expense is measured by the amount of the decrease in assets or the increase in liabilities related to the production and delivery of goods and the rendering of services. ... In its broadest sense expense includes all expired costs which are deductible from revenues. In income statements, distinctions are made between various types of expired costs by captions or titles including such terms as cost, expense, or loss: e.g. cost of goods or services sold, operating expenses, marketing and administrative expenses, and loss on sale of property.[19]

The four cases indicate that events occur in the following sequences:

1. Acquisition creates an asset;
2. Manufacturing creates a cost of a product or activity;
3. Equation-matching or allocation creates an expense;
4. Misuse creates a loss.

The three central accounting techniques to create an expense are matching, allocation, and expiration. Basically, there are three possible cases:[20]

1. Costs that are directly associated with the revenue of the period and are matched against revenue;
2. Costs that are associated with the period in some basis other than a direct relationship with revenue and are allocated to the period;
3. Costs that cannot, as a practical matter, be associated to any period and are expired and expensed immediately.

While the third case is straightforward, the first two cases require the use of two important accounting techniques: matching and allocation.

Matching and Allocation

Matching is an accounting procedure that requires first, a determination of revenues, and second, a matching with expenses that represent the effort needed for the generation of the revenues:

The problem of properly matching revenues and costs is primarily one of finding satisfactory bases of association—clues to relationships which unite revenue deductions and revenues. . . . Observable physical connections often afford a means of tracing and assigning. It should be emphasized, however, that the essential test is reasonableness, in the light of all the pertinent conditions, rather than physical measurements.[21]

The problem is corrected by a reliance on three basic principles of matching: (1) association of cause and effect, (2) systematic and rational allocation, and (3) immediate recognition.

The association of cause and effect requires that matching be made on the basis of some discernible positive correlation of costs with revenues. One expression of this principle is the *cost attach concept*. As stated by William Paton and A. C. Littleton:

Ideally, all costs should be viewed as ultimately clinging to definite items of goods sold or service rendered. If the conception could be effectively realized in practice, the net accomplishment of the enterprise could be measured in terms of units of output rather than intervals of time. . . . In the more typical situation the degree of continuity of activity obtaining tends to prevent the basis of affinity which will permit convincing assignments, of all classes of costs incurred, to particular operations, departments, and—finally—items of product. Not all costs attach in a discernible manner, and this fact forces the accountant to fall back upon a time-period as the unit for associating certain expenses with certain revenues.[22]

As the statement indicates, the association of cause and effect constitutes a difficult principle, if not an impossible one.

The allocation of costs over time is another way of implementing that matching principle. It is a partitioning process to separate classifications or periods of time, so that the periods receive the correct benefits or services of the asset and, in the process, bear their share of the costs of the benefits received. A systematic and rational allocation is presumed to be used so that "the allocation method used should appear reasonable to an unbiased observer and should be followed systematically."[23]

To be theoretically justified, allocations are expected to meet the following three criteria:

1. *Additivity*: the total amount is allocated, so that the sum of the allocated amounts is equal to the whole.
2. *Unambiguity*: the allocation method should result in a unique allocation, i.e., should result in only one set of parts.
3. *Deferrability*: the allocation method selected is clearly superior to other methods on the basis of convincing arguments.[24]

The three criteria are generally difficult to meet, which renders most allocations arbitrary and impossible. They are incorrigible because they can't be verified or refuted by objective, empirical means. They do not correspond to anything in the real world. As Arthur Thomas states,

Conventional allocation assertions do not refer to real-world partitioning: when an incorrigible allocation divides an accounting total, there is no reason to believe that this reflects the division of an external total into dependent parts. . . . Conventional allocation assertions do not refer to real-world economic phenomena, but only to things in asserters' and readers' minds.[25]

One solution to this dilemma is to use allocation-free financial statements such as cash-flow statements, exit-price systems, and certain types of replacement-cost systems. In spite of these criticisms and limitations, in practice, costs continue to be allocated to serve a variety of needs, such as inventory value determination, income determination, pricing and production determination, and meeting regulatory requirements.

The immediate recognition of expenses is used for costs viewed in the current period or in previous periods that are assumed to no longer provide future benefits, or because there is a high degree of uncertainty about the existence of future benefits.

CURRENT OPERATING VERSUS ALL-INCLUSIVE INCOME

Income is generally measured for short periods of time, to provide users with useful information about the financial performance of the firm. What is to be included in the income figure has led, however, to two basic concepts of income—*the current operating concept* and *the all-inclusive concept.*

The *current operating concept* of income includes in the income statement only the results of decisions of the current period and arising from normal operations and reports nonoperating items in the retained earnings statement. The focus on the operating items in the current operating concept of income derives from their characteristics as recurring, regular, and predictable features of the operations of the firm. The advocates of the current operating concept of income argue that the end result is more meaningful and useful for interperiod and interfirm companies and for predicting possible future income and dividend flows if items extraneous to operating decisions are excluded. There is less risk of the financial statement users being misled or confused if the irregular, nonoperating items are excluded from the income statement.

The *all-inclusive concept* of income includes all the components of comprehensive income in the income statement, i.e., all the items that affected the net increase or decrease in stockholders' equity during the period, with the exception of capital transactions. The advocates of the all-inclusive concept of income argue that the concept is viable because

1. Net income of the firm for the life of the firm should be equal to the sum of the annual report net incomes;
2. Income smoothing may be checked by the inclusion of all income charges and credits;
3. A better picture of the total performance of the firm is conveyed, especially when both recurring and unusual, infrequently occurring items are displayed separately in the same income statement.

The official position in the issue has varied over time. Prior to the issuance of APB Opinion 9, the AICPA favored the current operating concept of income. With the issuance of APB Opinion 9, *Reporting the Results of Operations*, the trend went toward the all-inclusive concept of income, with the opinion's conclusions that income should include all items of profit or loss during the period, with the exception of certain material prior-period adjustments that should be reflected as adjustments of the beginning retained earnings balance. The tilt toward the all-inclusive concept of income continued with the issuance of APB Opinions Nos. 15, 20, and 30, requiring disclosure of the earnings per share, cumulative effects of changes in accounting principles, extraordinary items, and results from discontinued operations on the income statement. The FASB has definitely adopted an all-inclusive concept of income in its definition of "comprehensive income" as part of its conceptual framework. FASB Statement of Concepts No. 6 defines "comprehensive income" as follows:

Comprehensive income is the change in equity of a business entity during a period from transactions and other events and circumstances from nonowner sources. It includes all changes in equity during a period except those resulting from investments by owners and distributions to owners.[26]

FORMAT APPROACHES

The display of the operating section of the income statement differs from one firm to another, using variations of two basic forms, the *single-step format* and the *multiple-step format*.

The single-step income statement includes two broad groups, revenues and expenses. The total revenues include operating revenues, other revenues, and gains not meeting the criteria of being extraordinary. The total expenses include the cost of goods sold, operating expenses, other expenses, and income tax expenses. The difference between the total revenues and total expenses is the income from continued operations. An example of a single-step format is shown in Exhibit 2.1. The single-step format is favored because of its simplicity and flexibility in reporting.

The multiple-step format proceeds through several steps to arrive at income from continuing operations. In the first step the cost of goods sold is deducted from net sales, to produce gross profit or gross margin on sales. In the second step, the operating expenses are deducted from gross profit to arrive at operating income. The "other revenues and expenses," the nonoperating items, are then deducted (or added) to operating income to derive the pretax income from continuing operations. In the final step, income tax expenses are deducted from the pretax income from continuing operations to arrive at income before continuing operations. An example of a multiple-set income statement is shown in Exhibit 2.2.

These additional sub-classifications on the multiple-step income statement are deemed more informative and useful to investors, creditors, and other users. The multiple-step income statement is becoming more popular, in spite of two potential limitations. The first limitation pertains to the potential different classifications of operating and nonoperating items by different firms, leading to noncomparable income statements. The second limitation pertains to the potential misleading inference from the multiple-step income statement that the recovery of expenses is essential.[27]

EXTRAORDINARY ITEMS

The ability to distinguish between normal recurring components of comprehensive income and nonrecurring items is essential to a sound evaluation of the results of current and past activities and the prediction of future results. And there lies the importance of extraordinary items, as they may affect that ability. The first explicit guidance on accounting for extraordinary items came in APB Opinion No. 9, which required the explicit display in a specifically designated

Exhibit 2.1

Oliver Corporation: Single-Step Income Statement for the Year Ended Dec. 31, 1999

Revenues:		
Sales revenue (net of $5,000 discounts and $2,000 returns and allowances)	153,000	
Interest Revenue	2,000	
Dividend Revenue	1,000	
Total Revenue		156,000
Expenses		
Cost of Goods Sold	80,000	
Selling Expenses	10,000	
General and Administrative Expenses	15,000	
Depreciation Expense	7,000	
Loss on Sale of Equipment	5,000	
Interest Expense	2,000	
Income Tax Expense	7,000	
		126,000
Income from Continuing Operations		30,000
Results from Discontinued Operations		
Income from operations of discontinued segment A (net of $2,000 income taxes)	4,500	
Loss on disposal of segment A (net of $3,000 income tax credit)	(2,000)	(2,500)
Income before extraordinary items		27,500
Extraordinary Loss from explosion (net of $700 income tax credit)		(2,000)
Cumulative Effect on prior years' income of change in depreciation method (net of $800 income taxes)		2,400
Net Income		27,900

Components of Income	Earnings per Share
Income from continuing operations	6.00
Results from discontinued operations	(0.50)
Extraordinary Loss from explosion	(0.40)
Cumulative effect on prior years' income of change in depreciation method	0.48
Net Income	5.58

Exhibit 2.2
Oliver Corporation: Multiple-Step Income Statement for the Year Ended Dec. 31, 1999

Sales Revenue		160,000
Less Sales returns and allowances	5,000	
sales discounts	2,000	7,000
Net Sales		153,000
Cost of Goods Sold		80,000
Gross Profit		73,000
Operating Expenses		
Selling Expenses	10,000	
General and Administrative Expenses	15,000	
Depreciation Expense	7,000	32,000
Operating Income		41,000
Other Revenues and Expenses		
Interest Revenue	2,000	
Dividend Income	1,000	
Loss on Sale of equipment	(5,000)	
Interest Expense	(2,000)	(4,000)
Pretax Income from continuing operations		37,000
Income tax expenses		7,000
Income from continuing operations		30,000
Results from discontinued operations		
Income from operations of discontinued segment A		
(net of $2,000 income taxes)		4,500
Loss on disposal of segment A		
(net of $3,000 income tax credit)		(2,000)
Income before extraordinary items		27,500
Extraordinary loss from explosion		
(net of $700 income tax credit)		(2,000)
Cumulative effect on prior years' income of change in		
depreciation method (net of $800 income taxes)		2,400
Net Income		27,900

Components of Income	Earnings per Share
Income from continuing operations	6.00
Results from discontinued operations	(0.50)
Extraordinary loss from explosion	(0.40)
Cumulative effect on prior years' income of	
change in depreciation method	0.48
Net Income	5.58

section of the income statement.[28] The following definition of "extraordinary items" was provided:

events and transactions of material effect, which would not be expected to recur frequently and which would not be considered as recurring factors in any evaluation of the ordinary operating processes of the business.[29]

The ambiguity of the definition, as well as the need to ensure a more uniform interpretation of the provisions, led the Accounting Principles Board to issue APB No. 30, *Reporting the Results of Operations*, where extraordinary items were characterized as both unusual in nature and infrequent in occurrence.[30] These characteristics were defined as follows:

Unusual in nature—The underlying event or transaction should possess a high degree of abnormality and be of a type clearly unrelated to, or only incidentally related to, the ordinary and typical activities of the entity, taking into account the environment in which the entity operates.

Infrequency of occurrence—The underlying event or transaction should be of a type that would not reasonably be expected to recur in the foreseeable future, taking into account the environment in which the entity operates.[31]

Items and transactions defined as not meeting this definition included write-downs and write-offs of receivables, inventories, equipment leased to others, deferred research and development costs, or other intangible assets; gains and losses in foreign currency transactions or devaluations; gains and losses on disposal of segments of a business; other gains and losses on the sale or abandonment of property, plant, and equipment used in business; effects of strikes; and adjustments of accruals on long-term contracts. The new criteria for extraordinary items made such items rare for a while. However, some FASB pronouncements are bringing them back. Examples include

1. *FASB Statement No. 4* requirement that a gain or loss on the extinguishment of debt be shown separately as an extraordinary item;
2. *FASB Statement No. 15* requirement that a gain on restructuring debt be reported as an extraordinary item by the debtor;
3. *FASB Statement No. 44* requirement that the initial write-off of unamortized costs of interstate operating rights impaired by the Motor Carrier Act of 1980 be reported as an extraordinary item.

RESULTS FROM DISCONTINUED OPERATIONS

A segment of a business refers to a component of an entity whose activities represent a separate major line of business or class of customers. By discontinued operations, it is meant the operations of a segment that has been sold, abandoned, spun off, or otherwise disposed of. A gain or loss is expected to be made from the discontinued operations at the measurement date. It includes two factors:

1. the income (or loss) from operations of discontinued segment from the measurement date until disposal date,
2. the loss (or gain) on the disposal.

APB Opinion No. 30 requires that the results from discontinued operations be reported net of tax on the income statement after the income from continuing operations, but before extraordinary items. The timing of the recognition of the deferrals is dependent upon whether the results are a gain or a loss. If a loss is expected, it is recognized at the measurement date, whereas a gain is deferred and recognized on the disposal date, which is in accordance with the general principle of conservatism.

PRIOR PERIOD ADJUSTMENTS

To be classified as prior period adjustments, APB Opinion No. 9 required events and transactions to be

a. specifically identified and directly related to the business activities of particular prior periods,
b. not attributable to economic events occurring subsequent to the date of the financial statements for the prior period,
c. dependent primarily on determination by persons other than management,
d. not susceptible of reasonable estimation prior to such determinations.[32]

In response to the restrictive nature of these requirements, the Securities and Exchange Commission (SEC) released on June 8, 1976, Staff Bulletin No. 8, which excluded charges or credits resulting from litigation from being treated as prior period adjustments. Subsequently, the FASB issued its Statement No. 16, *Prior Period Adjustments*, in which it limited prior period adjustments to the following:

a. correction of an error in the financial statements of a prior period,
b. adjustments that result from the realization of income tax benefits of preacquisition operating loss carry-forwards of purchased subsidiaries.[33]

With regard to certain changes in accounting principles, prior period restatement (adjustment) is required, instead of a cumulative effect of adjustment for the following cases:

1. a change from the last-in, first-out (LIFO) inventory cost flow method to another method,

2. a change in the method of accounting for long-term construction-type contracts,

3. a change to or from the "full cost" method of accounting used in the oil and gas industry,

4. a change from retirement-replacement-betterment accounting to depreciation accounting from railroad track structures,

5. a change from the cost method to the equity method for investments in common stock.

ACCOUNTING CHANGES

Three types of accounting changes and errors are identified in APB Opinion No. 20, as follows:

1. *Change in accounting principle*: this type of change occurs when a firm adopts a generally accepted accounting principle that differs from the one previously used for reporting purposes. Examples include a change from first-in, first-out (FIFO) and LIFO inventory cost flow assumptions or a change from straight line to accelerated depreciation.

2. *Change in accounting estimate*: these changes are a result of the periodic presentation. The preparation of financial statements requires estimation of future events, and such estimates are subject to periodic review. Examples of such change include the changes in the life of depreciable assets and the estimated collectibility of receivables.

3. *Changes in reporting entity*: this type of change is caused by changes in the reporting units, which may be the result of consolidations, changes in specific subsidiaries, or a change in the number of companies consolidated.

4. *Errors*: errors are not accounting changes. They are the results of mistakes or oversights such as the use of incorrect accounting methods or mathematical miscalculations.[34]

All changes in accounting principles, except those specifically excluded by APB Opinion 20 and other APB Opinions and FASB statements, are accounted for as a cumulative effect change in the comprehensive income on the income statement of the period of change in a separate section entitled "accounting changes." The effect of adopting the new accounting principle on income before extraordinary items and on net income (and on related per share amounts) of the period of change is disclosed in the notes to the financial statements. Furthermore, income before extraordinary items and net income computed on a pro forma basis are shown on the income statements of all periods presented as if the newly adopted accounting principles were applied during all periods affected.[35]

A change in accounting estimates is accounted for in the period of change if the change affects that period only, or in the period of change and future periods if the change affects both.[36]

A change in accounting entity is accounted for retroactively by prior period restatement of all financial statements as if the new reporting entity had existed for all periods. A description of the change, the reason for it, as well as the effect of the change on income before extraordinary items, net income, and related earnings per share, are disclosed for all periods presented.[37]

An error is accounted for retroactively as prior period adjustments and therefore is excluded from the determination of net income for the period, under the provisions of FASB Statement No. 16.[38]

EARNINGS PER SHARE

Earnings per share is a summary indicator that can assuredly communicate considerable information about a firm's performance. To establish consistency in earnings per share computations and promote comparability of accounting information, APB Opinion No. 15 was issued to require the disclosure of earnings per share and provide guidelines for computation.[39] The calculations arc examples that the AICPA published shortly after a 189-page document that contains unofficial accounting interpretations for the computation of earnings per share.[40]

The computation of earnings per share is different for two types of capital structures—the simple and the complex. A simple capital structure is one that consists of "only common stocks or includes no potentially dilutive convertible securities, options, warrants, or other rights that upon conversion or exercise could in the aggregate dilute earnings per share."[41] In the case of the simple capital structure, the earnings per share is computed by dividing the actual earnings applicable to the common shares by the weighted average number of shares outstanding.

A complex capital structure includes in addition to common stocks such items as convertible preferred stocks and bonds, stock options and warrants, participating securities and two-class stocks, and contingent shares that are potentially a common stock equivalent. In the case of the complex capital structure, two earnings per share figures are required:

1. A primary earnings per share that is based on the outstanding common shares and the common stock cquivalents that have a dilutive effect.
2. A fully diluted earnings per share that reflects the dilution of earnings per share that would have occurred if all contingent issuances of common stock that would have individually reduced earnings per share had taken place.[42]

The primary earnings per share is computed by dividing the earnings applicable to the common shares by weighted average number of shares of common stock and common stock equivalents (convertibles that met a yield test plus warrants and stock options). The fully diluted earnings per share are equivalent to the earnings that would result if all potential dilution took place.[43]

Earnings per share is not, however, the only summary indicator that can be provided to users. An FASB report identified the potential for other summary indicators that can communicate considerable information about both a firm's performance and its financial position. Examples include return on investment and cash flow per share.

CONCLUSIONS

This chapter covered the conceptual and practical issues associated with the income statement prepared on the basis of a transactional approach. Although the FASB seems to be refining the document in the direction of a clear determination of comprehensive income, a lot remains to be done, with a steady move towards an asset-liability approach to the financial statements.

NOTES

1. Financial Accounting Standards Board (FASB), Statement of Financial Accounting Concepts No. 5, *Recognition and Measurement in Financial Statements of Business Enterprises* (Stamford, CT: FASB, 1984), para. 5.

2. Ibid., para. 12.

3. Ibid., para. 23.

4. Robert R. Sterling, *An Essay on Recognition*, R. J. Chambers Research Lecture 1985 (Sydney: The University of Sydney, Accounting Research Center, 1987), p. 82.

5. Ibid., pp. 57–58.

6. Accounting Principles Board, Statement No. 4, *Basic Concepts and Accounting Principles Underlying Financial Statements of Business Enterprises* (New York: AICPA, 1970), para. 34.

7. FASB, Statement of Financial Accounting Concepts No. 6, *Elements of Financial Statements* (Stamford, CT: FASB, 1985), para. 16.

8. Committee of Terminology, Accounting Terminology Bulletin No. 2, *Proceeds, Revenue, Income, Profit and Earnings* (New York: AICPA, 1955), para. 5.

9. FASB, Statement No. 6, para. 88.

10. Robert T. Sprouse and Maurice Moonitz, Accounting Research Study No. 3, *A Tentative Set of Broad accounting Principles for Business Enterprises* (New York: AICPA, 1968), p. 47.

11. Committee on Accounting Procedure, Accounting Research Bulletin (ARB) No. 43, *Restatement and Revision of Accounting Research Bulletin* (New York: AICPA, 1953), Chap. 1, para. 1.

12. Wilber E. Haseman, "An Interpretive Framework of Cost," *Accounting Review*, Oct. 1968, pp. 738–52.

13. American Accounting Association Committee on Cost Concepts and Standards, "Report of the Committee on Costs Concepts and Standards," *Accounting Review*, Apr. 1952, p. 176.

14. Accounting Principles Board, Statement No. 4, *Basic Concepts and Accounting Principles Underlying Financial Statements of Business Enterprises* (New York: AICPA, 1970), para. 12.

15. Committee on Terminology, Accounting Terminology Bulletin No. 4, *Proceeds, Revenue, Income, Profit, and Earnings* (New York: AICPA, 1955), para. 31.

16. Accounting Principles Board, Statement No. 4, para. 134.

17. Financial Accounting Standards Board, Statement of Financial Accounting Concepts No. 6, *Elements of Financial Statements* (Stamford, CT: FASB, 1985), para. 80.

18. Ibid.

19. R. T. Sprouse, and M. Moonitz, Accounting Research Study No. 3, *A Tentative Set of Broad Accounting Principles for Business Enterprises* (New York: AICPA, 1962), p. 25.

20. Accounting Principles Board, Statement No. 4, para. 19.

21. William Paton, and A. C. Littleton, *An Introduction to Corporate Accounting Standards* (Sarasota, FL: American Accounting Association [AAA], 1940), p. 71.

22. Ibid., p. 15.

23. Accounting Principles Board, Statement No. 4, para. 19.

24. Arthur L. Thomas, "The Allocation Problem in Financial Accounting Theory," *Studies in Accounting Research No. 3* (Sarasota, FL: AAA, 1969), pp. 6–15.

25. Arthur L. Thomas, "The Allocation Problem: Part Two," *Studies in Accounting Research No. 9* (Sarasota, FL: AAA, 1969), p. 3.

26. FASB, Statement of Financial Accounting Concepts No. 6, *Elements of Financial Statements* (Stamford, CT: FASB, 1978), para. 45.

27. Ibid.

28. Accounting Principles Board, Opinion No. 9, *Reporting the Results of Operations* (New York: AICPA, 1966).

29. Ibid., para. 21.

30. Accounting Principles Board, Opinion No. 30, *Reporting the Results of Operations* (New York: AICPA, 1973).

31. Ibid., paras. 19–20.

32. Accounting Principles Board, Opinion 9, para. 23.

33. Financial Accounting Standards Board, Statement No. 16, *Prior Period Adjustments* (Stamford, CT: FASB, 1977), para. 11.

34. Accounting Principles Board, Opinion No. 20, *Accounting Changes* (New York: AICPA, 1971).

35. Ibid., paras. 18–21.

36. Ibid., para. 31.

37. Ibid., paras. 34–35.

38. Financial Accounting Standards Board, Statement No. 16.

39. Accounting Principles Board, Opinion No. 15, *Earnings Per Share* (New York: AICPA, 1969).

40. J. T. Ball, "Computing Earnings Per Share," *Unofficial Accounting Interpretations of APB Opinion No. 15* (New York: AICPA, 1970).

41. Accounting Principles Board, Opinion No. 15, para. 14.

42. Ibid., para. 15.

43. P. A. Boyer, and C. H. Gibson, "How About Earnings Per Share?" *The CPA Journal*, Feb. 1979, p. 23.

REFERENCES

The Accounting Review, Apr. 1965, 368–72. "The Matching Concept."
———, Apr. 1965, 312–22. "The Realization Concept."

Accounting Terminology Bulletin No. 4. *Cost, Expense and Loss*. New York: AICPA, 1957.

American Accounting Association. *A Tentative Statement of Accounting Principles Underlying Corporate Financial Statements*. Sarasota, FL: AAA, 1936.

APB Opinion No. 9. *Reporting the Results of Operations*. New York: AICPA, 1966.

APB Opinion No. 17. *Intangible Assets*. New York: AICPA, 1970.

APB Opinion No. 20. *Accounting Changes*. New York: AICPA, 1971.

APB Opinion No. 30. *Reporting the Results of Operations*. New York: AICPA, 1973.

APB Statement No. 4. *Basic Concepts and Accounting Principles Underlying Financial Statements of Business Enterprises*. New York: AICPA, 1970.

Committee of Accounting Procedure. *Restatement and Revision of Accounting Research Bulletins*. ARB No. 43. New York: AICPA, 1953.

Committee of Terminology. Accounting Terminology Bulletin No. 2. *Proceeds, Revenue, Income, Profit, and Earnings*. New York: AICPA, 1955.

FASB Discussion Memorandum. *An Analysis of Issues Related to the Conceptual Framework of Financial Reporting: Elements of Financial Statements and Their Measurement*. Stamford, CT: FASB, 1976.

Financial Accounting Standards Board. Statement of Financial Accounting Concepts No. 6. *Elements of Financial Statements*. Stamford, CT: FASB, 1985.

———. Statement of Financial Accounting Standards No. 2. *Accounting for Research and Development Costs*. Stamford, CT: FASB, 1974.

———. Statement of Financial Accounting Standards No. 7. *Accounting and Reporting by Development Stage Enterprises*. Stamford, CT: FASB, 1975.

———. Statement of Financial Accounting Standards No. 12. *Accounting for Certain Marketable Securities*. Stamford, CT: FASB, 1975.

———. Statement of Financial Accounting Standards No. 96. *Accounting for Income Taxes*. Stamford, CT: FASB, 1975.

Frishkoft, Paul. *Reporting of Summary Indicators: An Investigation of Research and Practice*. Stamford, CT: FASB, 1981.

Horngren, Charles T. "How Should We Interpret the Realization Concept?" *Accounting Review*, Apr. 1965, 323–33.

Jaenicke, Henry R. *Survey of Present Practices in Recognizing Revenues, Expenses, Gains, and Losses*. Stamford, CT: 1981.

Mobley, Sybil C. "The Concept of Realization: A Useful Device." *Accounting Review*, Apr. 1966, 292–96.

Myers, John H. "Revenue Realization, Going-Concern and Measurement of Income." *Accounting Review*, Apr. 1959, 232–38.

Philips, G. Edwards. "The Accretion Concept of Income." *Accounting Review*, Jan. 1963, 14–25.

Sprouse, R. T., and M. Moonitz. Accounting Research Study No. 3. *A Tentative Set of Broad Accounting Principles for Business Enterprises*. New York: AICPA, 1962.

Thomas, Arthur L. Michigan Business Reports No. 49. *Revenue Recognition*. Ann Arbor, MI: Bureau of Business Research Graduate School of Business Administration, University of Michigan, 1966.

———. Michigan Business Reports No. 3. *The Allocation Problem*. Sarasota, FL: AAA, 1974.

Chapter 3

The Statement of Cash Flows

INTRODUCTION

The balance sheet reflects the financial structure of the firm at a point in time. The profit and loss statement reflects the financial performance of a firm over a period of time. What is missing is a statement reflecting the financial conduct of the firm in managing the funds available. The concern gave rise to various calls and pronouncements for some form of funds statement, resulting in the mandatory disclosure of a statement of cash flows. This new statement provides a view of the financial conduct of the firm and is a step toward a form of cash flow accounting. Accordingly, this chapter explores both the nature of the statement of cash flows and the nature of cash flow accounting.

THE STATEMENT OF CASH FLOWS

Historical Development

The first recommendation of the funds statement as an important component of the annual reports was made by Perry Mason in Accounting Research Study No. 2.[1] Following Mason's recommendation, the Accounting Principles Board (APB) issued APB Opinion No. 3 that recommended that a statement of source and application of funds be presented as supplementary information in financial reports.[2] An all-financial resources concept of funds was suggested for use in this statement, so that "the statement will include the financial aspects of all significant transactions, e.g., 'non-fund' transactions such as the acquisition of property through the issue of securities."[3] The reaction to the issuing of Opinion No. 3 was favorable, as evidenced by (a) the combined endorsement of the New York Stock Exchange and the Directors of the Financial Analysts Federation, (b) the inclusion of a funds statement in the annual reports of many U.S. companies between 1964 and 1971, and (c) a 1970 Securities and Exchange Commission (SEC) requirement that an audited funds statement be included in the annual reports filed with the Commission. That was a signal strong enough to make the American Institute of Certified Public Accountants (AICPA) act, publishing in 1971 APB Opinion No. 19, *Reporting Changes in Financial Position.*[4] It required that a "Statement of Changes in Financial Position" be presented for each period for which an income statement is included in the annual reports. An all-resources concept of funds was suggested in order to include interfirm transactions not affecting working capital, such as the acquisition of long-term assets through the issuance of securities. The Opinion called for flexibility in form, content, and terminology, leading to a variety of applications and a total lack of comparability across companies. This total flexibility was not without its benefits, however, as it generated discussions and debates, as well as applications of a concept of funds as cash flows. This movement and support for a concept of cash flows resulted ultimately in official endorsement. In 1987, the FASB issued its Statement No. 95, *Statement of Cash Flows*, requiring that companies present a statement of cash flows for the accounting period, along with an income statement and balance sheets.[5]

Concepts of Funds Flow

From the historical perspective, it is apparent that the concept of funds flow has been changing over time. The alternatives used have included (a) short-term monetary asset flows, (b) net monetary asset flows, (c) working capital concept of funds, (d) all-financial resources concept of funds, and (e) cash. Each is examined below.

1. A first concept of funds used is the short-term monetary assets, hence representing resources easily convertible into cash.

2. A second concept of funds used is the net monetary asset flows obtained by deducting short-term obligations from the current monetary assets. It is different from the first concept by considering both the net constructive inflows and outflows of cash.

3. A third concept of funds used is the working capital concept of funds. It differs from the net monetary asset flows concept by including nonmonetary assets, such as inventories and prepaid expenses, and some nonmonetary liabilities, such as advance receipts for services not yet performed.

4. The fourth concept of funds used is the all-financial resources concept of funds. It differs from the working capital concept of funds by disclosing the effects of all significant interfirm transactions.

5. The fifth concept of funds, adopted by FASB Statement No. 95, is cash. It is generally defined to include cash in hand or on-demand deposits, plus cash equivalents.

Cash Flows and the Conceptual Framework

The conceptual framework has taken a definite position in favor of the production and disclosure of cash flow information. The position starts with a definition of the needs of potential users. Investors, lenders, suppliers, and employees are assumed to perceive the business enterprise as a source of cash in the form of dividends or interests, appreciated market prices, repayment of borrowing, payments for goods and services, or salaries or wages.[6] It follows that general purpose external financial reporting which is to be directed towards the common interest of all these potential users will focus on the ability of firms to generate favorable cash flows. More specifically, in its Statement of Financial Accounting Concepts No. 1, the Financial Accounting Standards Board (FASB) stated,

Financial reporting should provide information about how an enterprise obtains and spends cash, about borrowing and repayment of borrowing, about its capital transactions, including cash dividends and other distributions of enterprise resources to owners, and about other factors that may affect an enterprise's liquidity or solvency. . . . [I]nformation about cash flows or other funds flows may be useful in understanding the operations of an enterprise, evaluating its financing activities, assessing its liquidity or solvency, or interpreting earnings information provided.[7]

This statement is the best signal that the FASB was ultimately going to make the move to a cash flow statement and to its Statement No. 95. The FASB's move is also evident in their belief that

[the] market's assessment of an enterprise's expected success in generating favorable cash flows affects the relative market prices of its securities although the level of market prices of its securities is affected by numerous factors—such as general economic conditions, interest rates, market psychology, and the like—that are not related to particular enterprises.[8]

It is also interesting that in its Statement of Financial Accounting Concepts No. 5, the FASB makes the following favorable assessments of a statement of cash flow:

It provides useful information about an entity's activities in generating cash through operations to repay debt, distribute dividends, or reinvest to maintain or expand operating capacity; about its financing activities, both debt and equity; and about its investing or spending of cash. Important uses of information about an entity's current cash receipts and payments include helping to assess factors such as the entity's liquidity, financial flexibility, profitability, and risk.[9]

This is further reinforced in Statement No. 95 itself, as follows:

The information provided in a statement of cash flows, if used with related disclosures and information in the other financial statements, should help investors, creditors, and others to (a) assess the enterprise's ability to generate positive future net cash flows; (b) assess the enterprise's ability to meet its obligations, its ability to pay dividends, and its needs for external financing; (c) assess the reasons for differences between net income and associated cash receipts and payments; and (d) assess the effects on an enterprise's financial position of both its cash and noncash investing and financing transactions during the period.[10]

Nature of the Cash Flow Statement

The statement of cash flows is intended to provide information on the change during an accounting period in cash and cash equivalents that can be useful in evaluating the firm's liquidity, financial flexibility, operating capability, and risk. By cash equivalents is meant the short-term, highly liquid investments that are both (a) readily convertible to known amounts of cash and (b) so near their maturity that they present insignificant risk of changes in value because of changes in the interest rate.[11] The statement of cash flows classifies the cash inflows and cash outflows as resulting from investing, financing, or operating activities. This follows from the FASB's argument that analysis by external users to predict the amount, timing, and uncertainty of future cash flows requires financial information to be segregated into reasonably homogeneous groups.[12] As a result, the statement of cash flows must clearly show

1. net cash flow from operating activities,
2. cash flows from investing activities,
3. cash flows from financing activities,
4. the net increase or decrease in cash,
5. a reconciliation of the beginning cash balance to the ending cash balance,
6. a supplemental schedule of noncash investing and financing activities.

The statement of cash flows can be prepared using either the direct or indirect method. Under the direct method, the operating cash flows are deducted from the operating cash inflows resulting in the net cash flow from operating activities. Under the indirect method, net income is adjusted for differences between income flows and cash flows for operating activities to determine the net cash provided by operating activities. FASB Statement No. 95 requires, however, that the reconciliation of net income to net cash flow from operating activities be provided regardless of whether the direct or indirect method of reporting net cash flow from operating activities is used. An example of the suggested format is illustrated in Exhibit 3.1.

Exhibit 3.1
Illustration of the Cash Flows Statement

Presented below is a statement of cash flows for the year ended December 31, 19X1 for

Company M, a US corporation engaged principally in manufacturing activities. This statement of

cash flows illustrates the direct method of presenting cash flows from operating activities, as

encouraged in paragraph 27.

COMPANY M

CONSOLIDATED STATEMENT OF CASH FLOWS

FOR THE YEAR ENDED DECEMBER 31, 19X1

Increase (Decrease) in Cash and Cash Equivalents

Cash flow from operating activities:		
Cash received from customers	$13,850	
Cash paid to suppliers and employees	(12,000)	
Dividend received from affiliate	20	
Interest received	55	
Interest paid (net of amount capitalized)	(220)	
Income taxes paid	(325)	
Insurance proceeds received	15	
Cash paid to settle lawsuit for patent infringement	(30)	
Net cash provided by operating activities		$1,365
Cash flows from investing activities:		
Proceeds from sale of facility	600	
Payment received on note for sale of plant	150	
Capital expenditures	(1,000)	
Payment for purchase of Company S, net of cash acquired	(925)	
Net cash used in investing activities		(1,175)
Cash flows from financing activities:		
Net borrowings under line-of-credit agreement	800	
Principal payments under capital lease obligation	(125)	

Exhibit 3.1 (*Continued*)

Proceeds from issuance of long-term debt	400	
Proceeds from issuance of common stock	(200)	
Net cash provided by financing activities		875
Net increase in cash and cash equivalents		1,065
Cash and cash equivalents at beginning of year		600
Cash and cash equivalents at end of year		$1,665

Reconciliation of net income to net cash provided by operating activities:

Net income		$760
Adjustments to reconcile net income net cash provided by operating activities		
Depreciation and amortization	$445	
Provision for losses on accounts receivable	200	
Gain on sale of facility	(80)	
Undistributed earnings of affiliate	(25)	
Payment received on installment note receivable for sale of inventory	100	
Change in assets and liabilities net of effects from purchase of Company S:		
Increase in accounts receivable	(215)	
Decrease in inventory	205	
Increase in prepaid expenses	(25)	
Decrease in accounts payable and accrued expenses	(250)	
Increase in interest and income taxes payable	50	
Increase in deferred taxes	150	
Increase in other liabilities	50	
Total adjustments		605
Net cash provided by operating activities		$1,365

Supplemental schedule of noncash investing and financing activities:

The company purchased all of the capital stock of Company S for $950. In conjunction

with the acquisition, liabilities were assumed as follows:

Fair value of assets acquired	$1,580
Cash paid for the capital stock	(950)
Liabilities assumed	$630

Exhibit 3.1 (*Continued*)

A capital lease obligation of $850 was incurred when the Company entered into a lease for new equipment.

Additional common stock was issued upon the conversion of $500 of long-term debt.

Disclosure of accounting policy:

For purposes of the statement of cash flows, the Company considers all highly liquid debt instruments purchased with a maturity of three months or less to be cash equivalents.

NATURE OF CASH-FLOW ACCOUNTING

The Problems with Accrual Accounting

The call for cash-flow accounting does not originate solely from the academic world. A good example is the following statement, made in 1982 by a commissioner of the Securities and Exchange Commission:

Over time, the accounting equation requires, of course, that accrual earnings equal cash earnings, but in the short term timing variations between accruals and cash flows may be quite significant; they may even make the crucial difference between continuing operations and bankruptcy. In other words, although accrual accounting, with its matching of revenues and expenses, may be important to the analysis of long-term profitability, cash flow is vital to survival.[13]

The most serious interest in cash-flow accounting was created by the limitations of accrual accounting. The advocates of cash-flow accounting questioned the importance and efficiency of accrual accounting and identified a shift to the cash-flow approach in security analysis.[14] The efficacy of the accrual system was severely questioned in general as well. A. L. Thomas stated explicitly that all allocations, which are the basis of accrual accounting, are arbitrary and incorrigible.[15]

To be precise about allocation, Thomas defined it as follows:

1. The assignment of costs, revenues, income, cash flows, or funds flows to individual inputs or groups of inputs to the firm, including assignment to individual periods of time, divisions of the firm, etc.
2. The division of any total into parts.
3. The assignment of costs to revenues, called matching.[16]

Thomas claimed that many of the allocations used in conventional accounting are arbitrary and theoretically unjustified, in that they are unable to meet the following criteria:

1. *Additivity*: the whole should equal the parts; the allocation should exhaust the total, dividing up whatever there is: no more and no less.

2. *Unambiguity*: once the allocation method has been specified, it should be impossible to divide the total into more than one set of parts.

3. *Defensibility*: any choice among allocation methods should have a conclusive argument backing it, defending the methods against all possible alternatives.[17]

Thomas then concluded that no legitimate purpose for financial accounting that has been advanced to date is furthered by making allocations, urging that financial accounting allocations should cease.[18]

Amounts reported on income statements are allocations of input cost to the expenses of individual years, and most of what appears in the nonmonetary portions of the balance sheet are the cumulative result of allocation. Three kinds of conventional allocations are distinguished: (1) annual contribution, (2) input contribution, and (3) annual profit (annual rate of return). The matching allocation of individual input costs to individual years (allocation methods 1 and 2) can result in the amount assigned to any specified year varying anywhere between zero and the total cost itself. It is also easy to prove that the annual profit allocation (method 3) is ambiguous, because any such allocation requires making an assumption about the input's book rate of return during each year.

All these problems arise because revenues are joint outputs of all inputs. Conventional matching attempts to associate joint revenue with cost. Actually, both joint revenue and all kinds of financial allocation have an identical form. In each case the fallacies of allocation are also identical.

Finally, Thomas concluded that we should forswear "matching fantasies," stop allocating, and prepare allocation-free financial statements. He recommended three possible kinds of such allocation-free statements:

1. current exit value reporting,

2. current entry value reporting,

3. net quick asset reporting or cash-flow accounting.

The principles Thomas proposed for the preparation of allocation-free "cash-flow" financial (funds) statements are as follows:

1. The category of funds should be net quick assets, i.e., total cash, receivables, and any other current monetary assets less current monetary liabilities.

2. A statement of current activities (a combination of conventional income and fund statements) should be prepared. It would begin with a detailed calculation of funds from operations and would make whatever distinction between ordinary and extraordinary items was appropriate. This would be followed by a report of purchases of nonmonetary assets, less proceeds from nonoperating sales of such assets, leading to

a figure for funds from operations less funds consequent to transactions in nonmonetary assets. The latter figure corresponds to conventional net income. Comparative funds statements would be disclosed.

3. The subtotal for funds from operations less funds consequent to transactions in non-monetary assets would be followed by the dividend and other data which customarily appear on a funds statement.

4. The conventional balance sheet would be replaced by (a) a statement of monetary assets and liabilities and (b) a statement of unamortized magnitudes of all nonmonetary assets presently in service.

5. There would be minor departures from conventional income statement and balance sheet reporting, consistent with the use of funds statements. For example, tax allocation would cease.

6. Insofar as possible, a rigorous orientation of inflow and outflow of net quick assets would be preserved throughout the reports; they would not be attempts to match or otherwise allocate.

7. Introduction of the new-style reports should require a lengthy transition period during which the old (accrual) reports would continue to be prepared.

The Meaning of Cash-Flow Accounting

Thomas's call was heard, because the Study Group established by the American Institute of Certified Public Accountants stated in its report published in 1973, "An objective of financial statements is to provide information useful to investors and creditors for predicting, comparing, and evaluating potential cash flow to them in terms of amount, timing, and related uncertainty."[19] Thomas A. Lee also identified three common needs of the users of accounting information:

1. Each group is concerned with how well the company has survived in the past and how well it is likely to survive in the future.

2. Each group is concerned with making and monitoring decisions. Each of these decisions has financial consequences, and suitable information is needed to aid the decision makers.

3. There are common features to be found, the main one being that each group is concerned with the most basic resource in business—cash.[20]

These needs were to be met by cash-flow accounting. Although there are various definitions of cash-flow accounting, the best definition needs to differentiate it from other forms of accounting, namely, (a) the cash basis of accounting, (b) the accrual basis of accounting, and (c) the allocation basis of accounting. Barry E. Hicks provides a good definition of each as follows:

• The cash basis of accounting means reflecting only transactions involving actual cash receipts and disbursement occurring in a *given period* with no attempt to record unpaid bills (or amounts) owed to or by the entity.

- The accrual basis of accounting means keeping records, so that in addition to recording transactions resulting from the receipt and disbursements of cash, the firm also records the amount it owes others and others owe it.
- The cash-flow basis of accounting means recording not only the cash receipts and disbursements of the period (the cash basis of accounting), but also the future cash flows owed to or by the firm as a result of selling and transferring title to certain goods.
- The allocation basis of accounting not only does all that the cash-flow basis of accounting does, but it goes beyond and subjects these cash flows to an allocation process. The allocation basis of accounting means (a) taking the "real" cash flows and dividing them into parts until the parts no longer represent "real" cash flows or (b) assigning the real cash flows or parts thereof to some period(s) other than the one in which they actually occur.[21]

Cash-Flow Accounting Systems

Various cash-flow accounting proposals have been made, as evidenced by a survey of articles by Lee.[22] Most of these systems share to a certain extent the same components and the same general philosophy. These major elements include the following:

N = Net cash inflow or outflow from operations

R = Replacement investment

G = Growth investment

RG = R + G = Total cash investment

T = Cash payments for taxation

D = Cash payments for dividends

I = Loan interest payments

E = New equity receipts

B = Borrowing

F = Residual financing charge

C = Residual change in cash resources of the period (usually cash and bank balances and deposits, but could include some near-cash items such as accounts receivable if these credit transactions are included with cash transactions).[23]

Using the above components, the cash-flow system proposed by G. H. Lawson[24] would appear along the lines of

$$N - R - G - T - I + E + B - C = D$$

The Lawson system focuses on the determination of D, the disposable income or net surplus the firm can generate from its trading and productive (or service) activity. In addition, it makes a distinction between replacement and growth investment.

Using the same components, the cash-flow system proposed by Lee[25] would appear along the lines of

$$N - [R + G] - T - I - D + E + B = C$$

which focuses on the cash residual, or

$$N - [R + G] - T - I - D = F$$

where $F = C - E - B$, which focuses on F, the residual financing charge during the period.[26] If the firm's transactions were financed internally, F would be positive; if they were financed out of cash balances and/or external sources, F would be negative.

Under both systems N could be expanded along these lines:

$$N = S - M - W = O$$

where

S = Cash sales

M = Cash payments for goods and services for resale

W = Wage payments

O = Overhead cash payments.

Another refinement would be to dichotomize T, to distinguish foreign from nonforeign transactions.

Other variations on the above two proposals include approaches which would report both past and forecast cash flows.[27] Yuji Ijiri makes the point for past and forecast cash-flow disclosure as follows:

Of course, if forecasted future cash flows can be obtained, they will certainly provide a useful supplement to a statement of past cash flows. The two should be clearly separated so as not to mix hard figures and soft figures. The two statements on cash flows, one on past, the other on forecast, can provide a complete picture of what has happened and what is expected to happen in the future under the best estimate available now, all based on cash flows. Forecasts can then be checked with actual performance as time passes, as mentioned earlier. A reliability indicator may be prepared based on past discrepancy between forecast and actual. I think that this is a better approach than trying to capture the financial status of a company at one point in time in terms of a still picture of all of its assets and liabilities based on their current cost or current value. The latter covers all noncash assets, but is static. The cash flow approach concentrates on cash flows only, but is dynamic in the sense that its focus extends over time and is most realistic since the statements are based on what has happened and what is expected to happen.[28]

Another proposal made would link C (the residual change in cash resources) to a statement of changes in net realizable value of resources, thereby transforming a simple cash-flow system to one including a profit figure. The combination of cash-flow and net-realizable-value accounting is the subject of the proposal. It would be accomplished by the mere segregation of net-realizable-value accounting data into realized cash flows, as in cash-flow accounting, and unrealized cash flows, as in net-realizable-value accounting.

Evaluation of Cash-Flow Accounting

Like any accounting system, cash-flow accounting has its supporters and detractors. It has generated a debate in the profession and in research which has finally resulted in some of the standard setters paying attention to the concept.

The advantages attributed to cash-flow accounting are numerous. They include the following:

1. Cash-flow accounting would rely on the price/discounted flow ratio as a more reliable investment indicator than the present price/earnings ratio, because of the arbitrary allocations used to compute the present accrual earnings per share figure and the international differences in the computation of earnings per share.

2. As stated earlier, cash-flow accounting may be allocation-free.

3. Cash-flow accounting retains money as the unit of measurement, which is familiar and not confusing to people.

4. Cash-flow accounting, when expanded to include projected cash flows, may help the investor to assess the ability of the firm to pay its way in the future and also its planned financial policy.

5. If the investor's interest is in the survival of the firm, together with the ability to provide a stream of dividend, then cash-flow accounting will prove more useful by providing accounting information about the current and anticipated cash positions of the firm. Liquidity assessment is a critical aspect of performance evaluation in the sense that cash flow and net profit are the end result of a firm's activities.[29]

6. Cash flow does not require price level adjustments, because cash transactions reflect prices of the period in which they occur. It is, however, appropriate to note that some general price level adjustment is needed for cash plans occurring in different periods.

7. Cash-flow information fits as an important variable in the decision models of various users because of the concerns associated with the firm's ability to pay dividends to investors, interest and capital to lenders and bankers, amounts due to suppliers, wages and other benefits to employees, rectification and maintenance services for customers, and taxation to governments.[30]

8. Cash-flow information is argued to be more objective and relevant than accrual-based information. According to Lee,

   First, in its historic form, it is perhaps the most objective information possible, avoiding most of the subjectiveness which enters into the technical adjustments involved in the traditional accrual accounting, it is the most relevant information for purposes of comparison with forecast information should this be measured on a cash basis. Second, forecast cash flows, although involving a great deal of uncertainty (however, no more so than budgeted profits on the accrual basis), clearly avoid the necessary subjectiveness of accrual judgments and opinions. Therefore, they appear to be far less subjective in a *total* sense than profit forecasts.[31]

9. There is the suspicion that the popularity of the all-embracing measures of performance such as profit may well have caused firms to underestimate the importance of performance measures such as market domination, productivity, and quality of products and services.[32]

10. Cash-flow accounting is the ideal system to correct the gaps in practice between the way in which an investment is made (generally based on cash flows) and the ways the results are evaluated (generally based on earnings).

Naturally, those opposed to cash-flow accounting question each of the above advantages, which leaves the debate at the hand of the researchers.

CONCLUSIONS

Cash-flow accounting is emerging internationally as a subject of research and interest to academics, practitioners, and/or standard setters. Although its alleged benefits, its impact on users' reactions, and its predictive ability are in need of more empirical evidence, its implementation seems to be gaining favor with the standard setters, who express fervent interest in its use. Cash-flow accounting has always been with us. It lost credibility for a while to the advantage of accrual accounting. Now it is making an international return. The return of cash-flow accounting to its well-deserved place of importance is best stated by Lee as follows:

Cash-flow accounting and reporting has a long and honorable history in the development of business enterprises. It was superseded by the sophisticated statements of allocated data which are by now such a familiar part of financial reporting practice. Perhaps, with liquidity such a vital issue in business today, the wheel will turn full circle, and cash-flow accounting will again be restored to its rightful place as a useful and relevant source of financial information about business enterprises for a variety of report users.[33]

NOTES

1. Perry Mason, Accounting Research Study No. 2, *"Cash Flow" Analysis and the Funds Statement* (New York: AICPA, 1961).

2. Accounting Principles Board, APB Opinion No. 3, *The Statement of Source and Application of Funds* (New York: AICPA, 1963).

3. Ibid., para. 9.

4. Accounting Principles Board, APB Opinion No. 9, *Reporting Changes in Financial Position* (New York: AICPA, 1971).

5. Financial Accounting Standards Board (FASB), Statement of Financial Accounting Standards No. 95, *Statement of Cash Flows* (Stamford, CT: FASB, 1987).

6. FASB, Statement of Financial Accounting Concepts No. 1, *Objectives of Financial Reporting by Business Enterprises* (Stamford, CT: FASB, 1978), para. 25.

7. Ibid., para. 49.

8. Ibid., para. 37.

9. FASB, Statement of Financial Accounting Concepts No. 5, *Recognition and Measurement in Financial Statements of Business Enterprises* (Stamford, CT: FASB, 1984), para. 52.

10. FASB, Statement of Financial Accounting Standards No. 95, p. 5.

11. Ibid., p. 7.

12. FASB, Statement of Financial Accounting Concepts No. 5, p. 20.

13. Barbara S. Thomas, "Reporting Cash Flow Information," *Journal of Accounting*, November 1982, p. 99.

14. D. Hawkins and W. Campbell, *Equity Valuation: Models, Analysis and Implications* (New York: Financial Executives Institute, 1978).

15. A. L. Thomas, Studies in Accounting Research No. 3, *The Allocation Problem in Financial Accounting Theory* (Sarasota, FL: American Accounting Association, 1969); idem, Studies in Accounting Research No. 9, *The Allocation Problem, Part Two* (Sarasota FL: American Accounting Association, 1974).

16. Thomas, *The Allocation Problem in Financial Accounting Theory*, p. 25.

17. Ibid., p. 30.

18. Ibid., p. 42.

19. American Institute of Certified Public Accountants, Study Group on the Objectives of Financial Statements, *Objectives of Financial Statements* (New York: AICPA, 1973), p. 16.

20. T. A. Lee, "The Simplicity and Complexity of Accounting," in *Accounting for a Simplified Firm Owning Depreciable Assets*, ed. R. R. Sterling and A. L. Thomas (Lawrence, KS: Scholars Book Co., 1979), p. 4.

21. Barry E. Hicks, "The Cash Flow Basis of Accounting," in *Cash Flow Accounting*, ed. Barry E. Hicks and Pearson Hunt (Sudbury, Ontario: School of Commerce and Administration, 1981), p. 30.

22. Thomas E. Lee, "Cash Flow Accounting and Reporting," in *Essays in British Accounting Research*, ed. M. Bromwich and A. Hopwood (London: Pitman, 1981), pp. 63–78.

23. The potential inclusion of near cash items is raised in Thomas A. Lee, "Cash Flow Accounting and Reporting," in *Developments in Financial Reporting*, ed. Thomas A. Lee (London: Philip Allan, 1981), p. 150.

24. G. H. Lawson, "The Cash Flow Performance of UK Companies," in *Essays in British Accounting Research*, ed. M. Bromwich and A. Hopwood (London: Pitman, 1981), pp. 79–100.

25. T. A. Lee, "A Case for Cash Flow Reporting," *Journal of Business Finance*, Summer 1972, pp. 27–36.

26. T. A. Lee, "What Cash Flow Analysis Says about BL's Finances," *Financial Times*, 23 Oct. 1981, p. 15.

27. R. J. Briston and R. A. Fawthrop, "Accounting Principles and Investor Protection," *Journal of Business Finance*, Summer 1971, pp. 9–10; C. J. Jones, "Accounting Standards: A Blind Alley?" *Accounting and Business Research*, Autumn 1975, pp. 273–79;

T. A. Climo, "Cash Flow Statements for Investors," *Journal of Business Finance and Accounting*, Autumn 1976, pp. 3–14.

28. Yuji Ijiri, *Historical Cost Accounting and Its Rationality*, Research Monograph No. 1 (Vancouver, BC: Canadian Certified General Accountants' Research Foundation, 1981), p. 75.

29. T. A. Lee, "Cash Flow Accounting, Profit and Performance Measurement: A Response to a Challenge," *Accounting Business Research*, Spring 1985, p. 93.

30. Lee, "Cash Flow Accounting and Reporting," p. 152.

31. Lee, "A Case for Cash Flow Reporting," p. 31.

32. R. S. Kaplan, "Measuring Manufacturing Performance: A New Challenge for Managerial Accounting Research," *Accounting Review*, Oct. 1982.

33. Lee, "Cash Flow Accounting and Reporting," p. 169.

REFERENCES

Anton, Hector R. *Accounting for the Flow of Funds*. New York: Houghton Mifflin, 1968.

Accounting Standards Committee. Statement of Standard Accounting Practice No. 6, *Extraordinary Items and Prior Year Adjustments*. London: Accounting Standards Committee, 1974, 15–25.

Arnold, J., and A. Hope. "Reporting Business Performance." *Accounting and Business Research*, July 1975, 96–105.

Barlev, B., and H. Levy. "On the Variability of Accounting Income Numbers." *Journal of Business Finance and Accounting*, Summer 1983, 305–15.

Beaver, W. H., and R. E. Dukes. "Interperiod Tax Allocation, Earnings Expectations, and the Behavior of Security Prices." *Accounting Review*, Apr. 1972, pp. 320–32.

Beaver, W. H., and D. Morse. "What Determines Price-Earnings Ratios?" *Financial Analysts Journal*, July–Aug. 1978, 65–76.

Belkaoui, Ahmed. *Accounting Theory*, 1st ed. New York: Harcourt Brace Jovanovich, 1981.

———. "Accrual Accounting and Cash Accounting: Relative Merits of Derived Accounting Indicator Numbers." *Journal of Business Finance and Accounting*, Summer 1983, 299–312.

Bird, Peter. "Objectives and Methods of Financial Reporting: A Generalized Search Procedure." *Accounting and Business Research*, Fall 1975, 162–67.

Bodenhorn, Diran. "Balance Sheet Items as the Present Value of Future Cash Flows." *Journal of Business Finance and Accounting*, Winter 1984, 493–510.

———. "An Economic Approach to Balance Sheets and Income Statements." *Abacus*, June 1978, 3–30.

Bromwich, Michael. "Standard Costing for Planning and Control." *Accountant*, Apr.–May 1969, 16–21.

Canning, J. *The Economics of Accountancy*. New York: Ronald Press, 1929.

Chambers, R. J. *Accounting, Evaluation and Economic Behavior*. Englewood Cliffs, NJ: Prentice-Hall, 1966.

———. "Continuously Contemporary Accounting: Additivity and Action." *Accounting Review*, October 1967, 751–57.

———. "Income and Capital: Fisher's Legacy." *Journal of Accounting Research*, Spring 1971, 137–49.

————. "Second Thoughts on Continuously Contemporary Accounting." *Abacus*, Sept. 1970, 39–55.

————. "Third Thoughts." *Abacus*, Dec. 1974, 129–37.

Climo, T. A. "Cash Flow Statements for Investors." *Journal of Business Finance and Accounting*, Autumn 1976, 3–14.

Daily, R. A. "The Feasibility of Reporting Forecast Information." *Accounting Review*, Oct. 1971, 686–92.

Edey, H. C. "Accounting Principles and Business Reality." *Accountancy*, Nov. 1963, 998–1002.

Edwards, E. O. "The Fundamental Character of Excess Current Income." *Accounting and Business Research*, Autumn 1980, 375–94.

Edwards, E. O. and P. Bell. *The Theory and Measurement of Business Income*. Berkeley: University of California Press, 1961.

Eggington, D. A. "Cash Flow, Profit and Performance Measures for External Reporting: A Rejoinder." *Accounting and Business Research*, Spring 1985, 109–112.

————. "In Defense of Profit Measurement, Some Limitations of Cash Flow and Value Added as Performance Measures for External Reporting." *Accounting and Business Research*, Spring 1984, 99–111.

Fama, E. F., and M. H. Miller. *The Theory of Finance*. New York: Holt, Rinehart and Winston, 1972.

Ferrara, W. L. "A Cash Flow Model for the Future." *Management Accounting*, June 1981, 12–17.

Financial Accounting Standards Board. *Statement of Financial Accounting Concepts No. 1*. Stamford, CT: FASB, November 1978.

Glautier, M. W. E., and B. Underdown. *Accounting Theory Practice*. London: Pitman, 1976.

Gombola, M. L., and J. E. Ketz. "A Note on Cash Flow and Classification of Patterns of Financial Ratio." *Accounting Review*, Jan. 1983, 105–14.

Gordon, M. J. "Postulates, Principles and Research in Accounting." *Accounting Review*, Apr. 1964, 221–63.

Grimlund, Richard A., and Robert Capettini. "Sign Tests for Actual Investments with Latter Period Net Cash Outflows." *Journal of Business Finance and Accounting*, Spring 1983, 83–193.

Gross, M. J., Jr. *Financial and Accounting Guide for Nonprofit Organizations*. New York: Ronald Press, 1972.

Hawkins, D., and W. Campbell. *Equity Valuation: Models, Analysis and Implications*. New York: Financial Executives Institute, 1978.

Heath, Loyd. C. "Let's Scrap the Funds Statement." *Journal of Accountancy*, Oct. 1978, 94–103.

Hendriksen, E. S. *Accounting Theory*. Rev. ed. Homewood, IL: Irwin, 1970.

Hicks, Barry E. *The Cash Flow Basis of Accounting*. Sudbury, Ontario: Laurentian University, 1980.

Ijiri, Y. "Cash-Flow Accounting and Its Structure." *Journal of Accounting, Auditing and Finance*, May 1978, 331–48.

————. "A Simple System of Cash-Flow Accounting." In *Accounting for a Simplified Firm Owning Depreciable Assets*, edited by Robert R. Sterling and A. L. Thomas. Houston: Scholars Book Company, 1979.

Ketz, J. E., and J. A. Largay III. "Reporting Income and Cash Flows From Operations."
   Accounting Horizons, June 1987, 5–17.
Lawson, G. H. "Accounting for Financial Management: Some Tentative Proposals for a
   New Blueprint." In *Problems of Investment*, edited by R. Shone, 36–64. London:
   Blackwell, 1971.
———. "Cash-Flow Accounting I and II." *Accountant*, 28 Oct. and 4 Nov. 1971, 15–
   20.
———. "The Cash Flow Performance of UK Companies." In *Essays in British Account-
   ing Research*, edited by M. Bromwich and A. Hopwood, 79–100. London: Pit-
   man, 1981.
———. "Initial Reactions to ED 18." *Certified Accountant*, Dec. 1976, 13–20.
———. "The Measurement of Corporate Performance on a Cash Flow Basis: A Reply
   to Mr. Eggington." *Accounting and Business Research*, Spring 1985, 99–108.
———. "Measuring Divisional Performance." *Management Accountant*, May 1971, 147–
   52.
———. "Memorandum Submitted to the Inflation Accounting Committee." *Working
   Paper No. 12*. Manchester: Manchester Business School, 1975.
———. "Profit Maximization via Financial Management." *Management Decision*, Win-
   ter 1969, 6–12.
———. "The Rationale of Cash Flow Accounting." *Analyst*, Dec. 1976, 22–30.
Lee, T. A. "The Accounting Entity Concept, Accounting Standards and Inflation Ac-
   counting." *Accounting and Business Research*, Spring 1980, 176–86.
———. "A Case for Cash Flow Reporting." *Journal of Business Finance*, Summer 1972,
   27–36.
———. *Cash Flow Accounting*. London: Van Nostrand Reinhold, 1984.
———. "Cash Flow Accounting and the Allocation Problems." *Journal of Business
   Finance and Accounting*, Autumn 1982, 341–52.
———. "The Cash Flow Accounting Alternative for Corporate Financial Reporting." In
   Trends in Managerial and Financial Accounting, vol. 1, edited by C. Van Dam,
   63–84. London: Martinus Nijhoff, 1978.
———. "Cash Flow Accounting and Corporate Financial Reporting." In *Essays in British
   Accounting Research*, edited by M. Bromwich and A. Hopwood, 63–78. London:
   Pitman, 1981.
———. "Cash Flow Accounting, Profit and Performance Measurement: A Response to
   a Challenge." *Accounting and Business Research*, Spring 1985, 93–97.
———. "Cash Flows and Net Realizable Values: Further Evidence of the Intuitive Con-
   cepts." *Abacus*, Dec. 1984, 125–37.
———. "The Contribution of Fisher to Cash Flow Accounting." *Journal of Business
   Finance and Accounting*, Autumn 1979, 321–30.
———. "Goodwill: An Example of Will-o'-the-Wisp Accounting." *Accounting and Busi-
   ness Research*, Autumn 1971, 318–28.
———. "Laker Airways: The Cash Flow Truth." *Accountancy*, June 1982, 115–16.
———. "A Note on the Nature and Determination of Income." *Journal of Business
   Finance and Accounting*, Spring 1974, 145–47.
———. *The Private Shareholder and the Corporate Report*. London: Institute of Char-
   tered Accountants in England and Wales, 1977.
———. "Reporting Cash Flows and Net Realizable Values." *Accounting and Business
   Research*, Spring 1981, 163–70.

————. "A Survey of Accountants' Opinions on Cash Flow Reporting." *Abacus*, Dec. 1981, 130–44.

————. "Towards a Practice of Cash Flow Analysis." Discussion Paper 13. Edinburgh: University of Edinburgh, 1981.

————. "What Cash Flow Analysis Says About BL's Finances." *Financial Times*, 23 Oct. 1981, 15.

Lee, T. A., and A. W. Stark. "A Cash Flow Disclosure of Government-Supported Enterprises' Results." *Journal of Business Accounting*, Spring 1984, 1–11.

Lee, T. A., and D. P. Tweedie. *Institutional Use and Understanding of Corporate Financial Information*. London: Institute of Chartered Accountants in England and Wales, 1981.

Loscalzo, William. *Cash Flow Forecasting*. New York: McGraw-Hill, 1982.

Mason, Perry Empey. *Cash Flow Analysis and Funds Statement*. New York: American Institute of Certified Public Accountants, 1961.

Meyer, P. E. "The Accounting Entity." *Abacus*, Dec. 1973, 116–26.

Milling, Bryan E. *Cash Flow Problem Solver. Procedures and Rationales for the Independent Businessman*. Radnor, PA: Chilton, 1981.

Ortina, R. E., and J. A. Largay III. "Pitfalls in Calculating Cash Flow from Operations." *Accounting Review*, Apr. 1985, 314–26.

Paton, W. *Accounting Theory*. Chicago: Accounting Studies Press, 1962.

Revsine, L. *Replacement Cost Accounting*. Englewood Cliffs, NJ: Prentice-Hall, 1973.

Rutherford, B. A. "Cash Flow Reporting and Distributional Allocations: A Note." *Journal of Business Finance and Accounting*, Summer 1983, 313–16.

————. "The Interpretation of Cash Flow Reports and the Other Allocation Problems." *Abacus*, June 1982, 40–49.

Stamp, E. "Financial Reports on Entity: Ex Uno Plures." In *Accounting for a Simplified Firm Owning Depreciable Assets*, edited by R. R. Sterling and A. L. Thomas, 163–80. Houston: Scholar Books, 1979.

————. "Useful Arbitrary Allocations." *Accounting Review*, July 1971, 472–79.

Staubus, G. J. *Making Accounting Decisions*. Houston: Scholars, 1977.

————. "The Relevance of Cash Flows." In *Asset Valuation*, edited by R. R. Sterling. Houston: Scholars, 1971.

————. *A Theory of Accounting to Investors*. Berkeley: University of California Press, 1961.

Sterling, R. R. "In Defense of Accounting in the United States." *Abacus*, Dec. 1966, 180–83.

————. "Earnings Per Share Is a Poor Indicator of Performance." *Omega*, 1974, 11–32.

————. *Theory of the Measurement of Enterprise Income*. Lawrence: University of Kansas Press, 1970.

————. *Towards a Science of Accounting*. Houston: Scholars, 1979.

Thomas, A. L. *The Allocation Problem in Financial Accounting Theory*. Studies in Accounting Research No. 3. Evanston, IL: American Accounting Association, 1969.

————. *The Allocation Problem: Part Two*. Studies in Accounting Research No. 9. Sarasota, FL: American Accounting Association, 1974.

————. *A Behavioral Analysis of Joint-Cost Allocation and Transfer Pricing*. Houston: Stipes Publishing, 1970.

————. "Matching: Up From Our Black Hole." In *Accounting for a Simplified Firm*

Owning Depreciable Assets, edited by R. R. Sterling and A. L. Thomas. Houston: Scholars, 1979.

Tweedie, D. P. "Cash Flows and Realizable Values: The Intuitive Accounting Concepts? An Empirical Test." *Accounting and Business Research*, Winter 1977, 2–13.

Vatter, W. J. *The Fund Theory of Accounting and Its Implications For Financial Reports*. Chicago: University of Chicago Press, 1947.

Whittington, G. "Accounting and Economics." In *Current Issues in Accounting*, edited by B. Carsberg and T. Hope. London: Philip Allan, 1977.

Chapter 4

The Inflation Report

INTRODUCTION

With the ever changing prices of goods and services in the economy, the reliance on the historical cost principle in generally accepted accounting principles leads to a definite distortion of the measurement of the financial position, financial performance, and financial conduct of the firm. The inflation report will remediate these problems by offering the revaluation and a restatement of all the accounts to recognize the changing prices and better reflect the value and performance of the firm. Accordingly this chapter will illustrate the various methods that have been proposed to take into account the impact of changing prices on the financial statements of the firms by presenting the various possible inflation reports that can be reported and disclosed in the financial statements.

PRICE CHANGE MODELS

Various models have been proposed to deal with the effects of changing prices on a firm's financial statements. The debates centers on the merits of the conventional historical cost model versus some form of current value. The differences between the price change models arise from the different attributes to be measured and the units of measure to be used.

Attributes to Be Measured

The attributes of assets and liabilities refer to what is being measured. First we will define four attributes to be measured:

1. *Historical cost* refers to the amount of cash or cash-equivalent paid to acquire an asset, or the amount of cash-equivalent liability.
2. *Replacement cost* refers to the amount of cash or cash-equivalent that would be paid to acquire an equivalent or the same asset currently or that would be received to incur the same liability currently.
3. *Net realizable value* refers to the amount of cash or cash-equivalent that would be obtained by selling the asset currently or that would be paid to redeem the liability currently.
4. *Present or capitalized value* refers to the present value of net cash flows expected to be received from the use of the asset or the net outflows expected to be disbursed to redeem the liability.

Units of Measure

Financial accounting measurements can be made in one of two units of measure: (1) units of money or (2) units of general purchasing power. Similarly, each of the four attributes we have defined is measurable in either units of money or units of general purchasing power. In the United States and in most other countries, conventional financial statements are expressed in units of money. Given the continuous decline of the purchasing power of the dollar, however, another unit of measure—the unit of purchasing power—is frequently presented as a preferable alternative because it recognizes changes in the general price level.

Do not confuse the general price level with either the specific price level or the relative price level. A change in the general price level refers to changes in the prices of all goods and services throughout the economy; the reciprocal of such changes would be a change in the general purchasing power of the monetary unit. A change in the specific price level refers to a change in the price of a particular product or service. Current value accounting differs from historical cost accounting in that the former recognizes changes in the specific price level on the basis of either replacement cost or net realizable value.

Finally, a change in the relative price level of a commodity refers to the part of the specific price change that remains after the effects of the general price-level change have been eliminated. Thus, if all prices increase by 32 percent and the price of a specific good increases by 10 percent, the relative price change is only 20 percent, or $(132/110) - 1$.

All three types of price changes may be incorporated in the asset-valuation and income-determination models. Note that both historical cost and current value are expressed in units of money and that general price-level restatements may be made for both.

Alternative Inflation Reports

The four attributes of all classes of assets and liabilities that may be measured are (1) historical cost, (2) current entry price or replacement cost, (3) current exit price or net realizable value, and (4) capitalized or present value of expected cash flows. The two units of measure that can be used are units of money and units of purchasing power. Combining the four attributes and the two units of measure yields the following eight alternative inflation reports:

1. Inflation report based on historical cost accounting that measures historical cost in units of money.

2. Inflation report based on historical cost accounting that measures replacement cost in units of money.

3. Inflation report based on net realizable value accounting that measures net realizable value in units of money.

4. Inflation report based on present value accounting that measures present value in units of money.

5. Inflation report based on general price level historical cost accounting that measures historical cost in units of purchasing power.

6. Inflation report based on general price level replacement cost accounting that measures replacement cost in units of purchasing power.

7. Inflation report based on general price level net realizable value accounting that measures net realizable value in units of purchasing power.

8. Inflation report based on general price level present value accounting that measures present value in units of purchasing power.

Each of these inflation reports will be illustrated next.

EXAMPLE USED FOR THE ILLUSTRATION OF THE DIFFERENT INFLATION REPORTS

To illustrate the derivation of the inflation report under the different price change models let us consider the simplified case of the Hellenic Company, which was formed on January 1, 2000, to distribute a new product called "KOULA." Capital is composed of $3,000 in equity and $3,000 in liabilities carrying a five percent interest. On January 1, the Hellenic Company began operations by purchasing 600 units of KOULA at $10 per unit. On May 1, the company sold 500 units at $15 per unit. At the end of the year, the company made the following cash payments:

1. Interest = $150
2. Wages = $30
3. Taxes = $100
4. Dividends = $20

Changes in the general and specific price levels for the year 2000 are as follows:

	January 1st	May 1st	December 31st
Replacement Cost	$10	$12	$13
Net Realizable Value	—	$15	$17
General Price Level Index	100	130	156

ALTERNATIVE INFLATION REPORTS EXPRESSED IN UNITS OF MONEY

Inflation Report Based on Historical Cost Accounting

Historical cost accounting, or conventional accounting, is characterized primarily by (1) the use of historical cost as the attribute of the elements of financial statements, (2) the assumption of a stable monetary unit, (3) the matching principle, and (4) the realization principle. The derivation of the income statements and the balance sheet under historical cost accounting is shown, respectively, in Exhibits 4.1 and 4.2. The net profit is equal to $2,220, which is the profit generated by the firm using the assumption of historical costs expressed in units of money. It includes a plowback to the firm of $2,200. The $2,200 represents the income reinvested after distribution to shareholders, bondholders, employees, and the government. It contains $700 in timing errors because (1) it includes in a single figure the operating income and holding gains and losses that are recognized in the current period and that occurred in previous periods and (2) it omits the operating profit and holding gains and losses that occurred in the current period but are recognizable in future periods. It also contains measuring unit errors because (1) it does not take into account changes in the general price level that would have resulted in amounts expressed in units of general purchasing power and (2) by relying on historical cost as the attribute of the elements of financial statements rather than either replacement cost or net realizable value, it does not take into account changes in the specific price level. In summary, historical cost accounting contains timing and measuring unit errors.

Inflation Report Based on Replacement Cost Accounting

Replacement cost accounting is characterized by (1) the use of replacement cost as the attribute of financial statements, (2) the assumption of a stable unit, (3) the realization principle, (4) the dichotomization of realized and unrealized holding gains and losses. The derivation of the income statement and the balance sheet under replacement cost accounting is shown, respectively, in Exhibits 4.1 and 4.2. The net profit amounts to $2,520 which is the net wealth generated by the firm under the assumption of replacement cost expressed in units of money. It includes a plowback to the firm of $2,500. The $2,500 amount represents the income reinvested after distribution to shareholders, bondholders, employees,

Exhibit 4.1
Hellenic Company Income Statements Expressed in Units of Money

INCOME STATEMENTS	HISTORICAL COST	REPLACEMENT COST	NET REALIZED VALUE
REVENUES	$ 7,500(1)	$7,500	$9,200(2)
MINUS EXPENSES:			
A. COST OF MATERIALS	$5,000 (3)	$6,000 (4)	$7,300(5)
B. INTEREST	$150	$150	$150
C. WAGES	$30	$30	$30
OPERATING PROFIT	$2,320	$1,320	$1,720
REALIZED HOLDING GAINS & LOSSES	INCL. ABOVE	$1,000(6)	$1,000
UNREALIZED HOLDING GAINS & LOSSES	NOT APPLICABLE	$300(7)	$300
GENERAL PRICE LEVEL GAINS & LOSSES	NOT APPLICABLE	NOT APPLICABLE	NOT APPLICABLE
NET PROFIT BEFORE TAX	$2,320	$2,620	$3,020
-TAXES	$100	$100	$100
NET PROFIT AFTER TAXES	$2,220	$2,520	$2,920
- DIVIDENDS	$20	$20	$20
RETAINED EARNINGS	$2,200	$2,500	$2,900

(1) $500 \times \$15 = \$7500$
(2) $7500 + (\$17 \times 100) = \$9200$
(3) $500 \times \$10 = \$5000$
(4) $500 \times 12 = \$6000$
(5) $6000 + (\$13 \times 100) = \$7300$
(6) $500 (\$12 - \$10) = \$1000$
(7) $100 (\$13 - \$10) = \$300$

and the government. It contains $400 in timing errors because (1) it omits the operating profit that occurred in the current period but that is realizable in future periods, (2) it includes the operating profit that is recognized in the current period but that occurred in previous periods, (3) it does not take into account changes in the general price level that would have resulted in amounts expressed in units of general purchasing power, and (4) it does take into account changes in the specific price level because it relies on replacement cost as the attribute of the elements of financial statements. In summary, replacement cost accounting contains operation profit timing errors and measuring unit errors.

Exhibit 4.2
Hellenic Company Balance Sheet for the Year Ended December 31, 2000

	HISTORICAL COST	REPLACEMENT COST	NET REALIZABLE VALUE
ASSETS			
CASH	$7,200	$7,200	$7,200
INVENTORY	$1,000	$1,300 a	$1,700 b
TOTAL ASSETS	$8,200	$8,500	$8,900
EQUITIES			
BONDS (10%)	$3,000	$3,000	$3,000
CAPITAL	$3,000	$3,000	$3,000
RETAINED EARNINGS			
REALIZED	$2,200	$2,200 c	$2,200 c
UNREALIZED	(NOT APPLICABLE)	$300	$700 d
TOTAL EQUITIES	$8,200	$8,500	$8,900

a. $100 \times \$13 = \$1,300$
b. $100 \times \$17 = \$1,700$
c. May be divided into Current Operating Profit ($1,200) and Realized Holding Gains and Losses ($1,000)
d. Unrealized Operating Gain $400 ($1,700 − $1,300) + Unrealized Holding Gain $300

Inflation Report Based on Net Realizable Value Accounting

Net realizable value accounting is characterized primarily by (1) the use of net realizable value as the attribute of the elements of financial statements, (2) the assumption of a stable monetary unit, (3) the abandonment of the realization principle, and (4) the dichotomization of operating income and holding gains and losses. The derivation of the income statement and the value added statement under net realizable value accounting is shown, respectively, in Exhibits 4.1 and 4.2. The net profit amounts to $2,920. It includes a plowback to the firm of $2,900. The $2,900 amount represents the income reinvested after distribution to shareholders, bondholders, employers, and the government. It does not contain any timing errors because (1) it reports all operating profit and holding gains and losses in the same period in which they occur and (2) it excludes all operating and holding gains and losses occurring in previous periods. It contains measuring unit errors because (1) it does not take into account changes in the general price level and (2) it does take into account changes in the specific price level because it relies on net realizable value as the attribute of the elements of financial statements. In summary, net realizable value accounting contains no timing errors but contains measuring unit errors.

ALTERNATIVE INFLATION REPORTS EXPRESSED IN UNITS OF GENERAL PURCHASING POWER

Inflation Report Based on General Price-Level Adjusted Historical Cost Accounting

General price-level adjusted historical cost accounting is characterized primarily by (1) the use of historical cost as the attribute of the elements of financial statements, (2) the use of units of general purchasing power as the unit of measure, (3) the matching principle, and (4) the realization principle. The derivation of the income statement and the balance sheet under general price-level adjusted historical cost accounting is shown, respectively, in Exhibits 4.3, 4.4, and 4.5. The net profit amounts to $1,100. It includes a plowback of $1,080. The $1,080 amount represents the income reinvested after distribution to shareholders, bondholders, employees, and the government. It contains the same type of timing errors as under historical cost accounting. It contains no measuring unit errors because it does take into account changes in the general price level. It does not, however, take into account changes in the specific price level because it relies on historical cost as the attribute of the elements of financial statements rather than on replacement cost or net realizable value. In summary, the net value under general price-level adjusted historical cost accounting contains timing errors but does not contain measuring unit errors.

Inflation Report Based on General Price-Level Adjusted Replacement Cost Accounting

General price-level adjusted replacement cost accounting is characterized primarily by (1) the use of replacement cost as the attribute of the elements of financial statements, (2) the use of units of general purchasing power as the unit measure, (3) the realization principle, (4) the dichotomization of operating income and real realized holding gains and losses, and (5) the dichotomization of real realized and real unrealized holding gains and losses. The derivation of the income statement and the balance sheet under general price-level adjusted replacement cost accounting appears, respectively, in Exhibits 4.3 and 4.5. The net profit amounts to $840. It includes a plowback of $820. The $820 amount represents the income reinvested after distribution to shareholders, bondholders, employees, and the government. It contains the same type of timing errors found under replacement cost accounting. It contains no measuring unit errors because it takes into account changes in the general price level. In addition, it takes into account changes in the specific price level because it adopts replacement cost as the attribute of the elements of financial statements. In summary, general price-level adjusted replacement cost contains timing errors but contains no measuring unit errors.

Exhibit 4.3
Hellenic Company Income Statements Expressed in Units of Purchasing Power

INCOME STATEMENTS	HISTORICAL COST	REPLACEMENT COST	NET REALIZED VALUE
REVENUES	$ 9,000(1)	$9,000	$10,700(2)
MINUS EXPENSES:			
A. COST OF MATERIALS	$7,800 (3)	$7,200 (4)	$8,500(5)
B. INTEREST	$150	$150	$150
C. WAGES	$30	$30	$30
OPERATING PROFIT	$1,020	$1,620	$2,020
REALIZED HOLDING GAINS & LOSSES	INCL. ABOVE	($600) (6)	($600)
UNREALIZED HOLDING GAINS & LOSSES	NOT APPLICABLE	($260) (7)	($260)
GENERAL PRICE LEVEL GAINS & LOSSES	$180 (8)	$180	$180
NET PROFIT BEFORE TAX	$1,200	$940	$1,340
-TAXES	$100	$100	$100
NET PROFIT AFTER TAXES	$1,100	$840	$1,240
- DIVIDENDS	$20	$20	$20
RETAINED EARNINGS	$1,080	$820	$1,220

(1) $7,500 × 156/130 = $9,000
(2) 9,000 + ($17 × 100 units) = $10,700
(3) $5,000 × 156/100 = $7,800
(4) $6,000 × 156/130 = $7,200
(5) $7,200 + ($13 × 100 units) = $8,500
(6) [(12 × 156/130) − ($10 × 156/100)] × 500 = ($600)
(7) [13 − ($10 × 156/100)] × 100 units = ($260)
(8) See Exhibit 4.4.

Inflation Report Based on General Price-Level Adjusted Net Realizable Value Accounting

General price-level adjusted net realizable value accounting is characterized primarily by (1) the use of net realizable value as the attribute of the elements of financial statements, (2) the use of units of general purchasing power as the unit of measure, (3) the abandonment of the realization principle, (4) the dichotomization of operation income and real holding gains and losses, and (5) the dichotomization of the real realized and unrealized gains and losses. The

Exhibit 4.4
General Price Level Gain or Loss, December 31, 2000

	UNADJUSTED	CONVERSION FACTOR	ADJUSTED
NET-MONETARY ASSETS ON JAN. 1, 2000	$3,000	156/ 100	$4,680
ADD MONETARY RECEIPTS DURING 2000: SALES	$7,500	156/ 100	$9,000
NET- MONETARY ITEMS	$10,500		$13,680
LESS MONETARY PAYMENTS:			
PURCHASES	$6,000	156/ 100	$9,360
INTEREST	$150	156/ 156	$150
WAGES	$30	156/ 156	$30
TAXES	$100	156/ 156	$100
DIVIDENDS	$20	156/ 156	$20
TOTAL	$6,300		$9,660
COMPUTED NET- MONETARY ASSETS, DEC. 31, 2000			$4,020
ACTUAL NET- MONETARY ASSETS, DEC. 31, 2000			$4,200
GENERAL PRICE LEVEL GAIN			$180

derivation of the income statement and the value added statement under general price-level adjusted net realizable value accounting appears, respectively, in Exhibits 4.3, 4.4, and 4.5. The net profit amounts to $1,240. It includes a plowback of $1,220. The $1,220 amount represents the income reinvested after distribution to shareholders, bondholders, employees, and the government. It contains no timing errors and no measuring unit errors.

COMPARISON BETWEEN THE INFLATION REPORTS

The application of the different price change models resulted in different values for the net value added. As shown in Exhibit 4.6, there are six different values for net value added. These values are evaluated in terms of whether or not both timing error and measuring unit error are eliminated. The profit of $1,220 under general price-level adjusted net realizable value accounting contains nothing from the two errors. It is the ideal measure under a situation of organized and proper liquidation. Another useful measure is the net value added of $820 obtained under general price-level adjusted replacement cost accounting. It indicates the profit created under operating rather than liquidating conditions after accounting for both changes in the general and specific price level.

Exhibit 4.5
Hellenic Company General Price-Level Balance Sheet for the Year Ended December 31, 2000

	HISTORICAL COST	REPLACEMENT COST	NET REALIZABLE VALUE
ASSETS			
CASH	$7,200	$7,200	$7,200
INVENTORY	$1,560a	$1,300	$1,700
TOTAL ASSETS	$8,760	$8,500	$8,900
EQUITIES			
BONDS (10%)	$3,000	$3,000	$3,000
CAPITAL	$4680 b	$4,680	$4,680
RETAINED EARNINGS			
REALIZED	$900	$900	$900
UNREALIZED	(NOT APPLICABLE)	($260)	$140 c
GENERAL PRICE-LEVEL			
GAIN OR LOSS	$180	$180	$180
TOTAL EQUITIES	$8,760	$8,500	$8,900

a. $1,000 \times 156/100 = \$1,560$
b. $3,000 \times 156/100 = \$4,680$
c. Unrealized Operating Gain $400 ($1,700 - $1,300) -$ Unrealized Holding Loss $260 = \$140$

Whatever the choice made of these six measures, it is important for the student and the user to understand the various assumptions made in the choice of the attribute and the choice of the measuring unit.

TOWARD A SOLUTION TO THE PRODUCTION OF INFLATION REPORTS

Early Attempts

Long recognized as a problem in the accounting literature, the issue of accounting for changing prices has been extensively studied by the various accounting standard-setting bodies. The American Institute of Certified Public Accountants (AICPA) Committee on Accounting Procedures in 1947, 1948, and 1953[1] and Accounting Principles Board (APB) Opinion No. 6 entitled *Status of Accounting Research Bulletins*, all examined the problems related to changes in the general price level without success. These attempts were followed by the AICPA's publication of Accounting Research Study No. 6, *Reporting the Financial Effects of Price-Level Changes*, in 1963, and by APB Statement No. 3, *Financial Statements Restated for General Price-Level Changes*, in June 1969. Both documents recommended the supplemental disclosure of general price-level information without success. The Financial Accounting Standards Board

Exhibit 4.6
Error Type Analysis

| ACCOUNTING MODEL | NET INCOME | TIMING ERROR | | MEASURING UNIT ERRORS |
		OPERATING PROFIT	HOLDING PROFIT	
1. HISTORICAL COST ACCOUNTING	$2,200	YES	YES	YES
2. REPLACEMENT COST ACCOUNTING	$2,500	YES	ELIMINATED	YES
3. NET REALIZABLE VALUE ACCOUNTING	$2,900	ELIMINATED	ELIMINATED	ELIMINATED
4. GENERAL PRICE LEVEL ADJUSTED, HISTORICAL COST ACCOUNTING	$1,080	YES	YES	ELIMINATED
5. GENERAL PRICE LEVEL ADJUSTED, REPLACEMENT COST ACCOUNTING	$820	YES	ELIMINATED	ELIMINATED
6. GENERAL PRICE LEVEL ADJUSTED, NET REALIZABLE VALUE ACCOUNTING	$1,220	ELIMINATED	ELIMINATED	ELIMINATED

(FASB) approached the price-level issue at a time when inflation was a major concern in the economy. After issuing a Discussion Memorandum (*Reporting the Effects of General Price-Level Changes in Financial Statements*) on February 15, 1974, an Exposure Draft (*Financial Reporting in Units of General Purchasing Power*) on December 31, 1974, a Research Report (*Field Tests of Financial Reporting in Units of General Purchasing Power*) in May 1977, another Exposure Draft (*Financial Reporting and Changing Prices*) on December 28, 1978, and a supplemental Exposure Draft to the proposed statement on general purchasing-power adjustments (*Constant-Dollar-Purchasing*) on March 2, 1979, the Board issued FASB Statement No. 33, *Financial Reporting and Changing Prices*, in September 1979, calling for information on the effects of both general inflation and specific price changes.

Progress on Financial Reporting and Changing Prices

FASB Statement No. 33 is the result of years of attempts by the diverse standard-setting bodies to develop methods of reporting the effects of inflation on earnings and assets. In its deliberations, the FASB considered a variety of accounting systems[2] which can be grouped under the following headings:

1. Measuring of inventory and property, plant, and equipment

   a. historical cost

   b. current reproduction cost

   c. current replacement cost

   d. net realizable value

   e. net present value of expected future cash flows (value in use)

   f. recoverable amount

   g. current cost

   h. value of business (current cost of lower recoverable amount)

2. Concepts of capital maintenance

   a. financial capital maintenance

   b. physical capital maintenance (the maintenance of operating capacity)

3. Measuring units

   a. measurements in nominal dollars

   b. measurements in constant dollars

This list suggests that the FASB examined all of the alternative asset-value income-determination models presented in this chapter. The Board concluded, however, that supplementary information should be presented according to historical cost/constant-dollar accounting and current-cost accounting. More specifically, the FASB now requires major companies to disclose the effects of both general inflation and specific price changes as supplementary information in their published annual reports. Major companies are defined as companies with assets of more than $1 billion (after deducting accumulated depreciation) or with inventory and property, plant, and equipment (before deducting accumulated depreciation) of more than $125 million.

Specifically, FASB Statement No. 33 requires major firms to report

1. Constant-dollar disclosures (current year)

   a. Information on income from continuing operations for the current fiscal year, on a historical cost/constant-dollar basis

   b. The general purchasing-power gain or loss on net monetary items for the current fiscal year, the general purchasing-power gain or loss on net monetary items shall *not* be included in income from continuing operations

2. Current-cost disclosures (current year)

   a. Information on income from continuing operations for the current fiscal year, on a current-cost basis

   b. The current-cost amounts of inventory and property, plant, and equipment at the end of the current fiscal year

   c. Increases or decreases for the current fiscal year in the current-cost amounts of inventory and property, plant, and equipment, net of inflation; the increases or decreases in current-cost amounts shall *not* be included in income from continuing operations.

3. Five-year summary data

   a. Net sales and other operating revenues

   b. Historical cost/constant-dollar information

     (1) Income from continuing operations

     (2) Income per common share from continuing operations

     (3) Net assets at fiscal year-end

   c. Current-cost information (except for individual years in which the information was excluded from the current-year disclosures)

     (1) Income from continuing operations

     (2) Income per common share from continuing operations

     (3) Net assets at fiscal year-cnd

     (4) Increases or decreases for the current fiscal year in the current-cost amounts of inventory and property, plant, and equipment, net of inflation

   d. Other information

     (1) General purchasing-power gain or loss on net monetary items

     (2) Cash dividends declared per common share

     (3) Market price per common share at fiscal year-end

4. Limitation

   a. Recoverable amount used to value the asset whenever the recoverable amount of an asset is less than either the constant-dollar value or the current-cost value

   b. "Recoverable amount" means the current value of the net cash flow expected to be realized from the use or sale of the asset

5. Methodology

   a. The constant-dollar method should use the Consumer Price Index for All Urban Consumers

   b. The current-cost method may use internally or externally developed specific price indices or evidence, such as vendor invoice prices or price lists, to determine the current cost of an asset; the method selected should be based on availability and cost, and should be applied consistently

   c. The constant-dollar amounts should be based on average-for-the-year indices

   d. The current costs should be based on average current costs of the period for the restatement of items required to compute operating income (cost of goods sold, depreciation, and depletion), and should be restated at end-of-period current costs, net of general inflation, for the measurement of increases or decreases in inventory, plant, property, and equipment; the latter statement requires the use of year-end current costs restated in average-for-the-period constant dollars[3]

FASB Statement No. 33 also provides the following information to explain minimum disclosure requirements for constant-dollar and current-cost data:

1. *Income from continuing operations* is income after applicable income taxes, excluding the results of discontinued operations, extraordinary items, and the cumulative effects of accounting changes. If none of the foregoing is present for a business enterprise, income from continuing operations is identical to *net income.*

2. The general purchasing-power gain or loss on net monetary items and the increase or decrease in current-cost amounts are excluded from income from continuing operations.

3. Current-cost information need not be disclosed if it is not materially different from constant-dollar information. The reasons for the omission of current-cost information must be disclosed in notes to the supplemental information.

4. Information relating to income from continuing operations may be presented either in the format of a conventional income statement or in a reconciliation format that discloses adjustments to income from continuing operations in the historical cost/nominal-dollar income statement.

5. The *average* Consumer Price Index for All Urban Consumers (CPI-U) is used for business enterprises that present only the minimum constant-dollar data for a fiscal year. If an enterprise presents comprehensive financial statements on a constant-dollar basis, either the *average* or the *year-end* CPI-U may be used.

6. An enterprise that presents only the minimum data required by FASB Statement No. 33 need not restate any financial statement amounts other than inventories, plant assets, cost of goods sold, and depreciation, depletion, and amortization expenses.

7. If the historical cost/constant-dollar amounts or the current-cost amounts of inventories and plant assets exceed the recoverable amounts of those assets, all data required by FASB Statement No. 33 must be presented on the basis of the low recoverable amounts. The recoverable amount of an asset *expected to be sold* is the net realizable value of the asset (expected sales proceeds less costs of completion and disposal). The recoverable amount of an asset *in continuing use* is its value in use (net present value of future cash inflows, including ultimate proceeds on disposal). Thus, *value in use* is synonymous with *direct valuation.*

8. The current costs of inventories, plant assets, cost of goods sold, and depreciation, depletion, and amortization expense may be determined by one of the following methods:

   a. indexation by use of either externally or internally developed specific-pricing indices,

   b. direct pricing by use of current invoice prices; vendor price lists, quotations, or estimates; or standard manufacturing costs that reflect current cost.[4]

Exhibits 4.7, 4.8, and 4.9 illustrate these FASB requirements. Thus, FASB Statement No. 33 requires two supplemental income computations—one dealing

Exhibit 4.7
Statement of Income from Continuing Operations Adjusted for Changing Prices
for the Year Ended December 31, 19X6 (in thousands of average 19X5 dollars)

	As Reported in the Primary statements	Adjusted for General Inflation	Adjusted for Changes in Specific Prices (Current Costs)
Net sales and other operating revenues	$500,000	$500,000	$500,000
Cost of goods sold	$400,000	$450,000	$455,000
Depreciation and amortization expenses	$20,000	$25,000	$26,000
Other operating expenses	$40,000	$40,000	$40,000
Interest expense	$15,000	$15,000	$15,000
Provision for income taxes	$20,000	$20,000	$20,000
Total Expenses	$495,000	$550,000	$556,000
Income (loss) from continuing operations	$5,000	($50,000)	($56,000)
Gain from decline in general purchasing power of net amounts owed		$5,000	$5,000
Increase in specific prices (current costs) of inventories and property, plant, and equipment held during the year [a]			$30,000
Effect of increase in general price level			$20,000
Excess of increase in specific prices over increase in general price level			$10,000

a. As of December 31, 19X6, current cost of inventory is $55,000 and current cost of property, plant, and equipment, net of accumulated depreciation, is $80,000.

with the effects of general inflation and the other dealing with specific price changes. Both types of information are intended to help users make decisions about investment, lending, and other matters in the following specific ways:

1. *Assessment of future cash flows*: Present financial statements include measurements of expenses and assets at historical prices. When prices are changing, measurements that reflect current prices are likely to provide useful information for the assessment of future cash flows.

2. *Assessment of enterprise performance*: The worth of an enterprise can be increased as a result of the prudent timing of asset purchases when prices are changing. That increase is one aspect of performance, even though it may be distinguished from

Exhibit 4.8

Five-Year Comparison of Selected Supplemental Financial Data Adjusted for Changing Prices (in thousands of average 19X3 dollars)

| | Year Ended December 31 | | | | |
	19X1	19X2	19X3	19X4	19X5
Net sales and other operating revenues	$350,000	$400,000	$420,000	$450,000	$500,000
Historical-cost information adjusted for general inflation					
Income (loss) from continuing operations				$29,000	$20,000
Income (loss) from continuing operations per common share				($2)	($2)
Net assets at year-end				$100,000	$120,000
Current-cost information					
Income (loss) from continuing operations				($100,000)	($26,000)
Income (loss) from continuing operations per common share				($1)	($2.6)
Excess of increase in specific prices over increase in general price-level				$5,000	$10,000
Net assets at year-end				$120,000	$130,000
Gain from decline in general purchasing power of net amounts owed				$4,500	$5,000
Cash dividends declared per common share	$2.00	$2.05	$2.10	$2.15	$2.20
Market price per common share at year-end	$40	$30	$45	$40	$39
Average consumer price	$170.5	$181.5	$195.4	$205.0	$220.9

operating performance. Measurements that reflect current prices can provide a basis for creating opportunities for earning cash flows.

3. *Assessment of the erosion of operating capability*: An enterprise typically must hold minimum quantities of inventory, property, plant, equipment, and other assets to maintain its ability to provide goods and services. When the prices of those assets are increasing, larger amounts of money must be invested to maintain the previous levels of output. Information on the current prices of resources that are used to generate revenues can help users assess the extent to which and the manner in which operating capability has been maintained.

4. *Assessment of the erosion of general purchasing power*: When general price levels are increasing, larger amounts of money are required to maintain a fixed amount of purchasing power. Investors typically are concerned with assessing whether or not an enterprise has maintained the purchasing power of its capital. Financial information that reflects changes in general purchasing power can help investors make that assessment.[5]

Obviously, because it requires the presentation of both general price-level and specific price-level information, FASB Statement No. 33 is a step forward. It falls short, however, of a total solution, which would require the use of general price-level-restated/current-cost accounting in conjunction with general price-level-restated/replacement accounting or with general price-level-restated/net-realizable-value accounting. Moreover, some of the specific requirements discussed in FASB Statement No. 33 do not pertain to most situations.[6]

Exhibit 4.9

Statement of Income from Continuing Operations Adjusted for Changing Prices for the Year Ended December 31, 19X6 (in thousands of average 19X5 dollars)

Income from continuing operations, as reported on the income statement		$5,000
Adjusted to restate costs for the effect of general inflation	($50,000)	
Cost of goods sold	$5,000	$55,000
Depreciation and amortization expense		
Loss from continuing operations adjusted for general inflation		$50,000
adjusted to reflect the difference between general inflation and changes in specific prices (current costs)	($5,000)	
Cost of goods sold	($1,000)	($6,000)
Loss from continuing operations adjusted for changes in specific prices		($56,000)
Gain from decline in general purchasing power of net amounts owed		$5,000
Increase in specific prices (current costs) of inventories and property, plant, and equipment held during the year[a]		$30,000
Effect of increase in general price level		$20,000
Excess of increase in specific prices over increase in general price level		$10,000

a. As of December 31, 19X6, current cost of inventory is $55,000 and current cost of property, plant, and equipment, net of accumulated depreciation, is $80,000.

CONCLUSIONS

Given the existence of four measurable attributes of the elements of financial statements and two units of measure in which to express these attributes, eight alternative asset-valuation and income-determination models exist:

1. historical-cost accounting

2. replacement-cost accounting

3. net-realizable-value accounting

4. present-value accounting

5. general price-level-adjusted/historical-cost accounting

6. general price-level-adjusted/replacement-cost accounting

7. general price-level-adjusted/net-realizable-value accounting

8. general price-level-adjusted/present-value accounting

In this chapter, we have compared and evaluated six of these models on the basis of four criteria: (1) avoidance of timing errors, (2) avoidance of measuring-unit errors (3) interpretability, and (4) relevance as measures of command of goods (COG).

Although the present-value models are conceptually preferable, they were not included in our comparison and evaluation because their subjectivity and the uncertainty surrounding their use make their implementation currently impractical.

Our comparison of the remaining models revealed that general price-level-adjuster/net-realizable-value accounting is the only model to meet each of the four criteria set forth in the chapter and therefore most closely represents a preferred-income position. FASB Statement No. 33, *Financial Reporting and Changing Prices*, falls short of adopting this solution and, instead, requires the disclosure of supplemental information on the effects of both general inflation and specific price changes.

NOTES

1. AICPA Committee on Accounting Procedures, Accounting Research Bulletin No. 33, *Depreciation and High Costs* (New York: AICPA, Dec. 1944); AICPA Committee on Accounting Procedures, Accounting Research Bulletin No. 43, *Restatement and Revision of Accounting Research, Bulletins*, ch. 9, sec. A (New York: AICPA, June 1953).

2. FASB, Statement No. 33, *Financial Reporting and Changing Prices* (Stamford, CT: FASB, Sept. 1979), pp. 47–48.

3. Ibid., paragraphs 29, 30, 35, 51, and 52.

4. Ibid., paragraphs 9, 11, 12, 14, 17, 20, and 22.

5. Ibid., paragraphs 1–21.

6. Several FASB pronouncements dealing with specific situations have been issued subsequent to FASB Statement No. 33. These include FASB Statement No. 39, *Financial Reporting and Changing Prices: Specialized Assets-Mining and Oil and Gas* (Oct. 1980); FASB Statement No. 40, *Financial Reporting and Changing Prices: Specialized Assets-Timberlands and Growing Timber* (Nov. 1980); FASB Statement No. 41, *Financial Reporting and Changing Prices: Specialized Assets-Income-Producing Real Estate* (Nov. 1980), FASB Statement No. 46, *Financial Reporting and Changing Prices: Specialized Assets-Motion Picture Films* (Mar. 1981); and FASB Statement No. 89, *Financial Reporting and Changing Prices* (Dec. 1989).

REFERENCES

Basu, S., and J. R. Hanna. *Inflation Accounting: Alternatives, Implementation Issues, and Some Empirical Evidence*. Hamilton, Ontario: The Society of Management Accountants of Canada, 1977.

Chambers, R. J. *Accounting, Evaluation, and Economic Behavior.* Englewood Cliffs, NJ: Prentice-Hall, 1966.

———. "NOD, COG, and PuPu: See How Inflation Teases!" *Journal of Accountancy,* Sept. 1975, 56–62.

Edwards, E. O., and P. W. Bell. *The Theory and Measurement of Business Income.* Berkeley: University of California Press, 1961.

Gynther, R. S. "Capital Maintenance, Price Changes, and Profit Determination." *Accounting Review,* Oct. 1970, 712–30.

Hanna, J. R. *Accounting-Income Models: An Application and Evaluation.* Special Study No. 8. Toronto: The Society of Management Accountants of Canada, July 1974.

Kerr, Jean St. G. "Three Concepts of Business Income." In *An Income Approach to Accounting Theory,* edited by Sidney Davidson et al., 40–48. Englewood Cliffs, NJ: Prentice-Hall, 1964.

Louderback, J. G. "Projectability as a Criterion for Income Determination Methods." *Accounting Review,* Apr. 1971, 298–305.

Parker, P. W., and P.M.D Gibbs. "Accounting for Inflation: Recent Proposals and Their Effects." *Journal of the Institute of Actuaries,* Dec. 1974, 1–10.

Revsine, L. and J. J. Weygandt. "Accounting for Inflation: The Controversy." *Journal of Accountancy,* Oct. 1974, 72–78.

Rosen, L. S. *Current-Value Accounting and Price-Level Restatements.* Toronto: Canadian Institute of Chartered Accountants, 1972.

Rosenfield, Paul. "Accounting for Inflation: A Field Test." *Journal of Accountancy,* June 1969, 45–50.

———. "CPP Accounting: Relevance and Interpretability." *Journal of Accountancy,* Aug. 1975, 52–60.

———. "The Confusion Between General Price-Level Restatement and Current-Value Accounting." *Journal of Accountancy,* Oct. 1972, 63–68.

Sterling, Robert R. "Relevant Financial Reporting in an Age of Price Changes." *Journal of Accountancy,* Feb. 1975, 42–51.

———. *Theory of Measurement of Enterprise Income.* Lawrence: University of Kansas Press, 1970.

Wolk, H. L. "An Illustration of Four Price-Level Approaches to Income Measurement." In *Accounting Education: Problems and Prospects,* edited by J. Don Edwards, 415–23. Sarasota, FL: Amen Accounting Association, 1974.

Zeff, S. A. "Replacement Cost: Member of the Family, Welcome Guest, or Intruder?" *Accounting Review,* Oct. 1962, 611–25.

Chapter 5 _____

The Value Added Report

INTRODUCTION

Because of a general focus on the shareholder as the main target of financial information, the income statement, with its reporting of financial performance, has been at the center of corporate reporting culture in the U.S. A possible challenge to the income statement which has already found a certain degree of acceptance in the U.K., France, Germany, South Africa, and Australia, to name a few countries, is the value added report. Basically, the value added report is an accounting report of the wealth created by the firm and the manner in which this wealth has been distributed. It is, therefore, a report on wealth measurement and distribution that can be interesting not only to the shareholders but to all the other stakeholders, namely, the bondholders, the employees, and the government.[1-3] The value added report can be traced back to the U.S. Treasury in the eighteenth century.[4] It remained the subject of debate, and, at various times, attempts or suggestions were made to include it in financial accounting practice.[5] The emergence and introduction of value added taxation in the European countries gave impetus to value added reporting, although the new type of tax did not require the computation of a value added statement.

The value added concept was given serious attention in the late 1970s in various European countries. It reached great popularity in the United Kingdom with the publication of the Corporate Report, a discussion paper published by the Accounting Standards Steering Committee (now the Accounting Standards Committee) in August 1975.[6] The committee recommended, among other things, a statement of value added showing how the benefits of the efforts of an enterprise are shared by employees, providers of capital, the state, and reinvestment. The rationale for the value added statement is contained in the following paragraphs:

6.7. The simplest and most immediate way of putting profit into proper perspective vis-a-vis the whole enterprise as a collective effort by capital, management and employees is by presentation of a statement of value added (that is, sales income less materials and services purchased). Value added (that is, sales income less materials and services purchased) is the wealth the reporting entity has been able to create by its own and its employees' efforts. This statement would show how value added has been used to pay those contributing to its creation. It usefully elaborates on the profit and loss account and in time may come to be regarded as a preferable way of describing performance.[7]

6.10. The statement of value added provides a useful measure to help in gauging performance and activity. The figure of value added can be a pointer to the net output of the firm; and by relating other key figures (for example, capital employed and employee costs) significant indicators of performance may be obtained.[8]

The recommendation was obviously accepted; one of the legislative proposals contained in the 1977 U.K. government report, The Future of Company Reports, was for a statement of value added.[9] What followed was an increasing number of companies each year producing value added statements. One survey reported in 1980 that more than one-fifth of the largest U.K. companies disclosed value added statements.[10] The growth of value added reporting was helped by trade union support of the concept. A document produced by one of the trade unions stated, "The Federation therefor aims to encourage the use of the added value as a discipline, so that all managers, with or without experience of accounting practices, will appreciate the financial environment within which decisions affecting manpower are taken.[11]

To the labor movement, the value added report was deemed a good vehicle for information disclosure and a basis for determining wages and rewards— what is termed value added incentive payment scheme (VAIPS).[12] In addition to these uses, Stuart Burchell, Colin Clubb, and Anthony Hopwood[13] mention its occasional use in the context of the performance of British industry,[14] in reforming company-wide profit-sharing schemes,[15] and in facilitating financial performance analysis.[16] Aware of these developments, the Institute of Chartered Accountants in England and Wales,[17] the Institute of Chartered Accountants of Scotland,[18] the Institute of Cost and Management Accountants,[19] and the Association of Certified Accountants[20] produced research reports on the value added concept.

THE VALUE ADDED MODEL

The Value Added Concept

Value added refers to the increase in wealth generated by the productive use of the firm's resources before its allocation among shareholders, bondholders, workers, and the government. Thus, while the profit is the final return earned by the shareholders, the value added refers to the total return earned by the team of workers, capital providers, and the government. The value added can be determined by adding pretax profit to payroll costs and interest charges. Another way of computing value added is to deduct bought-in costs from sales revenues where these costs represent all costs and expenses incurred in buying goods and services from other firms. As an example of value added, let's assume that Manufacturer 1 has determined to sell a product at $100. The $100 does not constitute the value added if the manufacturer has bought goods and services from Manufacturer 2 for $40. In such as case, Manufacturer 1 should show a value added of $60 ($100 − $40) as a measure of wealth creation in his or her going concern. All things being equal, value added is an aggregation of all of the total wealth created in a given economy.

Value Added Equation and Examples

The value added statement may be conceived as a modified version of the income statement. Consequently, it can be derived from the income statement as follows:

Step 1: The income statement computes retained earnings as a difference between sales revenue, on the one hand, and costs and dividends, on the other hand:

$$R = S - B - DP - W - I - DD - T \tag{1}$$

where

R = retained earnings
S = sales revenue
B = bought-in materials and services
DP = depreciation
W = wages
I = interest
DD = dividends
T = taxes

Step 2: The value added equation can be obtained by rearranging the profit equation as

$$S - B = W + I + DP + DD + T + R \tag{2}$$

or

$$S - B - DP = W + I + DD + T + R \tag{3}$$

Exhibit 5.1
Deriving the Value Added Statement

A. The conventional income statement of a company for 19x8 was

Sales		$3,000,000
Less: Materials Used	$1,200,000	
Wages	400,000	
Services Purchased	600,000	
Interest Paid	120,000	
Depreciation	80,000	
Profit Before Tax		600,000
Income Tax (assume a 50% tax rate)		300,000
Profit After Tax		300,000
Less Dividend Payable		100,000
Retained Earnings for the Year		200,000

B. A value-added statement for the same year would be

Sales		$3,000,000
Less: Bought-in Materials and Services and Depreciation		1,880,000
Value Added Available for Distribution or Retention		1,120,000
Applied as Follows		
To Employees		$400,000
To Providers of Capital		
Interest	$120,000	
Dividends	100,000	220,000
To Government		300,000
Retained Earnings		200,000
Value Added		1,120,000

Equation 2 expresses the gross value added method. Equation 3 expresses the net value added method. In both cases, the left part of the equation shows the value added among the groups involved in the managerial production team (the workers, the shareholders, the bondholders, and the government). The right-hand side is also known as the additive method and the left-hand side the subtractive method. Given the lack of mandatory uniform guidelines, variations in the treatment of some items do, however, exist.

Exhibit 5.1 shows how the value added statement can be derived from a regular income statement. The company in this example deducted bought-in materials, services, and depreciation from sales to arrive at a value added of $1,120,000. The $1,120,000 was divided among the team of workers ($400,000), shareholders ($100,000), bondholders and creditors ($120,000), and the government ($300,000), leaving $200,000 for retained earnings.

Variations among countries depend on the construction of the income statement in each country as the value added report is just a restructuring of the income statement to determine the wealth created and how that wealth was distributed. Examples of British value added statements are shown in Exhibits

5.2 and 5.3. Similarly examples of French value added statements and income statement are shown in Exhibits 5.4, 5.5, and 5.6.

EVALUATION OF VALUE ADDED REPORTING

Although the concept of value added reporting has not yet been widely used, a number of authors have examined some of the benefits and limitations associated with it.

Advantages of Value Added Reporting

The advantages of value added reporting stem basically from the multidimensional scope of the technique when compared to the conventional mode of reporting the financial affairs of a going concern. Some of the most cited advantages follow.

Value added reporting generates a good organizational climate for workers by highlighting their importance to the final results of the firm. The disclosure of the value added statement should lead to an increased favorable and positive attitude by employees toward their companies. Employees who feel as if they are major participants in the firm may turn out higher-quality work, cooperate more fully, and identify with the company more closely.

Value added reporting may provide a more practical way of introducing productivity bonus increases and link rewards to changes in the value added amounts.[21]

Value added based ratios may act as good diagnostic and predictive cues. In other words, they may be useful in detecting or predicting economic events of importance to the firm.[22–25]

Value added reporting is more congruent with the concepts used to measure national income and may create a useful link to the macroeconomic databases and techniques used by economists. It is useful to government for measuring national income, which involves aggregating (among other things) the value added (net output) of firms. Basically,

the reason why value added rather than sales or the sales value of production (both measures of gross output) is used is to avoid "double counting" in the aggregation process, since the cost of materials and services which would be included in the gross output measures of one firm will probably already have been included in the gross output measures of its supplier. Hence national income, if it involved aggregating gross outputs would be a function of the degree of vertical integration in the economy. Thus, value added information from firms forms a useful function in macro-economic measurement and forecasting, from government's point of view.[26]

In line with this, value added reporting will presumably be useful to individual economists in constructing and testing explanatory models of the economy.

Exhibit 5.2
1985 Value Added Statement, Imperial Chemical Industries

SOURCES AND DISPOSAL OF VALUE ADDED

	Notes	1985 £m	1984 £m	Percentage change
SOURCES OF INCOME				
Sales turnover		10,725	9,909	+ 8%
Royalties and other trading income		142	116	+ 22%
Less: materials and services used		-7,560	-6,845	+ 10%
VALUE ADDED BY MANUFACTURING AND TRADING ACTIVITIES		3,307	3,180	+ 4%
Share of profits less losses of related companies and amounts written off investments		56	71	- 21%
TOTAL VALUE ADDED		3,363	3,251	+ 3%
DISPOSAL OF TOTAL VALUE ADDED				
EMPLOYEES[1]				
Pay, plus pension and national insurance		1,835	1,647	
contributions, and severance costs		48	58	
Profit-sharing bonus[2]		1,883	1,705	+ 10%
GOVERNMENTS		308	373	
Corporate taxes[3]		-28	-28	
Less: grants		280	345	- 19%
PROVIDERS OF CAPITAL		122	100	
Interest cost of net borrowings		214	186	
Dividends to stockholders		52	56	
Minority shareholders in subsidiaries		388	342	+ 13%
RE-INVESTMENT IN THE BUSINESS				
Depreciation and provisions in respect of		514	460	
extraordinary items		298	399	
Profit retained		298	399	
		812	859	- 5%
TOTAL DISPOSAL		3,363	3,251	

Notes:
1. The average number of employees in the Group worldwide increased by 3 percent. The number employed in the UK decreased by 2 percent.
2. 1985 UK bonus rate 8.1p per £1 remuneration (1984 10.1p).
3. Does not include tax deducted from the pay of employees. Income tax deducted from the pay of UK employees under PAYE amounted to £157m in 1985 (1984 £148m).
This table, which is used for calculating the bonus under the Employees' Profit-Sharing Scheme, is based on the audited historical-cost accounts; it shows the total value added to the cost of materials and services purchased from outside the Group and indicates how this increase in value has been disposed of.
Source: G. Meek and S. Gray, "The Value Added Statement: An Innovation for U.S. Companies," *Accounting Horizons* (June 1988): 76. Reprinted with permission of the American Accounting Association and Gary Meek.

Exhibit 5.3
1985 Income Statement, Imperial Chemical Industries

GROUP PROFIT AND LOSS ACCOUNT

For the year ended 31 December 1985

	1985 £m	1984 £m
TURNOVER	10,725	9,909
Operating costs	-9,917	-8,990
Other operating income	170	144
TRADING PROFIT (after providing for depreciation 1985 £474m, 1984 £440m)	978	1,063
Share of profits less losses of related companies and amounts written off investments	56	71
Net interest payable	-122	-100
PROFIT ON ORDINARY ACTIVITIES BEFORE TAXATION	912	1,034
Tax on profit on ordinary activities	-308	-373
PROFIT ON ORDINARY ACTIVITES AFTER TAXATION	604	661
Attributable to minorities	-52	-56
NET PROFIT ATTRIBUTABLE TO PARENT COMPANY	552	605
Extraordinary items	-40	-20
NET PROFIT FOR THE FINANCIAL YEAR	512	585
Dividends	-214	-186
PROFIT RETAINED FOR YEAR	298	399
EARNINGS BEFORE EXTRAORDINARY ITEMS PER £1 ORDINARY STOCK	86.4p	98.2p

Source: G. Meek and S. Gray, "The Value Added Statement: An Innovation for U.S. Companies," *Accounting Horizons* (June 1988): 77. Reprinted with permission of the American Accounting Association and Gary Meek.

There are, however, qualifications to the general rules equating the sum of the value added by all companies to national income. Michael F. Morley lists several:

1. National income includes Value Added by government and by other public bodies. For example, the Value Added [VA] by defense expenditure is assumed to be equal to its costs.

2. The VA of a company may rise partly in foreign territories. Similarly, Value may be Added in the domestic country by a foreign concern.

Exhibit 5.4
Vertical Presentation of the French Income Statement by Nature of Expenses

Revenues

Sales of goods purchased for resale	300
Sale of own production (products and services)	200
Production held as inventory (increase or decrease)	40
Production capitalised	20
Reversal of provisions	11
Operating subsidies	70
Other operating revenues	10
Total operating revenues (A)	651
Share of profits from joint enterprises	5
Financial income	100
Total financial revenues (B)	105
Exceptional income	50
Total exceptional revenues (C)	50
Total revenues (D) = (A) + (B) + (C)	806
Expenses	
Purchase of goods for resale	100
Inventory movements of goods purchased for resale	30
Purchase of raw materials and other supplies	110
Inventory movements of raw materials and other supplies	10
Other purchases and external expenses	40
Taxes and similar expenses (excluding income taxes)	20
Wages and salaries	80
Depreciation and provision expenses	26
Other operating expenses	15
Total operating expenses (E)	431
Share of losses from joint enterprises	6
Financial expenses	80
Total financial expenses (F)	86
Exceptional expenses	54
Total exceptional expenses (G)	54
Employee profit sharing (H)	34
Income taxes (I)	55
Total expenses (J) = (E) + (F) + (G) + (H) + (I)	660
Income after income taxes (K) = (D) - (J)	166

Exhibit 5.5
Computation of Value Added in France Using the Subtractive Method

Sales of goods purchased for resale (A)	300
Purchase of goods for resale	100
Inventory movements of goods purchased for resale	30
Acquisition cost of merchandise sold (B)	130
Commercial margin (gross margin) (C) = (A) - (B)	170
Sale of own production (products and services)	200
Production held as inventory (increase or decrease)	40
Production capitalized	20
Total production for period (D)	260
Purchase of raw materials and other supplies	110
Inventory movements of raw materials and other supplies	-10
Other purchases and external expenses	40
Consumption of goods and services from third parties (E)	140
Value added (F) = (C) + (D) - (E)	290

3. Economic measures of national income concentrate on production rather than on sales. Differences arise, therefore, in the valuation of increases/decreases in inventories.

4. National income conventions involve several major simplifying assumptions which are not used by financial accountants. For example, the output of durable consumer goods is assumed to have been consumed in the year of manufacture. In effect, the economist depreciates a car by 100 percent in the first year while the accountant would write off his company's fleet of vehicles at, say, 25 percent of cost in each year.[27]

Value added reporting may act as a good measure of the size and importance of companies. It is a better measure of the net creation of wealth a company has achieved. Both sales and capital, generally used as surrogate for size, may be misleading. This case is argued as follows:

When an accountant is asked "Is BP bigger than ICI?" his first reaction is to decide which is the best measure of size for the purpose in question. For some purposes sales might be appropriate, but that figure can give a false impression if a large proportion of a company's turnover is merely representing the passing on to customers of costs incurred in buying-in from other companies. For some purposes, net capital employed may be appropriate, but this can overstate the company's importance if the industry is a very capital intensive one.[28]

Value added reporting may be useful to the employee group because it could affect its aspirations and those of its negotiating representatives. Value added reporting may be used as measure of relative equity in relation to other stockholder groups. This argument has been made by K. T. Maunders:

Exhibit 5.6
Computation of Value Added in France Using the Additive Method

Income after income taxes	166
+ Taxes and similar expenses (excluding income Taxes)	20
+ Wages and salaries	80
+ Depreciation and provision expenses	26
- Reversal of provisions	-11
+ Other operating expenses	15
- Operating subsidies	-70
- Other operating revenues	-10
+ Share of losses from joint enterprises	6
- Share of gains from joint enterprises	-5
+ Financial expenses	80
- Financial income	-100
+ Exceptional expenses	54
- Exceptional income	-50
+ Employee profit sharing	34
+ income Taxes	55
= Value added	290

This is because such a statement reveals (or should reveal) the comparative shares of each of the stockholder groups in the firm's net output for a given period. For this purpose compared with, say the profit and loss account, it has the advantage that it shows explicitly what relative share each group takes. It should be noted, however, that its usefulness in this respect will be dependent on both its coverage and classification of group rewards.[29]

The rules may also be used as a measure of "ability to pay" and a measure of total productivity in the bargaining process. Some may think that the workers may object and ask for a greater share of value added. George Copeman argues that the objection can be met in two ways:

First, by providing adequate information: when employees regularly see the breakdown of value added, they will be better able to decide for themselves the point at which they would be eating the seed corn, and endangering their future livelihood, by taking in more cash.

Second, a way round the objection would be to provide for share participation by employees. This will give them a steadily increasing stake in the future. It thus demotes into a somewhat academic exercise the question of whether the present share of gains is about right or not.[30]

Value added reporting may be useful to equity investors. The argument would have validity in that the value added information could be related to the prediction of either the systematic risk of a firm's securities or the expected return and total risk of those securities, depending on which view of the efficiency of the market is considered relevant. The link can be made by the possible indirect impact of value added in the earnings of the firm. Maunders offers the following rationale:

Value added information can affect the conduct of collective bargaining and hence the company's future labor costs. Unless such changes in labor costs are exactly canceled by increases in the values of output (an unlikely coincidence), company earnings will also change. So, on the presumption that we are able to show . . . that value added information may affect collective bargaining, we can also deduce that it is potentially useful to investors for forecasting a company's earnings and, hence, the expected returns and total risk associated with securities.[31]

Value added appears to offer a useful tool for predicting earnings, expected returns, and total risk associated with securities. Maunders states,

Value added information can affect the conduct of collective bargaining and hence the company's future labor costs. Unless such changes in labor costs are exactly canceled by increases in the values of output (an unlikely coincidence), company earnings will also change. So, on the presumption that we are able to show . . . that value added information may affect collective bargaining we can also declare that it is potentially useful to investors for forecasting a company's earnings and, hence, the expected returns and total risk associated with securities.[32]

This argument follows from the evidence that indicates a relationship between earnings measures and security prices.[33]

Value added reporting may be useful to employees by revealing their share of the value added and signaling the extent of their importance to management.

Value added reporting offers a better picture of the firm's reinvestment policies by disclosing separately the funds generated internally to replace and separate fixed assets. Hence, the sum *of* depreciation and retained earnings signals the importance management attaches to the internal generation *of* funds for investment in renewal *of* productive assets and investment in new technologies.

The inclusion of a local value added statement in the host-country annual reports of multinationals would provide information to analyze the contributions of these firms to the process of national economic development.[34] Rahman offers the following equation for computing local value added (LVA):

$$LVA = (SR + CI) - (IP + RP + OPF + DIA)$$

where

SR = sales revenue (gross) consisting of local sales and freight-on-board value of exports

CI = change in inventory

IP = import payments (CIF—cost, insurance, and freight value) for raw materials and other inputs

RP = royalty payments to parent and/or other foreign parties

OPF = other payments to foreigners for services or equity and loan capital

DIA = depreciation on imported (fixed) assets[35]

Net value added (NVA) is a better index of performance than net profit (NP), especially in cases where arbitrary and incorrigible accounting techniques result in the recognition of an accounting loss rather than an accounting profit. Witness the following argument:

NP accrues to proprietors, and accordingly, if any organization incurs losses for a consecutive number of years, it would seem appropriate for the owners, in their own interests, to close the business. But the decision would be different from a social point of view. Every unit generates values that are shared by labourers and owners. So, even if the earnings of proprietors are negative, labourers earn their wages. As a result, from the social perspective, if the aggregate of labourers' share and owners' share is positive, it would be beneficial to run the business. Public utilities like Postal Services, Transport Services, etc. in rural or thinly populated areas would have never been introduced had the NP been considered the only decision criterion for the said purpose. If wages, besides input, are recovered it would be a sufficient ground for justifying the establishment of these service-concerns, because they would not only provide such services to the people but also generate the employment opportunities in a labour surplus economy.[36]

Disadvantages of Value Added Reporting

Among the disadvantages are the following.

Value added reporting relies on the erroneous assumption that a company is a team of cooperating groups. The facts may show that, in general, the groups implied have a basic conflict relationship as to the allocation of the firm's resources, the firm's increase in wealth, and the best way of managing the firm. Additionally, some may question the legitimacy of including the government as a cooperating or even invited member. Another point raised is that some legitimate member of the cooperating team may be excluded—for example, the specialist supplier to a sole customer who would be excluded from the team even though the supplier had no other outlet for his or her production.[37]

The value added statement can lead to confusion, especially in cases where the value added is increasing while earnings are decreasing. If the shareholders understand that the value added statement is not a report to them, the problem would be resolved. Some would then argue that there is still a need to use the earnings statement as a special report on the welfare of a more broadly defined team. This argument would lead to cries of information overload and information redundancy.

The inclusion of the value added statement may lead management to seek wrongly to maximize the firm's value added, an unwise objective that has already been advocated in some publications.[38,39]

The naive approach to the interpretation of a firm's value added may lead to the following five fallacies:

Increasing value added must increase profit.

Increasing value added per unit of labour must benefit shareholders.

It is possible to identify in advance an equitable distribution of changes in value added.

A relatively high value added per unit of labour represents a superior economic performance.

A labour force taking a high proportion of value added does not deserve even higher wages.[40]

USEFULNESS OF VALUE ADDED REPORTING: EMPIRICAL RESEARCH

The empirical research evaluating the usefulness of disclosing value added data—in addition to earning and cash flows data—has been conducted from three perspectives: (1) value added based performance of firms in different contexts, (2) the informational content of value added data in market valuation, and (3) the predictive ability of value added data. A review of each research perspective follows.

Value Added Performance of Firms

The value added performance of firms has been examined under different contexts which are summarized in Exhibit 5.7. The first context concerns the M-Form hypothesis; it stipulates a better performance following the implementation of the multidivisional structure. Most studies examining the M-Form hypothesis measured the economic performance of firms before and after implementation of M-Form using either earnings-based or market-based performance indicators.[41,42] The results were mixed. One study by Ahmed Riahi-Belkaoui[43] instead relied on a value added based measure of productivity as a measure of economic performance of the firm before and after the implementation of the M-Form. Values for a sample of U.S. firms found that following the implementation, productive efficiency decreased for vertically integrated firms and increased for related diversified firms. The increase in productivity was not significant for unrelated diversifiers. In sum, the adoption of the M-Form seems to be more beneficial in terms of productivity to those firms adopt-

Exhibit 5.7
Value Added Performance of Firms

Value Added Performance of Firms		
Study	**Context**	**Results**
1. Riahi-Belkaoui (1996)	Multidivisional structure and diversification strategy	Following the M-Form implementation, productive efficiency decreases for vertically integrated firms and increases for related diversified firms. The moderate increase in productivity is not significant for unrelated diversifiers.
2. Riahi-Belkaoui and Pavlik (1994)	Effects of ownership structure	There is a significant nonmonotonic relationship between value added performance and ownership structure.
3. Askren et al. (1994)	Performance plan adoption	Firms adopting accounting-based performance plan do not experience any greater gains in accounting return or productivity measure than do a set of control firms.
4. Riahi-Belkaoui (1996)	Performance plan adoption and ownership structure	Following performance plan adoption, profitability will increase in owner-controlled firms, but not manager-controlled firms.

ing a related diversification strategy. The strategy allows the realization of synergistic economies of scope through the joint use of input.

The second context concerns the effect of ownership structure on performance as reflected in the debate regarding the importance of stock ownership on corporate efficiency and strategic development. Empirical examination of the issue led to conflicting results that were attributed to data problems when attempting to construct meaningful measures of performance. The study by Riahi-Belkaoui and Ellen Pavlik[44] argued that the effects of ownership structure and performance are best examined when performance expressed total return rather than being restricted to accounting returns. Using a sample of U.S. firms, they found a significant noneconomic relationship between value added based performance and ownership structure. Value added based performance declines up to a turning point before increasing proportionally to the increases in ownership structure measures. The phenomenon held regardless of whether ownership structure is measured by management stockholding, stock concentration, or a sum of two measures. This result is compatible with (a) a dispersion ownership and nonvalue maximizing behavior where holdings are less than 10 percent ownership and (b) a convergence of interest for the maximization of value added based performance between managers and shareholders where there is more than 10 percent ownership.

The third context concerns the firm's performance resulting from the adoption of performance plans. This context follows from theoretical arguments indicating that long-term accounting-based performance plans motivate executives to improve firm performance in the long run. Barbara Askren et al.[45] present results based on a sample of U.S. firms indicating that firms adopting accounting-based performance do not experience any greater gains in accounting returns or value added based productivity measures than do a set of control firms. However, Riahi-Belkaoui[46] argued that the nature of the relation varies with the ownership structure of the firm. Using the same sample of firms, his results supported this contention with respect to owner-controlled but not manager-controlled firms.

Market Valuation and Value Added versus Conventional Data

The information content of value added data versus conventional earnings, cash flow, and abnormal economic earnings data has been examined in variation studies shown in Exhibit 5.8, using various market valuation models. The results in Exhibit 5.8 confirm the thesis, usually, that the association between firm value and value added measures of performance is stronger than the association between firm value and either earnings, cash flow, or abnormal economic earnings measures. The results, with one exception, hold for both linear and nonlinear valuation models. The exceptions are provided by C. J. Van Staden's analysis of the predictive power of value added in South Africa.[47] However, when the research question examined the functional specification relating earnings or net value added to market returns, the model relating accounting and market returns has more explanatory power under the following conditions: (a) the accounting returns are expressed by the relative change in net value added and (b) the relation is a nonlinear, convex-concave function.[48]

Predictive Ability of Value Added Data

The predictive ability of value added data has been examined in three studies that differ in terms of the nature of prediction or the economic event predicted (see Exhibit 5.9).

The first study by Karpik and Belkaoui[49] follows from earlier works establishing the empirical/theoretical relationship between accounting variables and market risk.[50] It tested the incremental abilities of value added measures to explain cross-sectional variation in market betas beyond that provided by risk measures which are either earnings or cash flow based. The results based on a

Exhibit 5.8
Market Valuation and Value Added versus Conventional Data

Study	Research Question	Model Used	Results
1. Bao and Bao (1989)	Association between productivity and firm value	Litzenberger and Rao (1971) valuation model	The association between firm value and productivity in the oil refining and apparel industries is stronger than between firm value and earnings measures.
2. Riahi-Belkaoui (1993)	Relative and incremental content of value added, earnings and cash flow	Earnings valuation model	Value added information can supply some explanatory power beyond that provided by earnings or cash flow measures.
3. Riahi-Belkaoui and Pavlik (1994)	Merits of derived accounting indicator numbers.	Accounting indicator numbers (Barlev and Levy, 1979)	The derived performance indicator numbers based on net value added had lower variability and higher persistency than corresponding numbers based on either earnings or cash flows.
4. Riahi-Belkaoui and Picur (1994)	Relative and incremental information content of value added and earnings	Combined earnings and value added valuation model	The study confirms an association between both relative changes in earnings and net value added and the relative changes in security prices.
5. Riahi-Belkaoui and Picur (1994)	Information content of level versus change in net value added	Book value and wealth models	Both the levels of net value added and the changes in net value added play a role in security valuation.
6. Riahi-Belkaoui (1996)	Functional specification relating unexpected earnings or net value added to market-adjusted returns.	Linear and nonlinear valuation models	Models relating accounting and market returns have more explanatory power when: (a) the accounting returns are expressed by the relative changes in net value added, and (b) the relation is a nonlinear convex-concave function.

Exhibit 5.8 (*Continued*)

Study	Research Question	Model Used	Results
7. Riahi-Belkaoui (1996)	Informational content of net value added components disclosed concurrently with earnings	Earnings valuation model	Earnings component of value added is viewed favorably by the market while the non-earnings components (interests, tax, and wages) are negatively related to market return.
8. Bao and Bao (1998)	Explanatory power of value added and abnormal economic earnings (EVA)	Linear valuation model	Value added has a higher explanatory issue through earnings while abnormal economic earnings are not a significant variable.
9. Kim et al. (1996)	Information content of productivity measures	Submartugab model as expectation model	Correlation between security, productivity changes, and unexpected earnings are not uniform across the sample countries.
10. Riahi-Belkaoui (1999)	The role of productivity in the prediction of firm profitability and firm valuation	Ohlson's valuation model	Productivity explains cross-structural differences in market value incremental to that explained by both value and current profit rate
11. Van Staden (2000)	Predictive and explanatory power of value added in South Africa	External indicator numbers: share price, price earnings ratio, and Altenan's Z-score	Value added information did not have significant predictive and explanatory power additional to that of earnings for the three relative external indicators.

sample of U.S. firms point to the superior explanatory power of value added variables in explaining the variability in market betas.

The second study by Bannister and Riahi-Belkaoui[51] follows from previous empirical endeavors to investigate the characteristics differentiating merger target firms from other firms.[52,53] This study instead relies on value added to (a) assess the differences in the characteristics of target firms compared to their industries and (b) explain target firms' abnormal returns during the takeover period. The results indicated that (a) takeover targets have lower value added ratios than other firms in their industries in the year preceding the completion of the takeover and (b) target firms' abnormal returns observed during the takeover period are positively related to the difference between target firm and average industry value added to total assets. The results suggest that while acquired

Exhibit 5.9
Predictive Ability of Value Added Data

Study	Nature of Prediction	Model Used	Results
1. Karpik and Riahi-Belkaoui (1989)	Explaining market risk	Market model	Value added variables process incremental information beyond accrual earnings and cash flows in the context of explaining market risk.
2. Bannister and Riahi-Belkaoui (1991)	Explaining target firm's abnormal returns during the takeover period	Market model	Takeover targets have lower value added to total ratios rather than other firms in their industries in the year preceding the completion of the takeover, and target firm abnormal returns observed during the takeover period are related to the difference between target firm and average industry value added.
3. Bao and Bao (1996)	Examining the structure and the forecasting accuracy of firm value added measure	Four time series models	The four value added measures can be diversified as a random walk model. The process/ model has the lowest forecast errors in terms of two error metrics.
4. Riahi-Belkaoui (2000)	Effects of accounting knowledge on the omission of value added in wealth measurement and distribution	Behavioral experiment	Accounting knowledge interferes with a decision-maker's ability to incorporate value added information in wealth measurement and distribution decisions.

firms are on the average underperformers, acquiring firms value the access to, and possibly the ability to redistribute, the resources of target firms.

The third study by Bao and Bao[54] is consistent with other studies regarding time series properties of accounting earnings. It examined the time series properties of value added based measures using four well-known time series models: the pure mean reverting model, the mean reverting model with a growth trend, the random walk model, and the random walk with a drift term. From a sample of U.S. firms, the results showed that the value added based measures can be described as a random walk process, which has the lowest forecast errors in terms of two error metrics: the autocorrelation coefficient test and a predictability test. The results are consistent with those of annual earnings and stock prices.

Finally, Riahi-Belkaoui[55] conducted an experiment to evaluate the behavioral effects of accounting knowledge on the omission of value added in wealth measurement and distribution. Its results indicate that accounting knowledge interferes with a decision-maker's ability to incorporate value added information in wealth measurement and distribution decisions.

VALUE ADDED REPORTING AND PRICE LEVEL CHANGE

The proceeding presentation of value added reporting was based on the assumption of the stability of price level. As suggested in Chapter 4, covering the inflation report, price levels are subjected to changes that require reevaluation and adjustment of the accounts. The same procedures of reevaluation and adjustment to reflect the changes in price levels are also necessary for the value added report. Similar to the presentation in the Chapter 4, combining the three attributes and the two units of measure yields the following six alternative value added reports:

1. A value added report based on historical cost accounting that measures historical cost in units of money.

2. A value added report based on historical cost accounting that measures historical cost in units of purchasing power.

3. A value added report based on replacement cost accounting that measures replacement cost in units of money.

4. A value added report based on replacement cost accounting that measures replacement cost in units of purchasing power.

5. A value added report based on net realizable value accounting that measures net realizable value in units of money.

6. A value added report based on net realizable value accounting that measures net realizable value in units of purchasing power.

To illustrate the derivation of the value added report under the different price change models, let us again consider the example used in Chapter 4: The Hellenic Company, which was founded on January 1, 2000, to distribute a new product called KOULA. Capital is composed of $3,000 equity and $3,000 liabilities carrying a five percent interest. On January 1, the Hellenic Company began operations by purchasing 600 units of KOULA at $10 per unit. On May 1, the company sold 500 units at $15 per unit. At the end of the year, the company made the following cash payments:

1. Interest = $150
2. Wages = $30
3. Taxes = $100
4. Dividends = $20

Exhibit 5.10
Hellenic Company Value Added Statements Expressed in Units of Money

Value Added Statement	Historical Cost	Replacement Cost	Net Realizable Value
A. Source of Net Value Added			
Revenues -	$7,500	$7,500	$9,200
Cost of Material	$5,000	$6,000	$7,300
Net Value Added before Gains & Losses	$2,500	$1,500	$1,900
Realized Holding Gains & Losses	INCL. ABOVE	$1,000	$1,000
Unrealized Holding Gains & Losses	NOT APPLICABLE	$300	$300
General Price Level Gains & Losses	NOT APPLICABLE	NOT APPLICABLE	NOT APPLICABLE
Net Value Added after Gains & Losses	$2,500	$2,800	$3,200
B. Distribution of Net Value Added			
Interest to Bondholders	$150	$150	$150
Wages to Employees	$30	$30	$30
Retained Earnings To Firm	$2,200	$2,500	$2,900
Taxes to Government	$100	$100	$100
Dividends to Shareholders	$20	$20	$20
Net Value Added after Gains & Losses	$2,500	$2,800	$3,200

Changes in the general and specific price levels for the year 2000 are as follows:

	January 1	May 1	December 1
Preplacement Cost	$10	$12	$13
Net Realizable Value	—	$15	$17
General Price Level Index	100	130	156

Exhibit 5.11
Hellenic Company Value Added Statements Expressed in Units of Purchasing Power

Value Added Statement	Historical Cost	Replacement Cost	Net Realizable Value
A. Source of Net Value Added			
Revenues -	$9,000	$9,000	$10,700
Cost of Material	$7,800	$7,200	$8,500
Net Value Added before Gains & Losses	$1,200	$1,800	$2,200
Realized Holding Gains & Losses	INCL. ABOVE	($600)	($600)
Unrealized Holding Gains & Losses	NOT APPLICABLE	($260)	($260)
General Price Level Gains & Losses	$180	$180	$180
Net Value Added after Gains & Losses	$1,380	$1,120	$1,520
B. Distribution of Net Value Added			
Interest to Bondholders	$150	$150	$150
Wages to Employees	$30	$30	$30
Retained Earnings To Firm	$1,080	$820	$1,220
Taxes to Government	$100	$100	$100
Dividends to Shareholders	$20	$20	$20
Net Value Added after Gains & Losses	$1,380	$1,120	$1,520

Based on the results shown in Exhibits 5.4. and 5.3, six different value added reports may be produced. They are the following:

1. A value added report based on historical cost accounting, in Exhibit 5.10, showing a net value added after gains and losses of $2,500.

2. A value added report based on replacement cost accounting, in Exhibit 5.10, showing a net value added after gains and losses of $2,800.

3. A value added report based on net realizable value accounting, in Exhibit 5.10, showing a net value added after gains and losses of $3,200.

4. A value added report based on general price-level adjusted historical cost accounting, in Exhibit 5.11, showing a net value added after gains and losses of $1,380.

5. A value added report based on general price-level adjusted replacement cost accounting. In Exhibit 5.11, showing a net value added after gains and losses of $1,120.

6. A value added report based on general price-level adjusted net realizable value accounting, in Exhibit 5.11, showing a net value added after gains and losses of $1,520.

CONCLUSIONS

Taken as a whole, the content of this chapter points to the relevance of value added reporting. Thus, the important accounting policy issue is the desirability of disclosing the underlying data needed to compute value added variables. The current disclosure system does not mandate the disclosure of some of the information needed to compute the value added. At present, less than 15 percent of the firms listed on Compustat consistently disclose labor expenses, a big variable. Supplementary financial statements are a practical way of introducing and gaining experience with new kinds of information. The value added concept is an example of the type of innovation in need of U.S. based experimentation. More research on the relevance of the value added concept is also needed.

NOTES

1. Ahmed Riahi-Belkaoui, *Value Added Reporting: The Lessons for the United States* (Westport, CT: Greenwood Publishing, 1994).

2. Ahmed Riahi-Belkaoui, *Performance Results in Value Added Reporting* (Westport, CT: Greenwood Publishing, 1996).

3. Ahmed Riahi-Belkaoui, *Value Added Reporting and Research* (Westport, CT: Greenwood Publishing, 1999).

4. B. Cox, *Value Added: An Application for the Accountant Concerned with Industry* (London: Heinemann and the Institute of Cost and Management Accountants, 1978).

5. W. W. Suojanen, "Accounting Theory and the Large Corporation," *Accounting Review*, July 1954, pp. 391–98.

6. Accounting Standards Steering Committee, *The Corporate Report* (London: Accounting Standards Steering Committee, 1975), p. 48.

7. Ibid.

8. Ibid.

9. Department of Trade, *The Future of Company Reports* (London: HMSO, 1977), pp. 7–8.

10. S. J. Gray and K. T. Maunders, *Value Added Reporting: Uses and Measurement* (London: Association of Certified Accountants, 1980).

11. Engineering Employers Federation, *Business Performance and Industrial Relations* (London: Kogan Page, 1977).

12. M. Woodmansay, *Added Value: An Introduction to Productivity Schemes* (London: British Institute of Management, 1978).

13. Stuart Burchell, Colin Clubb, and Anthony G. Hopwood, "Accounting and Its Social Context: Towards a History of Value Added in the United Kingdom," *Accounting, Organizations and Society* 10, no. 4 (1985): 387.

14. F. C. Jones, *The Economic Ingredients of Industrial Success* (London: James Clayton Lecture, Institution of Mechanical Engineers, 1976), "Our Manufacturing Industry: The Missing $100,000 Million," *National Westminster Bank Quarterly Review*, May 1978, pp. 8–17; C. New, "Factors in Productivity That Should Not Be Overlooked," *Times*, 1 Feb. 1978.

15. S. Cameron, "Added Value Plan for Distributing ICI's Wealth," *Financial Times*, 7 Jan. 1977.

16. Vickers da Costa, "Testing for Success" (London: 1979, mimeographed).

17. M. Renshall, R. Allan, and K. Nicholson, *Added Value in External Financial Reporting* (London: Institute of Chartered Accountants in England and Wales, 1979).

18. Michael F. Morley, *The Value Added Statement* (London: Gee and Co., for the Institute of Chartered Accountants of Scotland, 1978).

19. Cox, *Value Added.*

20. Gray and Maunders, *Value Added Reporting.*

21. Michael F. Morley, "The Value Added Statement in Britain," *Accounting Review*, July 1979, p. 62.

22. Ibid.

23. Ibid., p. 622.

24. Cox, *Value Added.* pp. 67–82.

25. Gokul Sinha, *Value Added Income* (Calcutta: Book World, 1983), pp. 130–37.

26. K. T. Maunders, "The Decision Relevance of Value Added Reports," in *Frontiers of International Accounting: An Anthology*, ed. Frederick D. Choi and Gerhard G. Mueller (Ann Arbor, MI: UMI Research Press, 1985), p. 241.

27. Morley, "Value Added Statement in Britain," p. 623.

28. Michael F. Morley, "Value Added Reporting" in *Developments in Financial Reporting*, ed. Thomas A. Lee (London: Philip Allan, 1981), p. 259.

29. Maunders, "Decision Relevance of Value Added Reports," pp. 225–45.

30. George Copeman, "Wages of Added Value," *Management Today*, June 1977, p. 138.

31. Maunders, "Decision Relevance of Value Added Reports," p. 229.

32. Ibid., p. 228.

33. B. Lev and J. A. Ohlson, "Market Band Empirical Research: A Review, Interpretation and Extension," *Journal of Accounting Research*, 1982, Supplement, pp. 239–322.

34. M. Zubaidur Rahman, "The Local Value Added Statement: A Reporting Requirement for Multinationals in Developing Host Countries," *International Journal of Accounting*, 2 Feb. 1990, pp. 87–98.

35. Ibid., p. 93.

36. Sinha, *Value Added Income*, p. 136.

37. Morley, "Value Added Statement in Britain," p. 624.

38. R. R. Gilchrist, *Managing for Profit: The Value Added Concept* (London: Allen and Unwin, 1977).

39. Michael F. Morley, "Value Added Statement: A British Innovation," *The Chartered Accountant Magazine*, May 1978 p. 30.

40. B. A. Rutherford, "Five Fallacies About Value Added," *Management Accounting*, Sept. 1981, pp. 31–33.

41. P. Karpik and Ahmed Riahi-Belkaoui, "The Effects of the Implementation of the Multidivisional Structure on Shareholders' Wealth: The Contingency of Diversification," *Journal of Business Finance and Accounting*, Apr. 1994, pp. 349–66.

42. A. Riahi-Belkaoui and J. W. Bannister, "Multidivisional Structure and Capital Structure: The Contingency of Diversification Strategy," *Managerial and Decision Economics* 15 (1994): 267–76.

43. A. Riahi-Belkaoui, "Multidivisional Structure and Productivity: The Contingency of Diversification Strategy," *Journal of Business Finance and Accounting*, June, 1997, pp. 615–27.

44. A. Riahi-Belkaoui and Ellen Pavlik, "The Effect of Ownership Structure on Value Added Performance," *Managerial Finance* 20, no. 9 (1994): 16–26.

45. Barbara J. Askren, J. W. Bannister, and E. Pavlik, "The Impact of Performance Plan Adoption on Value Added and Earnings," *Managerial Finance* 20, no. 9 (1994): 27–43.

46. A Riahi-Belkaoui, "Performance Plan Adoption and Performance: The Contingency of Ownership Structure," *Managerial Finance* 23, no. 5 (1997): 18–27.

47. C. J. Van Staden, "Aspects of the Productive and Explanatory Power of Value Added Information in South Africa," *SA Journal of Accounting Research* (Forthcoming).

48. Ahmed Riahi-Belkaoui, "Earnings-Return Versus Net-Value Added Returns Relation: The Case for Nonlinear Specification," *Advances in Quantitative Analysis in Finance and Accounting* 4 (1996): 175–85.

49. P. Karpik and Ahmed Belkaoui, "The Relative Relationship Between Systematic Risk and Value Added Variables," *Journal of International Financial Management and Accounting*, Autumn, 1989, pp. 259–76.

50. B. E. Ismael and H. K. Kim, "On the Association of Cash Flow Variables with Market Risk: Further Evidence," *Accounting Review*, Jan. 1989, pp. 125–36.

51. J. W. Bannister and Ahmed Riahi-Belkaoui, "Value Added and Corporate Control in the U.S.," *Journal of International Financial Management and Accounting*, Autumn 1991, pp. 241–57.

52. Ahmed Belkaoui, "Financial Ratios as Predictors of Canadian Takeovers," *Journal of Business Finance and Accounting*, Spring 1978, pp. 53–107.

53. Ahmed Belkaoui, "The Entropy Law, Information Decomposition Measures and Corporate Takeovers," *Journal of Business Finance and Accounting*, Fall 1976, pp. 45–57.

54. Ben-Hsien Bao and Da-Hsien Bao, "The Time Series Behavior and Predictive Ability Results of Value Added Data," *Journal of Business Finance and Accounting*, Spring 1978, pp. 93–107.

55. Ahmed Riahi-Belkaoui, "Effects of Accounting Knowledge on the Omission of Value Added in Wealth Measurement and Distribution" (Working paper, University of Illinois at Chicago, 2000).

REFERENCES

Accounting Standards Steering Committee. *The Corporate Report*. London: Accounting Standards Steering Committee, 1975.

American Accounting Association, Committee on Accounting and Auditing Measurement, 1989–90. *Accounting Horizons*, Sept. 1991, 81–105.

Askren, Barbara J., J. W. Bannister, and E. Pavlik. "The Impact of Performance Plan Adoption on Value Added and Earnings." *Managerial Finance* 20, no. 9 (1994): 27–43.

Ball, R. J. "The Use of Value Added in Measuring Efficiency." *Business Ratios*, Summer 1968, 5–11.

Banque de France. "Methodologie d'Analyse Financiere." Centrale de Bilan, 1988.

Bannister, James W., and Ahmed Riahi-Belkaoui. "Value Added and Corporate Control in the US." *Journal of International Financial Management and Accounting*, Autumn 1991, 241–57.

Bao, B. H., and D. H. Bao. "An Empirical Investigation of the Association between Productivity and Firm Value." *Journal of Business Finance and Accounting* 16 (1989): 699–717.

———. "The Time Series Behavior and Predictive Ability Results of Value Added Data." *Journal of Business Finance and Accounting*, Apr. 1996, 449–60.

———. "Usefulness of Value Added and Abnormal Economic Earnings: An Empirical Examination." *Journal of Business Finance and Accounting*, Jan./Mar. 1998, 251–64.

Barlev, Benzion, and Haim Levy. "On the Variability of Accounting Numbers." *Journal of Accounting Research*, Autumn 1979, 305–15.

Belkaoui, Ahmed. "Financial Ratios as Predictors of Canadian Takeovers." *Journal of Business Finance and Accounting*, Spring 1978, 93–107.

Belkaoui, Ahmed. "The Entropy Law, Information Decomposition Measures and Corporate Takeovers." *Journal of Business Finance and Accounting*, Fall 1976, 45–57.

Bentley, Trevor. "Value Added and Contribution." *Management Accounting*, Mar. 1981, 17–21.

Brodier, P. L. *Une Autre Approche de la Gestion: La Valeur Ajoutee Directe*. Paris: Afnor, 1988.

Burchell, Stuart, Colin Clubb, and Anthony Hopwood. "Accounting and Its Social Context: Towards a History of Value Added in the United Kingdom." *Accounting, Organizations and Society* 10 (1985): 381–413.

Chua, K. C. "The Use of Value Added in Productivity Measurements." In *Productivity Measurement and Achievement: Proceedings of Accountancy*. Victoria: University of Wellington, 1977.

Conseil National de la Comptabilite. *Plan Comptable General*. Paris: Imprimerie Nationale, 1986.

Cox, Bernard. *Value Added: An Application for the Accountant Concerned with Industry*. London: Heinemann, 1978.

Cruns, R. P. "Added-Value: The Roots Run Deep Into Colonial and Early America." *Accounting Historian Journal*, Fall 1982, 25–42.

Cubbin, J., and D. Leach. "The Effect of Shareholder Dispersion on the Degree of Control in British Companies: Theory and Measurement." *Economic Journal* 3 (1983): 351–369.

Deegan, C., and A. Hallman. "The Voluntary Presentation of Value Added Statements in Australia: A Political Cost Perspective." *Accounting and Finance*, May 1991, 1–29.

Dewhurst, James. "Assessing Business Performance." *Accountant*, 3 Mar. 1983, 17–18.

Dormagen, J. C. "Marge et Valeur Ajoutee." *Revue Francaise de Comptabilite*, Mai 1994, 12–14.

Easton, P. D., and T. S. Harris. "Earnings as an Explanatory Variable for Returns." *Journal of Accounting Research*, Spring 1991, 19–36.

Egginton, D. A. "In Defense of Profit Measurement: Some Limitations of Cash Flow and Value Added Data as Performance Measures for External Reporting." *Accounting and Business Research*, Spring 1984, 32–43.

Financial Accounting Standards Board (FASB). Statement of Financial Accounting Concepts No. 5. *Recognition and Measurement in Financial Statements of Business Enterprises*. Stamford CT: FASB, 1984.

Foley, B. J., and K. T. Maunders. *Accounting Information Disclosure and Collective Bargaining*. London: Macmillan, 1977.

Force, J. "Valeur Ajoutee et Analyse Financiere." In "La Valeur Ajoutee," *Supplement à la Revue Francaise de Comptabilite*, Juillet 1977, 12–14.

Gilchrist, R. R. *Managing for Profit: The Value Added Concept*. London: Allen and Unwin, 1971.

Gray, Sidney. *Value Added Reporting: Uses and Measurement*. London: Association of Certified Accountants, 1980.

Gray, Sidney, and K. T. Maunders. "Recent Developments in Value Added Disclosures." *Certified Accounting*, Aug. 1979, 255–56.

Haller, A. *Werschopfungsrechnung, Ein Instrumentaur Steigerung der Aussagefahigkeit von Unternehmensabschlussen im Internationalen Kontext*. Stuttgart: Schaffer-Poeschel Verlag, 1997.

Haller, Axel, and Herve Stolowy. "Value Added in Financial Accounting: A Cognitive Study of Germany and France." *Advances in International Accounting* 11 (1998): 23–51.

Harris, G. J. "Value Added Statement." *The Australian Accountant*, May 1982, 261–64.

Hill, C. W., and S. A. Snell. "Effects of Ownership Structure and Control on Corporate Productivity." *Academy of Management Journal* 32 (1989): 25–46.

Hoskisson, R. E. "Multidivisional Structure and Performance: The Contingency of Diversification Strategy." *Academy of Management Journal* 2 (1987): 625–44.

Ismail, B. E. and M. K. Kim. "On the Association of Cash Flow Variables with Market Risk: Further Evidence." *Accounting Review*, Jan. 1989, 125–36.

Karpik, P., and Ahmed Riahi-Belkaoui. "The Effects of the Implementation of the Multidivisional Structure on Shareholders' Wealth: The Contingency of Diversification Strategy." *Journal of Business Finance and Accounting*, Apr. 1994.

———. "The Relative Relationship Between Systematic Risk and Value Added Variables." *Journal of International Financial Management and Accounting*, Autumn 1989, 259–76.

Kim, Jee, and Joo Hong. In Ki Choi and Frederick D. S. Choi, "The Information Content of Productivity Measures: An International Comparison." *Journal of International Financial Management and Accounting*, Autumn 1996, 167–190.

Lev, B., and J. A. Ohlson. "Market Based Empirical Research: A Review, Interpretation and Extension." *Journal of Accounting Research*, 1982 Supplement, 239–322.

Litzenberger, R. H., and C. W. Rao. "Estimates of the Marginal Rate of Time Preference and Average Risk Aversion of Investors in Electric Utility Shares: 1960–66." *Bell Journal of Economics and Management Science*, Spring 1976, 265–77.

Maunders, K. T. "The Decision Relevance of Value Added Reports." In *Frontiers of*

International Accounting: An Anthology, edited by F. D. Choi and G. G. Mueller, 225–45. Ann Arbor, MI: UMI Research Press, 1985.

McLead, Charles C. "Use of Value Added." *Bests Review*, Jan. 1984, 80–84.

McSweeney, Brendan. "Irish Answer to Value Added Reports." In *Frontiers of International Accounting: An Anthology*, edited by Frederick K. Choi and Gerhard G. Mueller, 225–45. Ann Arbor, MI: UMI Research Press, 1985.

Meek, Gary K., and Sidney J. Gray. "The Value Added Statement: An Innovation for the US Companies." *Accounting Horizons*, June 1988, 73–81.

Morck, R. A., A. Shleifer, and R. W. Vishny. "Management Ownership and Market Valuation: An Empirical Analysis." *Journal of Financial Economics* 20 (1988): 293–315.

Morley, M. F. "Value Added Reporting." In *Developments in Financial Reporting*, edited by Thomas A. Lee, 251–69. London: Philip Allan, 1981.

———. *The Value Added Statement*. London: Gee and Co. for the Institute of Chartered Accountants of Scotland, 1978.

Morley, M. F. "The Value Added Statement: A British Innovation." *The Chartered Accountant Magazine*, May 1978, 31–34.

———. "The Value Added Statement in Britain." *Accounting Review*, May 1979, 618–89.

Ohlson, J. A., "Accounting Earnings, Book Value and Dividends: The Theory of Clear Surplus Equation." Working paper, Columbia University, 1988.

———. "Earnings, Book Value and Dividends in Security Valuation." *Contemporary Accounting Research*, Spring 1995, 661–87.

Pendrill, Davie. "Introducing a Newcomer: The Value Added Statement." *Accountancy*, Sept. 1981, 121–22.

Rahman, M. Zubaidur. "The Local Value Added Statement: A Reporting Requirement for Multinationals in Developing Host Countries." *International Journal of Accounting*, 2 Feb. 1990, 87–98.

Renshall, M., R. Allan, and K. Nicholson. *Added Value in External Financial Reporting*. London: Institute of Chartered Accountants in England and Wales, 1979.

Riahi-Belkaoui, Ahmed. "Earnings-Return versus Net Value-Added Returns Relation: The Case for Nonlinear Specification." *Advances in Quantitative Analysis in Finance and Accounting* 4 (1996): 175–85.

———. "Effects of Accounting Knowledge on Omission of Value Added in Wealth Measurement and Distribution." Working paper, University of Illinois at Chicago, 2000.

———. "An Empirical Case for Value Added Reporting in the United States." *Indian Journal of Accounting*, Dec. 1996, 40–47.

———. *Handbook of Management Control Systems*. Westport, CT: Greenwood Publishing, 1986.

———. "The Information Content of Value Added, Earnings and Cash Flows: US Evidence." *The International Journal of Accounting* 28, no. 2 (1993): 140–46.

———. "Multidivisional Structure and Productivity: The Contingency of Diversification Strategy." *Journal of Business Finance and Accounting*, June 1997, 615–27.

———. "Performance Plan Adoption and Performance: The Contingency of Ownership Structure." *Managerial Finance* 23, no. 5 (1997): 18–27.

———. *Performance Results of Value Added Reporting*. Westport, CT: Greenwood Publishing, 1996.

————. "Productivity, Profitability, and Firm Value." *Journal of International Financial Management and Accounting* 10, no. 3 (1999): 158–201.

————. *Value Added Reporting: The Lessons for the United States.* Westport, CT: Greenwood Publishing, 1992.

————. *Value Added Reporting and Research.* Westport, CT: Greenwood Publishing, 1999.

Riahi-Belkaoui, Ahmed, and J. W. Bannister. "Multidivisional Structure and Capital Structure: The Contingency of Diversification Strategy." *Managerial and Decision Economics* 15 (1994): 267–76.

Riahi-Belkaoui, Ahmed, and Ali Fekrat. "The Magic in Value Added: Merits of Derived Accounting Indicator Numbers." *Managerial Finance* 20, no. 9 (1994): 3–15.

Riahi-Belkaoui, Ahmed, and Ellen Pavlik. "Asset Management Performance and Reputation Building for Large US Firms." *British Journal of Management* 2 (1991): 231–38.

————. "The Effect of Ownership Structure on Value Added Performance." *Managerial Finance* 20, no. 9 (1994): 16–26.

Riahi-Belkaoui, Ahmed, and Ronald D. Picur. "Explaining Market Returns: Earnings versus Value Added Data." *Managerial Finance* 20, no. 9 (1994): 44–45.

Rutherford, B. A. "Easing the CCA Transition in Value Added Statements." *Accountancy*, May 1983, 121–22.

————. "Five Fallacies About Value Added." *Management Accountant*, Sept. 1981, 31–33.

————. "Published Statements of Value Added: A Survey of Three Years' Experience." *Accounting and Business Review*, Winter 1980, 15–28.

————. "Value Added as a Focus of Attention for Financial Reporting: Some Conceptual Problems." *Accounting and Business Research*, Summer 1972, 215–20.

Sinha, Gokul. *Value Added Income.* Calcutta: Book World, 1983.

Soujanen, W. W. "Accounting Today and the Large Corporation." *Accounting Review*, July 1954, 391–98.

Stainbank, L. J. "Value Added Reporting in South Africa: Current Disclosure Patterns." *SA Journal of Accounting Research* 11 (1997): 69–91.

Van Staden, C. J. "Aspects of the Predictive and Explanatory Power of Value Added Information in South Africa." *SA Journal of Accounting Research.* Forthcoming.

————. "The Usefulness of the Value Added Statement in South Africa." *Managerial Finance* 24 (1998): 44–58.

Van Staden, C. J., and Q. Voster. "The Usefulness of Value Added Statement: A Review of the Literature." *Meditari*, 1998, 337–51.

Chapter 6

The Employee Report

INTRODUCTION

The history of accounting for employees is unfortunately characterized by an early attitude of neglect going from polite ignorance to deliberate misleading. Witness the following comment made in 1963 by an official of the United Auto Workers:

In other cases, corporations, with or without the collaboration of accountants, have used accounting data to prepare special financial reports for employees which were deliberately designed not to enlighten them but to mislead them. I have in my briefcase one which portrays the corporation in question as Old Mother Hubbard. She has an income from sales and the distributes this income—all of it. She distributes a good big chunk of it in the form of retained profits. Old Mother Hubbard's cupboard is bare and so, the worker obviously is supposed to conclude, there is no room for a wage increase. On this basis, of course, there would never be any room for a wage increase in any corporation.[1]

While the question of the final identity of users of financial reports continues to plague the accounting world, it is now a well-accepted fact in the literature and in practice that employees deserve to be considered as important users of financial reports during their recruitment and years of employment and prior to their retirement. Unions as representative of employees also qualify as important users of accounting information especially with the purpose of finding convincing arguments for their collective-bargaining positions. With the emergence of employees and unions as potential users of accounting information, it also appears, and for a good many reasons, that the annual report to shareholders is not the all inclusive document suitable for all unions. The solution lies in the production of a special report to employees and unions. This solution has been accepted in a lot of country members of the Organization of Economic Cooperation and Development, including the United States, West Germany, Canada, France, Denmark, Norway, Sweden, and the United Kingdom. The idea has been accepted not only operationally but conceptually. For example, in the United Kingdom, the *Corporate Report* identifies employees as a user group of published company annual reports.[2] Therefore, the objective of this chapter is to review the literature on employee reporting with the purpose of explaining the factors influencing the phenomenon, the information needs of employees and unions, the content of this special report, and the role of the accountant.

FACTORS INFLUENCING EMPLOYEE REPORTING

This section elaborates on the factors influencing employee reporting. Because different factors apply for employees and unions, each group will be reviewed separately. In fact, a sample employment report, included as an appendix to the *Corporate Report*, showed quantitative data under the following headings:

1. Number employed (analyzed in various ways),
2. Location of employment,
3. Age distribution of permanent work force,
4. Hours worked during the year (analyzed),
5. Employee costs,
6. Pension information,
7. Education and training (including costs),
8. Recognized trade unions,
9. Additional information (race relations, health and safety statistics, etc.), and
10. Employment ratios.[3]

Similarly, in Canada, the Canadian Institute of Chartered Accountants published a research study in June 1980 entitled *Corporate Reporting: Its Future Evolution.*[4] The report identified employees (past, present, and future), explicitly as users of corporate reports.

Employee reporting and the general disclosure of information to employees have definite implications for the relationship between management on one hand and the employees and their representatives on the other hand. A definite trust can be established through the power of employee reporting. Witness the following comment:

[It] is not conductive to the creating of an atmosphere of mutual trust in which effective honoring of agreements depends that the workpeople's representative should have to depend on inadequate or imperfect sources of information. The more intimate and friendly are your relations with the employer, the more it becomes the common desire to settle and then the more advantageous it is for each side to be completely honest about what is going on. There is nothing which interferes more with the general disclosure.[5]

The "efficiency wage theory" suggests that the provision of information to employees working for a high-wage firm may reduce shirking and encourage monitoring costs.[6] Efficiency wage theory also suggests that workers may evaluate their managers more highly when more information is provided.[7]

It is the impact on productivity and profitability that may be the ultimate justification for reporting to employees. Most studies have generally concluded that increases in the amount of information provided to employees would result in some productivity increases.[8,9] However, this information-sharing was found to have a significant negative relationship to profits and cash flows in nonunion employees.[10] More research on the effects of employee reporting on profitability and liquidity is needed.

The approaches to employee reporting may be characterized along three different lines: (a) the pragmatic, (b) abstract analytical or (c) empirical.[11] The pragmatic approach is based on a "shopping list" or "consumer sovereignty approach," where a drawing up of lists of information defined what information could be or is made available irrespective of its appropriateness for the needs of employees. The abstract analytical approach is based on a user needs approach where the needs of the employee were determined on the basis of a rational approach such as economic models.[12,13] The empirical approach is based on a descriptive approach where the needs of employees were taken from books of models of employee decision making[14] or learned through experience.[15]

Anthony Hilton, however, identified three specific approaches to the preparation of the employee report, namely (a) the shareholder approach, (b) the demand approach and (c) the business planning approach.[16] The shareholders approach is based on the belief that

1. both shareholders and employees should be aware of the financial status of the firms as perceived by management,

2. no groups should be deprived of information provided to the other groups, and

3. management needs to provide employee reports.[17]

The demand approach to preparation rests on the idea that employees should be provided with what they want. Finally, the business planning approach rests on the belief that employees should be provided the information that will allow them to adapt their behavior towards a performance improvement.

Factors Influencing Disclosure to Employees

Firms do have a continuous communication process with employees through various media including plant-level discussions, quality circles, audiovisual presentations, and in-house journals and notices. The purpose of the formal employees annual report is to provide an integrative and exhaustive report rather than a piecemeal approach. The same point is argued as follows:

It must be a report, capable of satisfying additional information needs of employees, rather than simply duplicating information already provided through alternative internal channels, or providing unwanted information. Unless the preparers of an annual report to employees can identify a genuine information void left by other internal communication media, and can justifiably believe that such a report can fill this void, then the report has no real justification.[18]

The literature has identified various aims and reasons for reporting to employees. A survey of the literature on financial reporting to employees between 1919 and 1979 identified the following reasons: (a) heralding changes, (b) presenting management propaganda, (c) promoting interest in understanding of company affairs and performance, (d) explaining management decisions, (e) explaining the relationship between employees, management, and shareholders, (f) explaining the objectives of the company, (g) facilitating greater employee participation, (h) responding to legislative or union pressure, (i) building company image, (j) meeting information requirements peculiar to employees, (k) responding to management fear of wage demands, strikes, and competitive disadvantages, and (l) promoting a higher degree of employee interest.[19]

The same survey shows that the level of interest in reporting to employees reached a higher level when the following four socioeconomic factors were also present: (a) the use of new technology in the workplace, (b) increased mergers in the corporate sector, (c) the emergence of anti-union sentiment, and (d) fears of economic recession.[20] It seems that management may have increased the level of employee reporting in reaction to the potential consequence of each of these factors or a combination of these factors. N. R. Lewis, L. D. Parker, and P. Sutcliffe, the authors of the survey, speculated that management may have hoped to

1. allay fears of lost rank, skill or employment through technological advances;
2. counter fears of "bigness," monopoly power, employee relocation and loss of identity through corporate mergers;
3. take advantage of community anti-union sentiments by bypassing union communication channels (reporting directly to employees), emphasizing management prerogatives and the need to control wages and associated costs and generally weakening the unions' potential to disrupt operations; and
4. prepare employees for hard times, confirm or dispel rumors of imminent company

failure, allay fears of unemployment and urge employees to greater efforts in difficult economic times.[21]

Dennis Taylor, Laurie Webb, and Les McGinley identified the following personal benefits which management might attempt to seek for itself by providing an annual report to employees in addition to using the conventional management-employee communication media: (a) building a favorable employee impression of the management group, (b) reducing the resistance of employees to changes initiated by management, and (c) providing a useful response to union pressure for more corporate financial information from management.[22] They also identified the following personal benefits which might accrue to employees with employee reporting: (a) having the basis for deciding whether to continue employment with the company or an organizational section of the company; (b) having the basis for assessing the relative position of the employees within the corporate structure, particularly in terms of getting a "fair go"; and (c) understanding the image of the company, as a basis for deciding at a personal level whether to identify with this image.[23]

Finally, B. J. Foley and K. T. Maunders identified arguments supporting disclosure directly to employees: (a) feedback of information to employees will improve job performance via learning effects and also serve to increase motivation; (b) the role of employee reporting is crucial to effective worker participation which will contribute to the efficiency of the company; (c) the fundamental change in the nature of the firm and its "social responsibility" legitimizes employee reporting; (d) employee reporting may be seen by some employers as a possible way of resurrecting the concept of joint consultation as a means of avoiding unionization; and finally, (e) the socialist tradition with its ultimate objective of changing the basis of ownership and the control of resources sees employee reporting as a step toward increasing "workers' control" and developing "workers' self confidence."[24] According to Foley and Maunders, the case for employee reporting using the socialist argument rests on two fundamental principles:

1. That it is a technique which helps employees to establish greater democratization of decision making in industry;

2. That is may usefully act as a check on those aspects of the market system which result in adverse external effects in the form of pollution and environmental degradation.[25]

Factors Influencing Disclosure to Unions

P. F. Pope and D. A. Peel rely on the rational expectations hypothesis to argue the desirability of disclosure to unions.[26] Basically, the argument goes that in the absence of a certain piece of information, the unions will form an expectation about it which, on the average, will be unbiased. If the forecast is biased, the variance of the forecast carries with it a cost due to the possible difference of opinion between the union and management. Therefore, disclosure of the information by management would reduce the variance and eliminate the forecast error. The interests of management should be in a more liberal disclosure policy to unions. "The bargaining process is not costless since it involves the commitment of considerable managerial resources. If a more liberal disclosure policy is adopted the differences in initial perceptions will be reduced immediately, confidence in outcomes will be increased, and the length of the subsequent negotiations will decrease."[27] Thus the disclosure of information can be expected to affect the bargaining process to the relative advantage of both labor and management. Foley and Maunders identified two major arguments favoring greater disclosure of company information to trade unions: a means of shifting bargaining power from management to union negotiators and a necessary condition if integrative bargaining is to develop.[28] The same point had been made earlier by R. B. McKersie and L. C. Hunter as follows:

The more information the parties share, the better the problem-solving is apt to function. Some companies still feel reluctant to reveal the "inner-workings" of the enterprise. Such hesitation makes the definition of problems, the development of alternatives and the selection of solutions difficult to execute. Without basis data and the overture of trust that is involved in sharing sensitive information, problem solving cannot be effective and attitudes will remain frozen.[29]

James A. Craft identified some specific factors that will influence the needs of a firm to disclose information to the union in collective bargaining.[30]

1. The discretion management enjoys regarding information disclosure beyond that required by the law which is related to its bargaining power vis-à-vis the union. More specifically, Craft reasons

   If management has substantial bargaining power, it will usually enjoy much discretion regarding disclosure of financial and other management information. It can obtain a settlement favorable to itself in any case, and the amount and type of disclosure will be determined by management's objectives and its relationship with the union.[31]

2. The independence an organization enjoys in collective-bargaining decision making, with a more independent employer feeling greater pressures for disclosure because of the increased need to justify a negotiating position arising from the absence of specific settlement or general pattern to be followed.

3. The nature of the collective-bargaining relationship with the union, with little incentive to disclose beyond that which is required by the law in relationships characterized by extensive conflict and with strong incentive to fully inform the union by providing nonselective disclosures in cooperative relationships between the union and management.

4. The political stability of the union with strong leadership creating a situation for more opportunities for disclosure in collective bargaining, in addition to what is required by law or accepted and supported by management.

5. The level of sophistication of union leaders and membership regarding financial accounting and related information, with higher sophistication leading to better disclosure.

Not all the arguments are in favor of disclosure of information to unions. Foley and Maunders cite the following arguments:

1. Lack of expertise and training in financial accounting of most union negotiators and particularly shop stewards can result in misunderstanding, mistrust, and damage to the bargaining process.

2. The disclosure of information will strengthen the bargaining position of shop stewards and trade unions, leading to more aggressive bargaining and earlier pay settlements in those cases where industrial relations are already in poor conditions.

3. The disclosure of sensitive information to unions—especially when the information deals with cost structure, efficiency indicators, pricing policy, and future development plans—may reach competitors.

4. The disclosure of information to unions presents a problem of confidentiality where the rights of shareholders are concerned, especially if these shareholders have not been consulted.

5. The disclosure of information to unions may negatively affect management's right to manage as it hinders the legitimacy of managerial authority.

6. The disclosure of information to unions rather than contributing to a better industrial relations atmosphere may lead to *"greater militancy and more inflationary trade union wage demands."*[32]

INFORMATION NEEDS IN EMPLOYEE REPORTING

Information Needs of Employees

Employee reporting is concerned with the provision of information that is useful to the decisions. Relevance of the information is naturally important to guard the credibility of the information with employees. Two approaches may be used: the consumer sovereignty approach and/or the decision oriented approach. The consumer sovereignty approach consists of merging the information needs of employees and evaluating the present disclosures to correct any discrepancies. This approach may suffer from the failure of employees to determine the appropriate information needed and from their tendency to demand information similar to what is currently available.

The decision oriented approach focuses on defining the decision models of the employees and determining the information needs in terms of the decision models' variables and parameters. Those models are either deductive or descriptive. Deductive models are subject to a number of limitations. These have been identified by David Cooper and Simon Essex as follows:

1. The difficulty and lack of an operational single measure of utility;

2. The difficulty of summarizing and synthesizing individual and inconsistent desires into a practical bargaining strategy;

3. The constantly changing values of the probabilities of the identified outcomes, the utility associated with each outcome, and the range of alternative actions specified in the basic subjective expected utility maximization model;

4. The cognitive limitations and the limited information processing capabilities of individual employees.[33]

Descriptive models focus on a correct portrayal of the real world and decision making, taking into account the idea that individuals and organizations are intentionally rational but limited by the complexity of the environment in which they operate. Various authors have provided descriptive models of employee decision making with the aim of identifying their information needs. David Cooper and Simon Essex provided a model centering on the shop steward's role, decision models, and information needs. Various authors identified employee need for information as evidenced by demands or suggested needs. Exhibit 6.1 provides a detailed list of types of information which have been either suggested by an author as potentially useful to employees or observed as employee demands by an author.[34] Lewis, Parker, and Sutcliffe identified the following employee decisions: (a) acceptance or rejection of entity offer of retaining/ relocation/promotion/new position, (b) level of productivity, (c) job satisfaction, stay or leave, retirement planning, (d) personal investment, saving levels, insurance (non-entity superannuation), employee shares, debentures in entity, (e) union membership or nonmembership, (f) level of involvement of member, and (g) personal expenditure: general organization's products, new products.[35] Exhibit 6.2 provides the information deemed useful to those decisions.

Four major categories of information needs of employees are identified by Foley and Maunders: (a) financial and economic information relating to job security, (b) information on working conditions, (c) information on achievement and performance indicators, and (d) information on equity or fairness in the distribution of economic reward.[36]

Finally, N. H. Cuthbert and A. Whitaker suggest the following information as potentially useful to shop stewards:

1. Individual plant operating accounts, particularly relating to levels of profitability.

2. Details of the costing process.

   a. The types of costing systems used and their impact on cost structure.

   b. How these affect returns at the level of a given plant.

3. Budgets and the variances produced.

Exhibit 6.1

Employee Need for Information as Evidenced by Demands or Suggested Needs

Presented below are types of information which have been either suggested by an author as potentially useful to employees or observed as employee demands by an author. Information types are grouped according to the publication in which they were discussed.

Information on productivity and efficiency data at plant level; manpower plans; benefits; intragroup payments; transfer prices; company's future plans. (Lafferty, 1977)

Pricing policy, especially transfer prices; advice re imminent collapse; social auditing (Swedish style). (Jenkins, 1975)

Future employment levels and work conditions; plans for expansion or contraction; effects of technological changes; training schemes; health and safety practices; pay conditions; terms of employment of various groups including managers; contribution made by employees in different plants and divisions; is adequate provision being made for pension payments?; can company afford higher wages?; can company succeed against competition?; is the company's overall product/cost/price structure right?. (Thompson, 1975)

Costings; performance indicators; manpower statistics. (Miller, 1975)

Details of past, present and planned capital spending; unit Costs of inputs (operating costs and overheads); details of sources and uses of funds; changes in value of fixed assets and trade investments; details of individuals' earnings and hours. (GMWU, 1976)

Performance detail of their own particular unit, be it factory, department, or company. (Holmes, 1977)

Matters directly affecting their own work and conditions on the shop floor; information about future developments. (ICAEW, 1976)

Performance, pay prospects. (ICMA, 1978)

Reporting on health and safety of the workplace; reporting on the effect of productivity bargaining and the monitoring of profit-sharing schemes; reporting on planning, agreements made between entity and government and the effect of these on job security; reporting on current and alternative distributions of income and the effect these have on the efficient allocation of resources; reporting for the purpose of negotiating a wage settlement. (Climo, 1976)

State of the order book; sales campaigns; exports; contracts entered; proposed capital expenditure and the reasons for it; fixed assets; the state of the cash flow; employment figures; changes in working practices and manpower requirements; productivity and proposed acquisition and disposals of segments of the company together with details of reasons for decisions taken; production, selling and distribution costs; costs of machinery; cost of management; costs of materials; health and safety costs and benefits; customer complaints; information re conduct of industrial relations; information on future plans. (Jones, 1975)

Production and marketing plans; difficulties likely to be met; research and development activity; future capital investment plans in terms of profit and equity; new facilities and the influence of these on employment and deployment of labor; information on success against previous objectives and identification of reasons for failure; changes in operating costs; details of cash flow situations; analysis of profit/loss generation; profit compared with sales and its disposition; capital employed performance; stock policy; plant utilization; overtime; absenteeism; sickness; etc. (Gogarty, 1975)

Monetary rewards; promotion opportunities; stability of employment; justice in distribution of rewards; identification with company's image. (Taylor et al., 1979)

Exhibit 6.1 (*Continued*)

Individual plant spending accounts, particularly relating to levels of profitability; details of costing process; the types of costing systems used and their impact on cost structure; how these affect returns at the level of the given plant; budgets and variances produced; the transfer pricing systems; stock levels; state of the order book. (Cuthbert and Whitaker, 1977)

Local factory and departmental accounts, cost structures, forecasts, and budgets. (ICAEW and IPM, 1978)

Company's safety records; investment plans; product performance; employee benefits; pension rights; progress with factory plans; outlook for future. (Martin, 1977)

Source: N. R. Lewis, L. D. Parker, and P. Sutcliffe, "Financial Reporting to Employees: Towards a Research Framework," *Accounting and Business Research* (Summer 1984): 237–38. Reprinted with permission.

4. The transfer pricing system (already a major topic in international trade union circles with respect to the policies of multinational corporations).

5. Stock levels.

6. State of the order book.[37]

Disclosure Policy in Labor Relations

Craft suggests a disclosure policy in labor relations conceptualized in terms of the extent of information disclosed to the union and the usefulness of the information to the union in dealing with specific collective-bargaining issues and questions.[38] The extent of information to unions ranges from low to high. What results are five disclosure policies in collective bargaining. They are basically (1) limited disclosure, (2) selective disclosure, (3) judgmental disclosure, (4) ineffective disclosure, and (5) complete disclosure. *Selective disclosure, limited disclosure, ineffective disclosure*, and *complete disclosure* are definable in terms of either high or low or both, the extent of information disclosed, and the usefulness of the information to the union. *Judgmental disclosure* policy refers to the decision of management to choose information for disclosure with broader objectives than simply conforming to the law and substantiating its own bargaining position. More specifically, "The information management does provide is chosen to help the union bargain within a meaningful framework, but due to cost and collection problems, may not be as detailed and specific as the union might desire."[39]

CONTENT OF THE EMPLOYEE REPORT

The content of the report to employees has not been standardized yet. Consequently, the alternatives available vary in the level of qualification and so-

Exhibit 6.2
Table of Possible Employee Decisions and Information Useful to Those Decisions

Employee Decisions	Information Useful
Acceptance or rejection of entity offer of retraining/ relocation/ promotion/new position.	Profile of entity employees: age, sex, volume changes, location, hierarchical/ job type levels. Degree of employee welfare provisions. Management policy/attitudes. Technology changes. Capital or labour intensive comparisons. New business developments. Expansion or contraction plans.
Level of productivity.	Wage levels, perquisites, advancement possibilities, attitude of remote/close management, budgetary proposals. Imminent technological changes, safety of new machinery, working methods, accident and compensation record of entity, noise and toxicity levels, employee contribution to output, levels of workers in associated plants, product demand, stock level, cost structure of area/ section/plant/division.
Job satisfaction. Stay or leave. Retirement planning.	Pension availability, contribution levels, and performance. Merger or takeover likelihood. Profitability, sales volumes, production volumes, cash flows, liquidity, labour and capital ratios, job opportunities in entity. Future manpower plans and technological changes. New products or ventures planned.
Personal investment. Saving levels, insurance (nonentity superannuation), employee shares, debentures in entity.	Likely or occurring takeovers or mergers. Profitability, liquidity, sales projections, new products, or ventures, expansion or contraction plans. Employee pension fund availability and performance.
Union membership or non-membership; level of involvement if member.	Industrial relations statistics. Management policy/ attitudes. Open or closed shop. Corporate social responsibility attitudes. Attitudes of management re profit-seeking versus cost-cutting. Expansion, contraction, relocation, new technologies, retraining plans. Employee welfare provisions: canteens, health and safety bonus schemes. Employment terms and wages levels. Profitability, liquidity.
Personal expenditure: General Organization's products New products Product	Product knowledge of entity and its associated companies. New products. Employee purchase schemes. Product safety, performance and environment effects. Mergers and takeover developments. Wage levels. Liquidity. Gearing. Sales volumes. Profitability.

Source: N. R. Lewis, L. D. Parker, and P. Sutcliffe, "Financial Reporting to Employees: Towards a Research Framework," *Accounting and Business Research* (Summer 1984): 238–39. Reprinted with permission.

phistication. A survey of the relevant literature revealed the following report contents: (a) employee relationships, (b) future prospects (firm and employee), (c) statement of value added, (d) corporate-government relations, (e) corporate objectives, (f) cash flow, (g) where money came from and where it went, (h) profit and loss, (i) balance sheet, (j) social balance sheet, (k) break-even chart, (l) role of profits, (m) personnel-related information, (n) chairman's address, and (o) competitions to encourage readership.[40]

Similarly, the dissemination of the information varied. The same survey identified the following techniques used: (a) mailed directly to employees, (b) report issued plus a management meeting, (c) letter format, (d) newspapers, (e) slides and films, (f) radio, (g) notice boards, (h) video tapes, (i) pay packets, (j) a request, (k) through supervisors, (l) financial training, and (m) integration with total communication network.[41]

To be read and accepted by employees, the employee report should at all cost avoid offending the employees. Richard Martin has identified some of the pitfalls to avoid:

Don't be patronizing.

Aim at the above average employee. It is better for some not to be interested than for those who are interested to feel they are being treated like children.

Avoid "them" and "us" language. Refer to our business and what we own.

Don't try to avoid the word profit—no business can survive unless it makes a profit. When mentioning "extraordinary items," specify them.

Avoid the use of bowler hats and cloth caps in illustrations.

Don't discuss politics because you won't convince those with other views—you simply widen the rift.

Don't be afraid to repeat the message from year to year if it's worth it; it won't be remembered and there are always new employees.

Avoid jargon: use simple straightforward language but make sure it is not capable of misinterpretation or thought to be advertising or propaganda.

The report must be informative and motivational; it should provoke inquiry, explanation and subsequent action.

The report should encourage pride in the company's products and services. Charts should be simple and product related if possible.

Problems in the company should not be ignored but discussed openly and solutions proposed.

Personnel problems can be included but debate this aspect carefully before-hand. Headmasterly tickings-off should be avoided as they cause resentment. If the problem is very large, such as lateness, pilfering or absenteeism, it is difficult to ignore but must obviously be handled with tact. One major company produced an employee report concentrating on this subject with considerable candor; it discussed recruitment, labor turnover, absenteeism, days lost through strikes and lay-offs, and the company's safety record.[42]

Naturally, employees may well be required to learn some of the accounting jargon used in accounting reports. Such education is essential if the disclosure of employee information is going to be effective.

ROLE OF THE ACCOUNTANT IN EMPLOYEE REPORTING

Employee reporting presents a unique opportunity for accountants to expand their expertise beyond conventional accounting information, to investigate the information needs of unions and employees, and to provide new information of relevance to employees and unions. Some authors went even further by calling for a management bargaining team role for the cost accountant.[43] Firms, however, differ in terms of the role of the accountant and the data they use to evaluate labor contract proposals:

There are Type A firms that use primarily demographic data but make little use of either accounting or other financial data; Type B firms that use primarily demographic and accounting data; and Type C firms that use all these kinds of data. Demographic data are used to describe the vital statistics of an employee population, e.g., number of dependents, rates of pay, and years of service. Accounting data are used to describe information that can usually be obtained from payroll records, e.g., amounts paid in direct wages, overtime-premiums, military leave pay, vacation pay, holiday pay, etc. Other financial data are used to describe internal economic data that are not directly related to payroll costs. They would include information, such as past or estimated future revenues, production volume, product mix, and non-labor costs that are normally found in a corporate budget or profit report.[44]

Given these divergences, the Controllership Foundation suggested seven ways for the accountant to present accounting information for use in collective bargaining:

1. By compiling in advance a "fact book" or a series of tables and reports, but without concerning himself directly with the actual negotiations.
2. By acting as a consultant to the company negotiator, before and during the bargaining sessions—but again without becoming directly involved.
3. By obtaining close cooperation between his deputies and those of the negotiator to guide the presentation of facts for bargaining.
4. By serving as a member of a negotiating committee which attends all sessions, but not presenting any facts himself.
5. By making himself available for such presentations of facts as the negotiator desires.
6. By taking charge of the actual presentation of factual material, with the negotiator retaining control of the company's argument and the ultimate terms of agreement.
7. By forming special committees or task forces to collect, analyze and interpret data on certain provisions of the collective bargaining agreement.[45]

Craft also examined the role of the accountant in collective bargaining by presenting a conceptual framework in terms of the accountant's relationship to the parties in collective bargaining and the degree of his involvement in the labor relations process.[46] The relationship varies from neutral to partisan and the degree of the involvement from low to moderate/high. The resulting framework illustrates roles for the accountant in collective bargaining. The appropriate role of the accountant, given the range of alternatives, is made contingent on other factors including disclosure policy, qualifications and interest of the accountant, and role of financial issues in negotiations.

Exhibit 6.3
A Narrative Flowchart of Required Empirical Tests

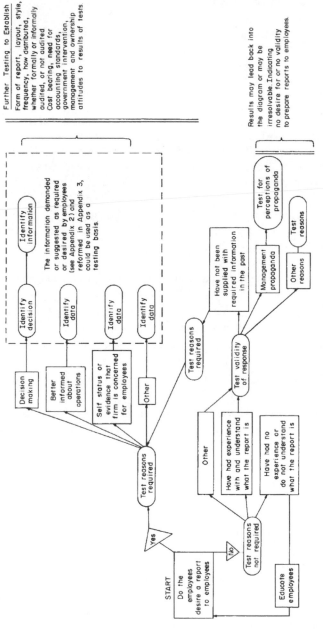

Source: N. R. Lewis, L. D. Parker, and P. Sutcliffe, "Financial Reporting to Employees: Towards a Research Framework," *Accounting and Business Research* (Summer 1984): 233. Reprinted with permission.

124

Exhibit 6.4
A Flowchart of Propositions

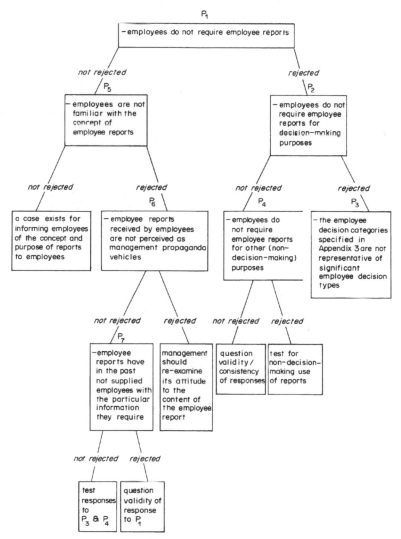

Source: N. R. Lewis, L. D. Parker, and P. Sutcliffe, "Financial Reporting to Employees: Towards a Research Framework," *Accounting and Business Research* (Summer 1984): 234. Reprinted with permission.

FUTURE RESEARCH IN EMPLOYEE REPORTING

The review of the literature in this chapter shows a general consensus among researchers that information should be reported to employees and unions in a separate report, giving definite benefits for both unions and employees on one hand and firms and managers on the other hand. It appears, however, from the same review that many remaining questions are unanswered with regard equally to the identity of the user groups, the information needs, the content and format of the report, and the behavioral and/or market impact that may follow such disclosure. To guide such research, Lewis, Parker, and Sutcliffe provided a research design that identifies the required empirical tests and the corresponding propositions (shown in Exhibits 6.3 and 6.4).[47] Empirical evidence in each of these propositions will provide more answers to the challenging subject of employee reporting.

NOTES

1. Nat Weinberg, "Factors Influencing Accounting: Employees," in *The Accounting Sampler: An Introduction*, ed. T. J. Burns and H. S. Hendrichosen (NY: McGraw-Hill Book Company, 1967), pp. 209–40.

2. Accounting Standards Steering Committee, *The Corporate Report* (London: Accounting Standards Steering Committee, 1975), p. 200.

3. Ibid., pp. 88–91.

4. Edward Stamp, *Corporate Reporting: Its Future Evolution* (Toronto: Canadian Institute of Chartered Accountants, 1980).

5. Trade Union Congress, Memorandum to the (Jenkins) Employment Law Committee (London: Trade Union Company, 1960), p. 941.

6. Larry Katz, "Efficiency Wage Theories: A Partial Evaluation," NBER Working Paper, Apr. 1986.

7. Oliver D. Hart, "Optional Labor Contracts Under Asymmetric Information: An Introduction," *Review of Economic Studies*, Jan. 1983, pp. 3–35.

8. J. S. Tracy, "An Investigation with the Determinants of U.S. Strike Activity," *American Economic Review*," June 1986, pp. 423–36.

9. A. Hollander and R. Laroix, "Unionism, Information Disclosure, and Profit Sharing," *Southern Economic Journal*, Jan. 1986, pp. 706–17.

10. M. M. Kleins and M. L. Bouillon, "Providing Business Information to Production Workers: Correlates of Compensation and Profitability," *Industrial Labor Relations Review*, July 1989, pp. 605–7.

11. J. Jackson-Cox, J. McQueeney, and J.E.M. Thirkell, *Strategies, Issues, and Events in Industrial Relations: Disclosure of Information in Context* (London: Routledge & Kegan Paul, 1987), p. 43.

12. T. Chrio, "Disclosure of Information to Employees' Representatives: A Wage Bargaining Decision Model" (Unpublished, University of Kent, 1971).

13. B. J. Foley and K. T. Maunders, *Accounting Information Disclosure and Collective Bargaining* (London: Macmillan, 1977).

14. D. Cooper and S. Essex, "Accounting Information and Employee Decision-Making," *Accounting, Organization and Society* 2 (1981): 97–107.

15. M. Cold, H. Levie, and R. Moore, *The Shop Stewards' Guide to the Use of Company Information*, (Nottingham: Spokesman Books, 1979).

16. Anthony Hilton, *Employee Reports: How to Communicate Financial Information to Employees* (Cambridge: Woodhead-Faulkner Ltd., 1978), p. 63.

17. Ibid., p. 24.

18. Dennis Taylor, Laurie Webb, and Les McGinley, "Annual Reports to Employees: The Challenge to the Corporate Accountant," *Chartered Accountant in Australia*, May 1979, p. 33.

19. N. R. Lewis, L. D. Parker, and P. Sutcliffe, "Financial Reporting to Employees: The Pattern of Development 1919 to 1979," *Accounting, Organizations and Society*, June 1984, p. 278.

20. Ibid., p. 281.

21. Ibid.

22. Taylor, Webb, McGinley, "Annual Reports to Employees," p. 35.

23. Ibid., p. 36.

24. Foley and Maunders, *Accounting Information Disclosure*, pp. 27–34.

25. Ibid., p. 34.

26. P. F. Pope and D. A. Peel, "Information Disclosure to Employees and Rational Expectations," *Journal of Business and Accounting*, Spring 1981, pp. 139–46.

27. Ibid., p. 142.

28. Foley and Maunders, *Accounting Information Disclosure*, pp. 39–40.

29. L. C. Hunter and R. B. McKersie, *Pay Productivity and Collective Bargaining* (London: Macmillan, 1973), p. 173.

30. James A. Craft, "Information Disclosure and the Role of the Accountant in Collective Bargaining," *Accounting, Organizations and Society* 6, no. 1 (1981): 99–101.

31. Ibid., p. 99.

32. Foley and Maunders, *Accounting Information Disclosure*, pp. 43–50.

33. David Cooper and Simon Essex, "Accounting Information and Employee Decision Making," *Accounting, Organizations and Society* 2, no. 3 (1977): 202–6.

34. N. R. Lewis, L. D. Parker, and P. Sutcliffe, "Financial Reporting to Employees: Towards a Research Framework," *Accounting and Business Research*, Summer 1984, pp. 237–38.

35. Ibid., pp. 238–39.

36. Foley and Maunders, *Accounting Information Disclosure*, p. 39.

37. N. H. Cuthbert and A. Whitaker, "Disclosure of Information and Collective Bargaining: A Reexamination," *Journal of Business Finance and Accounting* 4, no. 3 (1977): 374.

38. Craft, "Role of the Accountant in Collective Bargaining," pp. 101–2.

39. Ibid., p. 102.

40. Lewis, Parker, and Sutcliffe, "Financial Reporting to Employees: The Pattern of Development," p. 278.

41. Ibid., p. 279.

42. Richard Martin, "Providing the Employee Report," *Management Accounting*, Sept. 1977, p. 342.

43. Lee C. Shaw, "Company Labor Policy and the Accountant's Part," *NACA Bulletin*, Mar. 1954, p. 865; Robert E. Hess, "Labor Unions Look at Accountants," *Management Accounting*, Oct. 1967, p. 60; Harold H. Jack, "The Accountant's Role in Labor Rela-

tions," *Management Accounting*, Oct. 1970, p. 60; Michael F. Granof, "Financial Evaluation of Labor Contracts," *Management Accounting*, July 1973, p. 42.

44. Granof, "Financial Evaluation of Labor Contracts," p. 42.

45. Earl Brooks, N. Arnold Tolls, and Richard F. Dean, *Providing Facts and Figures for Collective Bargaining: The Controller's Role* (New York: Controllership Foundation, 1950), p. 26.

46. Craft, "Role of the Accountant in Collective Bargaining," pp. 103–6.

47. Lewis, Parker, and Sutcliffe, "Financial Reporting to Employees: Towards a Research Framework," pp. 233–34.

REFERENCES

Carlsberg, B. V., and A.J.B. Hope, eds. *Current Issues in Accounting*. London: Philip Allan, 1977.

Climo, T. "The Role of the Accountant in Industrial Relations." *Accountant*, 16 Dec. 1976, 702.

Cooper, D., and S. Essex. "Accounting Information and Employee Decision Making." *Accounting, Organizations and Society* 12, no. 3 (1977): 201–17.

Craft, J. A. "Information Disclosure and the Role of the Accountant in Collective Bargaining." *Accounting, Organizations and Society* 6, no. 1 (1981): 97–107.

———. "A Reply to Maunders and Foley." *Accounting, Organizations and Society* 9, no. 1 (1984): 107–8.

Cuthbert, N. H., and A. Whitaker. "Disclosure of Information and Collective Bargaining: A Reexamination." *Journal of Business Finance and Accounting* 4, no. 3 (1977): 373–78.

Dale, Ernest. *Sources of Economic Information for Collective Bargaining*. New York: American Management Association, 1950.

Foley, B. J., and K. T. Maunders. *Accounting Information Disclosure and Collective Bargaining*. London: Macmillan, 1977.

General and Municipal Workers Union (GMWU) (U.K.). *Law at Work*. London: GMWU, 1976.

Gogarty, J. P. "What Employees Expect to be Told." *Management Accounting* (United Kingdom), Nov. 1975, 359–60.

Granof, Michael F. "Financial Evaluation of Labor Contracts." *Management Accounting*, July 1973, 42.

Holmes, G. "How UK Companies Report," *Accountancy*, Nov. 1977, 66.

Horwitz, B., and R. Shalahang. "Published Corporate Accounting Data and General Wage Increases of the Firm." *Accounting Review*, Apr. 1971, 243–52.

Hussey, R. *Employees and the Employee Report*. London: Touche Ross, 1978.

Hussey, R., and R. J. Craig. *Keeping Employees Informed*. Sydney, Australia: Butterworth, 1982.

Institute of Chartered Accountants in England and in Wales (ICAEW). *The Reporting of Company Financial Results to Employees*. London: ICAEW, Dec. 1976.

——— and the Institute of Personnel Management (IPM). *Assisting Employees in the Understanding and Use of Financial Information*. London: IPM, 1978.

Institute of Cost and Management Accountants (ICMA). "Presentation of Information." London: ICMA, Dec. 1978.

Jack, Harold H. "The Accountant's Role in Labor Relations." *Management Accounting*, Oct. 1970, 60.

Jackson-Cox, J., J. E. Thirkell, and J. McQueeney. "The Disclosure of Company Information to Trade Unions: The Relevance of the ACAS Code of Practice on Disclosure." *Accounting, Organizations and Society*, June 1984, 253–73.

Jenkins, C. "A Trade Unionist's Viewpoint on Financial Information Requirements." *Management Accounting*, Nov. 1975, 359.

Jones, D.M.C. "Designing Accounts to Inform More Effectively." *Management Accounting*, March 1975, 359.

Lafferty, M. "Collective Bargaining." *Journal of Business Finance and Accounting*, Spring 1974, 109–27.

———. "How Much Should We Tell Trade Unions?" *Accounting Age*, 22 February 1974, 340–46.

———. "A Landmark for Union and the City." *Financial Times* (26 July 1977).

Martin, Richard. "Providing the Employee Report." *Management Accounting*, Sept. 1977.

Miller, J. "Financial Information for Employees." *Accountant*, 29 May 1975, 690.

Palmer, John R. *The Use of Accounting Information in Labor Negotiations*. New York: National Association of Accountants, 1977.

Parker, L. D. "Financial Reporting to Corporate Employees: A Growing Practice in Australia." *Chartered Accountant in Australia*, March 1977, 5–9.

Pope, P. F., and D. A. Peel. "Information Disclosure to Employees and Rational Expectations." *Journal of Business Finance and Accounting*, Spring 1981, 139–46.

Taylor, Dennis, Laurie Webb, and Les McGinley. "Annual Reports to Employees: The Challenge to the Corporate Accountant." *Chartered Accountant in Australia*, May 1979, 33–39.

Thompson, S. "Involving a Financial Policy and Strategy Which Includes Consideration of Employees' Information Needs." *Management Accounting*, November 1975, 360.

Chapter 7

The Social Performance Report

A firm's reputation is a very important asset that can generate future returns. Firms actively engage in reputation building through the measurement and disclosure of reputation signals that crystallize their status within an industrial social system. These reputation signals are generally accounting signals regarding the financial performance, structure, and conduct of the firm that trigger market responses and market signals of similar magnitude and sign.

Since the activities of corporations also impact their environment and various clienteles beyond market participants, however, corporations also engage in the measurement and production of nonaccounting reputation signals. These nonaccounting reputation signals are deemed as important as accounting signals in the production and reproduction of reputation. These nonaccounting reputation signals are of two kinds: (1) measures of social performance and (2) measures of organizational effectiveness. They are deemed extremely important in the evaluation of firms and in answering the questions "How is the company performing?" and "How much better should the company be performing?" Accordingly, this chapter explains the nature, rationale, and measurement of social performance.

CONCEPTS OF SOCIAL PERFORMANCE

Nature of Social Performance

The measurement of social performance falls in the general area of social accounting.[1] Under the general heading of social accounting, however, there are four various activities that can be delineated, namely (1) social responsibility accounting (SRA), (2) total impact accounting (TIA), (3) socioeconomic accounting, and (4) social indicators accounting.[2] The general concept and disclosure of social performance are products of SRA and TIA, and social accounting is appropriately defined as "the process of selecting firm-level social performance variables, measures and measurements procedures; systematically developing information useful for evaluating the firm's social performance, and communicating such information to concerned social groups, both within and outside the firm."[3] A good conceptual framework for social accounting, proposed by K. V. Ramanathan and comprising three objectives and six concepts, is shown in Exhibit 7.1. This framework applies equally to SRA and TIA. A question arises about who is "pushing" for corporate social reporting. Are they to the right or the left of the political spectrum? R. Gray et al. presented corporate social reporting (CSR) as a dialectic among four positions:

1. The extreme left-wing of politics ("left-wing radicals").
2. The acceptance of the *status quo*.
3. The pursuit of subject/intellectual property rights.
4. The extreme right-wing of politics (the "pristine capitalists" or "right-wing radicals").[4]

The second group appears to represent those true advocates of corporate social reporting. They are represented by people

(1) who assume that the purpose of CSR is to enhance the corporate image and hold the, usually implicit, assumption that corporate behavior is fundamentally benign; (2) who assume that the purpose of CSR is to discharge an organization's accountability under the assumption that a social contract exists between the organization and society (the existence of this social contract demands the discharge of social accountability); (3) who appear to assume that CSR is effectively an extension of traditional financial reporting and its purpose is to inform investors.[5]

Rationale for Social Performance

Various arguments are used for the measurement and disclosure of social performance. The first is the *social contract* argument. Implicitly, it is assumed that organizations ought to act in a manner that maximizes social welfare, as if a social contract existed between the organization and society. By doing so, organizations gain a kind of organizational legitimacy vis-à-vis society. While the social contract can be assumed to be implicit, various societal laws may render certain covenants of the contract more explicit. These laws, which constitute the rules of the game in which organizations choose to play, become the terms of the social contract.[6] Through these implicit and explicit laws, society defines the rules of accountability for organizations.

The state, however, plays a primary role in the formulation of these laws and

Exhibit 7.1
Proposed Objectives and Concepts for Social Accounting

Objective 1
An objective of corporate social accounting is to identify and measure the periodic net social contribution of an individual firm, which includes not only the costs and benefits internalized to the firm, but also those arising from externalities affecting different social segments.

Objective 2
An objective of corporate social accounting is to help determine whether an individual firm's strategies and practices, which directly affect the relative resources and power status of individuals, communities, social segments, and generations, are consistent with widely shared social priorities on the one hand and the individual firm's legitimate aspirations on the other.

Objective 3
An objective of corporate social accounting is to make available in an optimal manner to all social constituents relative information on a firm's goals, policies, programs, performances, and contributions to social goals. Relevant information is that which provides for public accountability and also facilitates public decision making regarding social choices and social resources allocation. Optimal implies a cost/benefit effective reporting strategy which also optimally balances potential information conflicts among the various social constituents of a firm.

Concept 1
A social transaction represents a firm's utilization or delivery of a socio-environmental resource which affects the absolute or relative interests of the firm's various social constituents and which is not processed through the marketplace.

Concept 2
Social overhead (returns) represents the sacrifices (benefit) to society from those resources consumed (added) by a firm as a result of its social transactions. In other words, social overhead is the measured value of a firm's negative externalities and social returns is the measured value of its positive externalities.

Concept 3
Social income represents the periodic net social contribution of a firm. It is computed as the algebraic sum of the firm's traditionally measured net income, its aggregate social overhead and its aggregate social returns.

Concept 4
Social constituents are the different distinct social groups (implied in the second objective and expressed in the third objective of social accounting) with whom a firm is presumed to have a social contract.

Concept 5
Social equity is a measure of the aggregate changes in the claims which each social constituent is presumed to have on the firm.

Exhibit 7.1 (*Continued*)

Concept 6
Net social asset of a firm is a measure of its aggregate nonmarket contribution to the
society's well-being less its nonmarket depletion of the society's resources during the
life of the firm.

Source: K. V. Ramanathan, "Toward A Theory of Corporate Social Accounting," *The Accounting
Review* (July 1976): 527. © 1976 by American Accounting Association. Reprinted with permission.

the specification of the rules of the game. In the U.S. contract, these laws and
the general concern with social performance created a need for tracking environmental risk. With the 1989 Securities and Exchange Commission (SEC)
requirement that companies disclose any potential environmental cleanup liabilities they may face under the Federal Superfund Law, the 1990 annual reports
of companies started the disclosure process. The 10-K disclosures, added to the
host of required filings with state and federal environmental agencies, led to the
creation of data banks that provided information on companies specializing in
the tracking of environmental risk. Examples of these companies include Ersite,
based in Denver; Environmental Audits in Lyonville, Pennsylvania; the Environmental Risk Information Center in Alexandria, Virginia; the Petroleum Information Corporation in Littleton, Colorado; Toxicheck in Birmingham,
Michigan; Vista Environmental Information in San Diego; and Environmental
Data Resources in Southport, Connecticut.[7] This new industry gives a glimpse
of a future characterized by concerned shareholders regarding the social performance of firms and by more accurate and reliable information on the environmental risks of U.S. corporations.

Second is the *social justice* argument. Three theories of justice, John Rawls's
theory of justice, as presented in his book, *A Theory of Justice*;[8] A. M. Nozick's
"entitlement theory;" as presented in his book *Anarchy, State and Utopia*;[9] and
A. Gerwith's theory of justice, as presented in *Reason and Morality*,[10] contain
principles for evaluating laws and institutions from a moral standpoint.

Rawls's contract theory—a theory of just social institutions—can be offered as
a concept of fairness in accounting. Applied to accounting, it suggests first the potential reliance on a veil of ignorance in all the situations calling for an accounting
choice to yield eventual solutions that are neutral, fair, and socially just. Second,
it suggests an expanded role of accounting in the making of just institutions and
the definition of the social minimum advocated by Rawls. This role, also espoused
by the advocates of social accounting, leads to the elimination of those aspects of
the social world in general, and the accounting world in particular, that seem arbitrary from a moral point of view. This view of fairness would be most welcome
by advocates of social accounting. As stated by Paul Williams,

Rawlsian principles also may prove to be a useful set of premises for speculation about
the alternative accounting system. For example, one plausible reason for the slow theo-

retical development of social accounting, at least in the United States, could be the constraining effect of conventional accounting premises about character and legitimacy of institutions, both public and private. Accounting scholars with interest in social accounting are certainly free to generate and test hypotheses about measuring accounting or reporting in Rawlsian, or any other, institutional setting.[11]

Fairness in accounting à la Nozick is essentially a libertarian theory of distribution, based on a principle of justice in acquisition and in transfer. This concept of distributive justice, with its reliance on a free market mechanism, does not allow for dealing adequately with fairness as a distributive function. It is assumed to fail to consider the social obligations of humans to each other, perpetuates past violations of principles of acquisition and transition, and distorts the meaning of well-offness in a world of scarcity.[12] The reliance on the market mechanism, the absence of a moral language to discuss social obligations, and the absence of a concept of redistributive justice are the basis of the cited failures of the libertarian theory of justice. In addition, the growing importance of mediocracy in the context of a basically market-driven system has created problems for a Nozickian theory of justice. The conflicting rules of distribution are not well accepted in our contemporary culture.[13]

Gerwith's theory of justice can also be offered as a concept of fairness in accounting. Applied to accounting, it suggests the primacy of the concern for the rights of freedom and well-being of all persons affected by the activities of the firm and for the creation of institutional and accounting arrangements to guarantee these rights. These arrangements call for some form of rectification through the creation of a "supportive system" and specific social rules to be followed by organizations and members within the organization.

Accounting may be called on to facilitate a drastic redistribution of wealth and to be an effective exercise of the fundamental rights to freedom and well-being of the stakeholders in organizations. Gerwithian principles may prove, for example, to be a useful set of premises for speculation about the merit of value added reporting. They support the emphasis in value added reporting to report the total return to all members of the "production team": shareholders, bondholders, suppliers, labor, government, and society. Since they are all given a place of importance in the measurement, reporting, and allocation of the total return of the firm, not one of these members is relegated to the position of "disadvantaged," as in other concepts of distributive justice.

Basically, the Gerwithian principles, as applied to fairness in accounting, include a recognition of the rights of all those affected by the activities of the organization and as stated by Gerwith himself, "a recognition of the rights of others, a positive concern for their having the objects of these rights, and a positive regard for them as persons who have rights or entitlement equal to his own as well as the rational capacity to reflect on their purposes and to control their behavior in light of such reflection."[14] This calls for action that is voluntary and purposive to affirm an egalitarian universalist moral principle.

Marx claimed, "man makes his own history." So too, the role of action in making moral judgments regarding efficiency and distribution protects the generic rights of all recipients of accounting information. Accounting will create its own history as a moral agent in the marketplace, an agent concerned with the rights of the recipients of accounting information. The merits of application of the principle of generic consistency (PGC) to the concept of fairness in accounting are derived from its capacity to present the accountant with rationally grounded answers to each of the three questions of moral philosophy:

1. The distributive question of which person's interests ought to be favorably considered is answered by calling for the respect of the generic rights of all recipients and for the equality of the rights of all prospective purpose agents.
2. The substantive question of which interests ought to be favorably considered is answered by focusing on the primacy of freedom and well-being.
3. The authoritative question of why should anyone be moral in the sense of taking favorable account of other people's interests is justified by the reason of avoiding self-contradiction. Basically an action that violates the PGC cannot be rationally justified.[15]

Third is the *users' needs* argument. Basically, users of financial statements need social information for their revenue allocation decisions. An argument can be made by some that shareholders are conservative and care only about dividends. In fact, according to a recent survey of shareholders, they want corporations to direct resources toward cleaning up plants, stopping environmental pollution, and making safer products.[16] As a result, Epstein advises corporations to do the following to manage expenditures on social concerns:

• Integrate corporate awareness of social, ethical and environmental issues into corporate decisions at all levels and make sure such concerns have representation on the board of directors;
• Develop methods to evaluate and report on the social and environmental impacts of corporate activities;
• Modify the corporate structure to set up a mechanism to deal with social, environmental, and ethical crises. Then a company can be a crisis-prepared organization rather than a crisis-prone organization. Companies that do not prepare themselves for crises simply flounder;
• Create incentives for ethical, environmental, and socially responsible behavior on the part of employees and integrate those incentives into the performance evaluation system and corporate culture. Unless this is institutionalized it never enters the corporate culture and significant, permanent change cannot occur;
• Recognize that if the environment is to be cleaned up, business must take a leadership role in the wise use of natural resources and the reduction of pollutants.[17]

There is, however, a lack of normative and/or descriptive models on the users' needs in terms of social information. One major exception identifies principal users, their major objectives, and the nature of useful information. Although the list of users appears intuitive and justifiable, there is a need for empirical research to evaluate the desirability of social information for various users and uses, and there is a demand for corporate social responsibility reporting.

Fourth is the *social investment* argument. Basically, it is assumed that an *ethical investor group* is now relying on social information provided in annual reports for making investment decisions. The disclosure of social information becomes, therefore, essential if investors are going to consider properly the negative effects of social awareness expenditures on earnings per share, along with any compensating positive effects that reduce risk or create greater interest from a particular investment clientele. Some argue that the risk-reducing effects will more than compensate for social awareness expenditures: "Between firms competing in the capital markets those perceived to have the highest expected future earnings in combination with the lowest expected risk from environmental and other factors will be most successful at attracting long term funds."[18]

Others believe that "ethical investors" form a clientele that responds to demonstrations of corporate social concern.[19] Investors of this type would like to avoid particular investments entirely for ethical reasons and would prefer to favor socially responsible corporations in their portfolios.[20] A survey by J. Rockness and P. F. Williams[21] identifies an emerging consensus on the primary character of social performance among fund managers. The performance factors that are considered investment criteria by most of the managers include environmental protection, treatment of employees, business relations with repressive regimes, product quality and innovation, and defense criteria.

An emerging theory of social investment is provided by S. T. Bruyn, who suggests that "[s]ocial and economic values can be maximized together, and this creative synergism is the practical direction taken by social investors today."[22] Bruyn's investor is assumed to contribute to the development of a social economy designed to promote human values and institutions as well as self-interests. The social investor bases investment decisions not only on economic and financial considerations but also on sociologically grounded considerations. Both "social inventions" and technological inventions hold an expectation of profit and economic development. Social investors, although concerned with the management of profits and scarce resources, are also interested in the corporation's accountability to other stakeholders in the environment besides stockholders.

THE MEASUREMENT OF SOCIAL PERFORMANCE

Microsocial Accounting

Microsocial accounting is that part of social accounting interested in the evaluation, measurement, and disclosure of social performance of firms. For example, microsocial accounting describes approaches used by practitioners and academicians studying the measurement and disclosure of the environmental effects of organizational behavior at the firm level. This section presents the diverse results of various institutional groups concerned with proposed approaches to and demand for microsocial accounting information.

Institute of Management Accountants (formerly National Association of Accountants)

Report of the Committee on Accounting for Corporate Social Performance. The objective of the Committee on Accounting for Corporate Social Performance was to develop systems of accountability for corporate social performance.[23] In doing so, four major areas of social performance were identified as community involvement, human resources, physical resources and environmental contributions, and product or service contributions. Community involvement included socially oriented activities designed to benefit the general public. Human resources included activities designed to benefit employees. The physical resources and environmental contributions category included activities designed to benefit the total environment of the firm, and product or service contributions included activities specifically directed toward benefiting customers.

Epstein, Flamholtz, and McDonough. Accounting for the social contributions of product and/or services was examined in a sample of 800 large U.S. corporations by M. Epstein, E. Flamholtz, and J. McDonough in *Corporate Social Performance.*[24] These corporations were surveyed to identify types of measures used to account for product and service contributions and to ascertain the respective levels of interest, involvement, and sophistication in accounting for these contributions.

The following measurement category framework was utilized, and respondents were asked to indicate their degree of involvement in these monitoring/measuring activities:

1. Descriptions: periodic reports made on the effects of product or service contributions on customers and/or society.

2. Inventories: records or classification of a firm's product or service contributions.

3. Time records: records of the amount of time spent by personnel in product and service contributions.

4. Cost allocations: costs that have been allocated by some criterion to product or service contributions.

5. Cost tracing: costs that have been traced directly to product or service contributions.

6. Nonmonetary benefits (costs): assessments of benefits or costs of product or service contributions in nonmonetary, quantitative terms.

7. Monetary benefits (costs): assessments of benefits or costs of product or service contributions in monetary terms.[25]

The study found that product and service contributions ranked uppermost among the four categories of social performance and that corporations do not, in most cases, account for the costs and benefits of activities dealing with social responsibility. Furthermore, corporations do not attempt to account for their involvement with product and service contributions. When benefits are measured, monetary terms are used most frequently followed by the use of descriptions and inventories. Banks and retail corporations appeared to be most involved in accounting for product and service contributions. Finally, the study indicated industry differences in the relative importance of product and service contributions to society.[26] Recognizing the limited development of corporate social accounting systems in practice, the authors state that the survey revealed "neither the existence of additional pioneering efforts nor any significant level of adoption of existing approaches."[27]

Nikolai, Bazley, and Brummet. Accounting for corporate environmental activity, another aspect of corporate social performance, was dealt with by L. A. Nikolai, J. D. Bazley, and R. L. Brummet in *The Measurement of Corporate Environmental Activity.*[28] Their study relied on three stages consisting of a questionnaire, an interview case study, and an integration stage.

The questionnaire, designed to ascertain the "state of the art" regarding measurement techniques used to evaluate the costs and benefits of corporate environmental activity and the effect on corporate decision making, resulted in two major findings. First, companies surveyed were much more involved in the monetary measurement of costs associated with environmental actions than with the measurement of benefits accruing to these factors. Second, the measurement activity was focused on areas such as equipment costs and research and development, where conventional measurement techniques can be used, as opposed to aesthetic and image-promotion costs.[29] The interview case study phase, designed to determine how "companies are organized to make environmental decisions, how they measure the specific costs and benefits associated with these decisions, and how they incorporate such measurements into their planning and control processes,[30] found that involvement in corporate environmental activity is generally the result of strong commitment and direction on behalf of top management.

The integrative stage, unlike the two previous stages, was a prescriptive stage designed to "review, synthesize, and integrate the existing organizational structures, environmental definitions, and measurement techniques along with the modification of information systems, as ascertained from the interview case study stage in order to develop recommendations for measurement and decision making concerning environmental activity."[31] The findings proposed definitions and suggestions on environmental costs, environmental benefits, environmental investment planning, and environmental organizational structure.

Nikolai, Bazley, and Brummet proposed four possible definitions of environmental cost: (1) the incremental traceable cost incurred for the environmental aspects of a project, (2) the total cost incurred for the environmental aspects of a project, (3) the incremental traceable cost incurred for a total project for which the primary motivation is to produce environmental benefits, and (4) the total cost incurred for the total project for which the primary motivation is to produce environmental benefits.[32] Citing the first definition as most acceptable, the authors concluded that initial costs should be recorded as land costs, equipment costs, engineering costs, research and development costs, and miscellaneous costs. Furthermore, operating costs should be categorized as equipment operating costs, additional production costs, maintenance costs, disposal costs, monitoring costs, depreciation, and miscellaneous costs. Finally, exit costs should be categorized as restoration costs.

Environmental benefits were defined as the benefits to the environment that result from an expenditure of an environmental cost and categorized as either internal or external. "Internal environmental benefits are those environmental benefits which directly benefit the company while indirectly benefiting society. External environmental benefits are those environmental benefits which directly benefit society while indirectly benefiting the company."[33] Internal environmental benefits included recyclable raw materials, energy production, by-product sales, development of salable processes, and improved working conditions in terms of reduced turnover, ability to attract new employees, reduced absenteeism, improved employee efficiency, and public acceptance. Examples of external water environment benefits include improvements in public water supply, in swimming and other sports, in fish and wildlife support, in agricultural and industrial water supply, in navigation, health, aesthetics, and overall impact.

Nikolai, Bazley, and Brummet recommended an environmental capital investment request form with respect to environmental investment policy. As to operational planning, they suggested the extension of corporate responsibility beyond traditional objectives to include social objectives, via "environmental responsibility accounting." Furthermore, they proposed the following three "environmental activity" variances:

Environmental Discharge Variance   = Standard Level of Pollutant Discharge–Pollutant Discharge

Environmental Effectiveness Variance   = Desired Level of Environmental Benefits–Actual Level of Environmental Benefits

Environmental Efficiency Variance   = Standard Cost for Actual Discharge Level–Actual Cost for Actual Discharge Level

The American Accounting Association

Report of the Committee on Measures of Effectiveness for Social Programs. The charge of the Committee on Measures of Effectiveness for Social Programs was to report on the implications of integrating various nonfinancial statistics and measures, essential to the evaluation of efficiency and effectiveness in social programs, into the formal accounting and reporting process.[34] A social program was defined as a plan of action, an experiment introduced into society for the purpose of producing a change in the status of the society or some of its members.[35]

Uniform principles or guidelines to facilitate comparisons of different social programs and a sound basis for evaluating effectiveness of such programs are scarce. However, there exists growing concern and interest in the evaluation of social programs, as evidenced by the call by various organizations and individuals for a concept of a "social report" and by an attempt to introduce a Senate bill known as the Full Opportunity and Social Accounting Act. The committee, however, identified four difficulties associated with obtaining social measures.

1. Often, there is inconsistency between a societal concept as theoretically formulated and the operational definition by which it is empirically measured. *Fractional measurement*, accordingly, appears since it is difficult to construct an operational definition that covers a concept in all its attributes.

2. A social accounting system relies often on *indirect* measurement, e.g., measuring societal concepts by using data originally collected for other purposes.

3. Social systems use *formalistic-aggregative measurement* of collective attributes.

4. Social systems are fluid, nonstationary systems where *over time* various indicators relevant at some point become outmoded and new problems emerge which require new indicators.[36]

These problems have implications for the evaluation of social programs.

1. With respect to the *fractional measurement* problem, it is recommended that the evaluation of social programs rely on more indicators of different dimensions, to consider the qualitative dimensions, avoid substituting the measurement of means for the measurement of goals, and focus on a social unit's success in terms of a system model versus a goal model. The difference between the two approaches is that the goal model expects organizational effectiveness to increase with the increase of more means (resources) to the organization (or social unit). The system model, on the other hand, perceives that these may be in balance in allocating a social unit's resources to the goal activities and indirect nongoal activities that have to be met first in order to attain the goals set for a social unit.[37]

2. With respect to the *indirect measurement* problem, it is recommended that the evaluation of social programs develop various indices for the different dimensions of a concept.

3. With respect to the problem of the *measurement of collective attributes*, it is recommended that the evaluation of social programs focus on the relevant social unit rather than on the formal social unit and on global measures (data characterizing the collectivity itself, apart from its members) rather than on aggregated measures (data based on the statistical manipulation of attributes of the members or attributes of their relationship).

4. With respect to the problem of *nonstationarity*, it is recommended that measurement of effectiveness be adaptive over time in order be relevant in dynamic systems.

The committee also found that the public accounting profession is either involved in or in favor of involvement in the effectiveness of social programs. Finally, the committee also examined the role of three central financial agencies—the Department of the Treasury, the General Accounting Office (GAO), and the Office of Management and Budget (OMB)—in providing information for planning and evaluating federal social programs. Examples given of account-auditor development of evaluation data and effectiveness measures given by the committee covered social issues including controlling industrial water pollution, preservation of wilderness area, programs for aiding educationally deprived children, effectiveness of the Economic Opportunity program, and job opportunity in the business sector. To aid these endeavors, with respect to the potential involvement of the accounting profession, the committee suggested participation of the accounting profession in the determination of society's goals and objectives, involvement of the accounting profession at the "criteria setting" or "surrogate development" level, involvement of the accounting profession as a data manipulation and data verification expert, and involvement of the accounting profession in auditing the disbursement of public funds.

Based on these suggestions, potential implications for the accounting profession cited by the committee were the following:

1. Development of a theoretical base for social accounting.
2. More specialization within the profession.
3. More interaction (formal or informal) with other professions, particularly statisticians and social scientists.
4. More education and professional schools.
5. More clearly defined ethical standards.
6. Greater separation between the audit and management services staff.
7. More legal problems.
8. More government intervention.
9. Research and development by accounting firms and governmental accountants.
10. Greater exposure to the public.
11. Growth in management services.
12. A control function over the statistics generated and disseminated by social programs and government agencies.[38]

Report of the Committee on Environmental Effects of Organizational Behavior. The Committee on Environmental Effects of Organizational Behavior was charged with the development of measurement and reporting methods useful in communicating to both internal and external users the effects of an organization's behavior on the physical environment.[39] To this end, the committee focused on the problem of pollution, including economic, international, and accounting aspects.

From an economic point of view, pollution creates externalities or social costs that are not internalized and, hence, are inflicted on individuals and society. From an international point of view, the extent of internalization of social costs in a particular country creates cost differentials and gives producers from other countries who are not active in pollution abatement a competitive edge. From an accounting point of view, the pollution issue creates problems with regard to financial reporting, internal reporting, the attest function, and decision making.

The related issues of internal reporting of environmental effects, external reporting of environmental effects, and the implications for accountants were explored by the committee. With respect to internal reporting, the committee called for a multidisciplinary approach to gathering and utilizing both financial and nonfinancial information. Although the committee agreed to the importance of the pollution problem, they were unable to discover reasonably accurate techniques for measuring the social costs of pollution with respect to external reporting. As reporting alternatives, the committee suggested (1) displaying environmental control expenses on a separate line in the income statement; (2) disclosing separately total environmental control expenditures in the statement of source and application of funds (now, cash-flow statement); (3) classifying separately environmental control facilities (and related depreciation) in the balance sheet; (4) estimating environmental controls that result in extraordinary losses or corrections in prior years, which presently call for separate disclosure under generally accepted accounting principles, whenever these are material in amount; and (5) using accrual accounting for environmental liabilities and disclosing material future pollution control outlays when they arise out of past transactions.[40] The committee also recommended that every firm be required to report, and its auditors to attest to, a verbal statement. Finally, with respect to the implications for accountants, the committee suggested a challenging and important research agenda.[41]

Report of the Committee on the Measurement of Social Costs. The Committee on the Measurement of Social Costs was charged with identifying critical accounting issues currently faced by those who are teaching and/or doing research in the area of social costs.[42] As a response to an overview of the changing climate in which businesses operate, the committee suggested the development of new measurement concepts "to enable management to identify issues, recognize implications of current and planned actions, set priorities and select specific activities."[43]

The changing business climate, as characterized by profit motivation, sensitivity to the natural and human environment, growth, responsiveness to consumer needs, equitable distribution of benefits, dynamic business structure, fair treatment of employees, and legal and ethical behavior, gives rise to two opposing views concerning the role of the accountant. The first view is one of total involvement of the accountant in the design and installation, administration and operation, and finally verification and attestation of detection and measurement systems in the social sphere. As a beginning, a taxonomy for the measurement of social performance to include both social costs and social benefits is needed. This measurement of organizational performance should be more inclusive than that which is provided by conventional accounting and should include

1. Net income, which benefits stockholders and provides resources for further business growth.
2. Human resource contribution, which assists the individual in the organization to develop new knowledge or skills.
3. Public contribution, which helps the organization's "community" to function and provide services for its constituency.
4. Environmental contribution (closely allied with public contributions), which affects "quality of life" for society.
5. Product or service contribution, which affects customer well-being and satisfaction.[44]

This classification requires extending performance measurement to transactions that would not normally be considered business transactions, such as

1. Human resource contributions such as employee training programs, changes in quality of life and attitudes of people who comprise the organization, employee recruiting programs, or safety programs.
2. Public contributions such as contributions to educational and cultural programs, support for urban housing or transportation programs, or support for volunteer community affairs.
3. Environmental contribution aspects of production operations, use of resources, or recycling operations.
4. Product safety, product durability, product utility, or consumer satisfaction.[45]

The opposing view calls for no involvement by the accountant in the area of social accounting. This view argues that accountants should be concerned with only "those costs which are imposed on the corporate (accounting) entity by law, public pressure, or by choice of the corporation itself.[46] Furthermore, accountants may not have the necessary measurement technology for social accounting.

Finally, the committee addressed the three facets of social reporting: internal social reporting, external social reporting, and social attestation. Internal social reporting was viewed as necessary to provide relevant information to be in compliance (minimum versus maximum) with social premises and legal requirements. External social reporting can lead to special disclosure to each of the major constituents, namely stockholders, employees, customers, and society at large. Attestation of social reports would add a desirable degree of credibility.

Report of the Committee on Social Costs. The Committee on Social Costs was also charged with identifying critical issues faced by those teaching and/or doing research in social accounting.[47] In particular, the committee examined the issues of social audits, types of measurement of socially relevant corporate activities, and cost concepts of social accounting.

With respect to social audits, the committee identified three measurement levels of activities:

Measurement Level I	Identified and described (or "inventoried").
Measurement Level II	Measured in terms of nonfinancial measures of cost/benefit to the firm's owners; measured in terms of nonfinancial measures of cost/benefit to constituents other than the owners of the firm (employees, customers, local and regional inhabitants, etc.)
Measurement Level III	Measured in terms of financial cost/benefit to the firm's owners; measured in terms of financial cost/benefit to constituents other than the owners of the firm (employees, customers, local and regional inhabitants, etc.).[48]

The committee identified four possible levels of measurement of socially relevant corporate activities. The first level identifies the set of activities that have social relevance. This is also labeled as taking an inventory. The second, or input, level consists of determining the extent of the efforts being expended in each of the identified socially relevant activities. The third level counts the immediate outputs of a social action or process. The fourth level evaluates the worth of the output in spite of the lack of and difficulty of assigning measurement values in most cases.

The committee distinguished between the way economists and social accountants use the concept of social cost. To an economist, social costs are the total cost to society of the production of a good or service, which is basically a concept of economic cost and opportunity cost. In social accounting, the cost measurement includes (1) those costs of business activities that are paid or borne by the firm and provide benefits to other entities (such as, employment of a work force, affirmative action programs, the portion of a firm's pollution control program that provides spillover benefits to other entities, philanthropy, taxes, etc.) and (2) those costs that arise from business activity that are paid or borne by entities other than the entity giving rise to the social impact (such as, damages to the environment, health and mortality effects from production and consumption of goods and services produced by the entity, use of public streets and property by the entity, etc.).[49]

The costs identified in the first group are relevant in social accounting as surrogates of social benefits, whereas those identified in the second group are considered social costs "in the sense of external diseconomies which arise from the activities of business entity, e.g., environment pollution."[50]

Report of the Committee on Accounting for Social Performance. The charges of the Committee on Accounting for Social Performance[51] were (1) to review current efforts in accounting for corporate social performance and provide an update of the previous committee's work in this area; (2) to review and develop a critical evaluation of the state of the art of social performance measurement; (3) to identify high potential areas for research in social measurement and, if feasible, to study in depth one or more of these identified areas; and (4) to cooperate with the Committee on Education and the director of education in exploring the possibilities for social measurement subject matter input to accounting curricula and the American Accounting Association (AAA) continuing education program.[52] The committee suggested 22 areas for research in accounting for social performance, constituting important areas in need of urgent answers.[53]

The American Institute of Certified Public Accountants

The attempts of the American Institute of Certified Public Accountants (AICPA) in the area of social accounting resulted in two publications, *Social Measurements*[54] and *The Measurement of Corporate Social Performance.*[55] The second attempt resulted in a three-part comprehensive treatment of the various aspects of the measurement of corporate social performance.

Part one served as an introduction to corporate social measurement and the examination of the major characteristics of an ideal system of social measurement, which the committee deemed unattainable in the near future. However, as best characteristics of an initial system, they offered "(1) that it is practical, (2) that it can be developed and implemented in stages, and (3) that almost from the onset, it can be useful."[56] This initial system is intended to measure the impacts on social conditions that significantly affect the quality of life.

Part two demonstrated how an initial system might be used in a number of areas of significant social concern. For each area, the committee identified the major constituencies, or publics, affected, the major impacts and actions that affect them, and the social conditions having a major effect on the quality of life. Then, the committee dealt with measurement methodologies for each area, suggested social measures appropriate for the areas of the environment—nonrenewable resources; human resources; suppliers of purchased goods and services; products, services, and customers; and the community.

The third part of the committee report covered the reporting and use of social information by both internal and external users, problems of credibility and assurance, and suggestions for making the initial system operational.

Proposed Approaches to Microsocial Accounting

Narrative Disclosure

The nature of the narrative disclosure is by definition nonquantitative. It is a necessary first step that allows firms to learn more about the best ways to measure and disclose environmental effects of organizational behavior. Narrative disclosure consists of verbal statements depicting these environmental effects. The verbal descriptions called for by the Committee on Environmental Effects of Organizational Behavior included (1) identification of environmental problems—specific organizational problems with regard to control, imposed control standards, compliance deadlines, penalties for noncompliance, environmental considerations contained in executory contracts, and other contingent aspects; (2) abatement goals of the organization—detailed description of plans for abatement, projection of time schedules, and estimates of cost and/or budgeted expenditures; (3) progress of the organization—description of tangible progress, cost to date, expected future costs, and pertinent nonmonetary information relative to the organization's attainment of environmental goals; and (4) disclosure of material environmental effects on financial position, earnings, and business activities of the organizations.[57]

Footnote Disclosure

While narrative disclosure is essentially nonquantitative and included in the descriptive, nonaccounting section of an annual report, footnote disclosure consists of quantitative measurements on the social involvement of the firm included as additions to the financial statement section of the annual report. Exhibit 7.2 shows an excerpt from the annual report of the Ansul Company for 1974, which describes a waste disposal reserve anticipated for future pollution costs. Footnote disclosure is a practical way of introducing financial statement readers to the voluntary expenditures and contingent liabilities facing a socially responsible firm, which may have more merit than the narrative disclosure in that it is covered by the auditor's opinion. It is, however, limited to voluntary "social awareness expenditures" and does not include the remaining social costs and benefits. Footnote disclosure can be used to accommodate the Floyd Beams and Paul Fertig proposal that resource impairment resulting from environmental pollution be recognized and reported on an accrual basis.[58] Their proposal explicitly includes disclosure of expected future outlays for environmental damages resulting from past and current production activities, legal liability that results from a firm's violation of existing laws, contingent liabilities from probable actions where firms are in violation, liabilities for those expected future outlays that will not create asset values for the firm, and liabilities for eventual land restoration during the stripping operations by mining companies.[59]

Other examples of footnote disclosures found in annual reports include the following on extraordinary items and pollution facilities:

Exhibit 7.2
Excerpt from the Ansul Company 1974 Annual Report, Notes to Consolidated Financial Statements

Notes – Deferred Items.

DEFERRED ITEMS AT DECEMBER 31, 1974 & 1973	1974 (DOLLARS)	1973 (DOLLARS)
Deferred currency exchange gains	740,369	1,137,595
Waste disposal reserve	1,915,000	1,000,000
Total	2,655,369	2,137,595

> The waste disposal reserve has been provided for anticipated costs that may be associated with the recycling or disposal of a salt waste byproduct of our domestic agricultural chemical production. During 1974, we determined that any recycling or disposal program probably will be completed over a period of time exceeding one year. As a result we have classified the waste disposal reserve and related future tax benefits as noncurrent items. The December 31, 1973, balance sheet and statements of changes in financial position have been restated to conform with 1974 classifications.

Source: Steven C. Dilley, "External Reporting of Social Responsibility," *MSU Business Topics* (Autumn 1975): 18. Reprinted by permission of the publisher, Division of Research, Graduate School of Business Administration, Michigan State University.

A reserve of $78 million before taxes ($39.6 million after tax effect) was provided in 1970 for estimated extraordinary losses to be incurred in connection with the anticipated abandonment of facilities which are unprofitable, obsolete, or unusable and which cannot, in the opinion of management, be made profitable by economically justifiable expenditures, and of facilities which do not meet environmental standards and which, in the opinion of management, cannot be brought into compliance for similar economic reasons.

In 1970, the . . . Water Department Authority sold $2 million of 7.5 percent Water Development Revenue Bonds (principal maturing $200,000 annually) to provide funds for the purchase and expansion of an existing stream pollution control facility of the company. . . .

Of this amount $1,552,781 was paid to the company for the existing facility, and the remaining $447,219 is held by the trustee to be used for the expansion of the facility. The company leases the facility for an annual amount sufficient to pay principal and interest on the bonds. The cost of the existing facility is included with property, plant, and equipment and long-term debt will be increased as funds held by the trustee and expended. The company has treated this transaction as a loan for both accounting and tax purposes.[60]

Additional Accounts

Beams proposed accounting procedures to deal with industrial site deterioration caused by pollution.[61] Site deterioration occurs when an efficient disposal of industrial waste is lacking. Failure to account for these site deteriorations can lead to misstatements in the financial reports of major polluters.

Beams suggested that charges for delayed site maintenance of prior years qualify as a prior-period adjustment as outlined in Accounting Principles Board (ABP) Opinion No. 9, giving rise to a corresponding credit to an allowance for industrial site deterioration in the financial statements. Furthermore, he proposed the recognition of two new expense accounts: industrial site maintenance expense for outlays to re-establish a deteriorated plant site and industrial site deterioration expense for charges stemming from air or water pollution or industrial waste accumulation.

From an auditing perspective, Beams notes that in light of existing legal requirements on pollution prevention and the increased responsibility of the auditor, a modification of the auditor's opinion may be necessary. Concerning taxation, Beams notes that the charges for industrial site and for prior-period adjustments are currently nondeductible and urged Congress to relax the present laws to allow these deductions as an incentive for better social concern from corporations.

Beams's proposal was along the same lines as those of the AAA Committee on Environmental Effects of Organizational Behavior, which recommended recognition of environmental expenses in the income statement, environmental expenditures in the statement of changes in financial position (now cash flow statement), environmental control facilities as assets in the balance sheet, and environmental liabilities as liabilities in the balance sheet. The committee specifically suggested three types of liabilities: (1) the liability for assessed but unpaid penalties or pollution taxes for noncompliance with standards, (2) the liability for estimated penalty or tax (not assessed) for noncompliance with standards or deadlines, and (3) the liability for the estimated cost of voluntary "restorations" of the environment for past or current damages.[62]

Both Beams's and the committee's proposals constituted a step forward toward a more comprehensive financial statement. Beams's proposal is, however, applicable for firms engaged in strip mining, agribusiness, resort development and management, and other industries where the condition of the soil, land surface, and still bodies of water is an important factor and may have limited applicability for accounting for the effects of air pollution and water pollution of flowing waterways.[63]

Pollution Reports

Initially, social reporting in annual reports was limited to disclosure of total pollution control expenses and compliance with environmental laws and regulations. Such disclosure does not tell the whole story according to John Tepper Marlin who proposed two additional reports on a company's pollution.[64]

An example of the first report compares the company's pollution controls with the state-of-the-art standards to be established jointly by the Ecology and Social Measurement committees of the AICPA and an Industry Institute Committee. The report is based on an internal audit conducted by accountants and engineers and may be accompanied by an auditor's opinion that reads

In addition to the financial statements, we have examined to the extent considered necessary in the circumstances all assertions in this report regarding the company's compliance with environmental regulations and the adequacy of its existing and planned pollution control equipment. In our opinion these assertions are consistent with independent inquiries made with regulatory authorities, equipment suppliers and outside scientific consultants; with inspection of company records of equipment purchased and periodic efficiency ratings; and with state-of-the-art standards developed by the AICPA committees on environmental accounting and social measurement and the committee on pollution control of the American Paper Institute.[65]

The second report would present the actual net pollution emissions and the federal standards by type of pollutant. In an example showing the performance of three paper companies in New York State in terms of oxygen demand, solid emissions, and eight other forms of pollution, along with the corresponding federal standards, the report is accompanied by the following (hypothetical) auditor's report:

In addition to company B's financial statements, we have examined to the extent considered necessary in the circumstances its assertions regarding the amount of pollution caused by its mills. In our opinion, based on consultation with plant staff and governmental authorities, and on an independent sampling of emissions by a private environmental consulting firm, the reported emissions fairly reflect the pollution caused by the mills at the time of our investigation, and the company has budgeted adequate operating expenses to maintain this level of control.[66]

The two pollution reports proposed by Marlin present a practical way to deal with the performance evaluation of a firm's polluting activities. This type of reporting can in fact be extended to all social areas where state-of-the-art standards can be produced and firm performance can be measured.

Social Responsibility Annual Report

Steven Dilley and Jerry Weygandt rightfully argue that companies will never permit disclosures of social data because the information will be too difficult to develop or the collection of data will cause internal hassle.[67] Accordingly, they have presented a social responsibility annual report (SRAR) based on a cost outlay approach. The report includes various unrelated reports and statements covering the performance of an actual midwestern gas and electric company in the areas of pollution, health and safety, minority recruitment, and promotion.

Environmental Exchange Report

A conceptual framework for reporting exchanges between a firm and its environment, known as an "environmental exchange report; was offered by Wayne Corcoran and Wayne Leininger.[68] Interaction between a firm and its environment involves the exchange of human, physical, and financial resources. The environmental exchange report divides the exchanges into input and output and includes both human and physical resources, since financial resources are already internalized in the statement of changes in financial position (now, cash flow statement).

Corcoran and Leininger define these inputs and outputs as follows:

Human resource input consists of all the human effort expended in the organization and includes, therefore, information such as number of employees, educational level, tenure with the firm; number of manhours used by the firm; and number of hours of paid vacations and sick leave. Other possibilities are measures of wage and productivity increases, promotions, and the profiles of new employees. Human resource outputs consist of such items as wages paid to employees as well as information about employee terminations.

Physical resource input includes all physical resources used (air, water, raw materials, and the physical output of other firms), and descriptive information should indicate the source, future availability, and amount of each resource employed in the production process. Physical output into the environment should describe the physical products marketed, the waste and residue resulting from the productive process, and the resources, such as water, that are returned to the environment.[69]

The environmental exchange report proposal is also a practical and easy approach to microsocial accounting. However, it is a rather restrictive report in that it fails to include the performance of the company in other areas of social concern.

Social Income Statement

The preparation of socially oriented financial statements and other accounting analyses in dollar terms has been suggested by Lee Seidler.[70] In particular, he proposed two social income statement formats, one for a profit-oriented company and one for a not-for-profit company. In essence, the format calls for an internalization of the social costs (external diseconomies) and the social benefits (external economies). The net result is a net social profit or loss for the company arrived at by adding to value added the socially desirable outputs not sold, and subtracting the socially undesirable effects not paid for.

The social income statement format for a not-for-profit organization, such as a university, is different from a conventional income statement. The revenues in the conventional statement represent the costs to society in terms of the payments by society to the university in exchange for educational services. The costs in the social income statement represent the benefits to society in terms of the cost of services the university has performed for society.

The two income statement formats provide another practical framework for social accounting experimentation. A more detailed list of social benefits and costs would, however, make the format more exhaustive and informative.

Comprehensive Social Benefit-Cost Model

An accounting model that systematically reflects the worth of all resources consumed, including those resources or values which are free to the consuming entity (noninternalized costs of external diseconomies), and the worth of all benefits produced, including those that provide no compensation to the produc- ing entity (external economies) was proposed by Ralph Estes.[71] Estes observed that the conventional accounting model excludes certain external economies and diseconomies and, in general, reflects a view of the entity looking out toward society. He proposed, alternatively, a view of society looking at the entity with social benefits equal to values or utilities actually received by society and social costs equal to the full detriments to society, paid and unpaid. This more rational resource allocation is based on the following model:

$$SS = \sum_{i=1}^{n} \sum_{t=1}^{\yen} \frac{B_i}{(1 + r)^t} - \sum_{j=1}^{m} \sum_{t=1}^{\yen} \frac{C_j}{(1 + r)^t}$$

where

SS = social surplus or deficit

B_i = the ith social benefit

C_j = the jth social cost

r = an appropriate discount rate

t = time period in which benefit or cost is expected to occur.[72]

The direct effects of a single entity on society are reflected in a comprehensive social report based on this model, whereas indirect effects are reported in foot- notes. The indirect effects could be reported in the social report itself if the following conditions were met: "(a) each element of society accurately measured and reported all social benefits and costs created, (b) each element was peri- odically assessed or rewarded an amount equal to its net social surplus or deficit, and (c) each element then adjusted the prices of its goods and services upward in response to assessments or downward for rewards."[73] The model takes soci- ety's point of view by reporting social costs and benefits in a comprehensive format for companies experimenting with microsocial accounting.

Exhibit 7.3

The Anonymous Corporation (1973 Equal Employment Opportunity Commission [EEOC]-1 Report)

EEOC REPORTING GROUPS	MINORITIES (present)	WOMEN (present)	TOTAL*
Group I -- Professionals	3.0	91.7	280
Group II -- Technicians	2.0	30.8	200
Group III -- Sales	5.4	86.8	9,597
Group IV -- Office and clerical	10.5	89.7	3,494
Group V -- Craftsmen	6.0	15.1	381
Group VI -- Operations	7.9	37.3	579
Group VII -- Laborers	7.0	28.8	828
Group VIII -- Services	18.4	68.5	3005
Group IX -- Officials and managers	3.8	43.1	1634
Total (all groups)	8.2	75.0	20,000

*In response to a desire for anonymity, the totals in this EEOC report were multiplied by a constant that forced the totals in 20,000 but did not change the proportions. All other data in this and other tables are those actually found in the corporation.

*In response to a desire for anonymity, the totals in this EEOC report were multiplied by a constant that forced the totals to 20,000 but did not change the proportions. All other data in this and other tables are those actually found in the corporation.

Source: Neil C. Churchill and John K. Shank, "Accounting for Affirmative Action Programs: A Stochastic Flow Approach," *The Accounting Review* (October 1975): 649. © 1975 by the American Accounting Association. Reprinted by permission.

Multidimensional Income Statement

Two types of income statements aimed at extending ordinary accounting and auditing in the private sector to social accounting have been suggested by Claude Colantoni, W. W. Cooper, and H. J. Dietzer.[74] Their first report presents conventional income statement items classified both conventionally and connected to other dimensions (social and physical environment) to pinpoint various aspects of social performance. Their second report presents a multidimensional extension highlighting the social performance of the company in areas of interest to selected constituencies of employees, suppliers, stockholders, and government.

A Stochastic Flow Format

Most of the techniques examined thus far have required some form of "balance sheet" or "stock" disclosure. Exhibit 7.3 shows an Equal Employment

Exhibit 7.4
Transition Probabilities Matrix for Promotion of Male Employees for a Selected Multilocation Retail Enterprise

JOB CATEGORY AT BEGINNING OF YEAR	JOB CATEGORY AT THE END OF THE YEAR								
	0	1	2	3	4	5	6	7	8
0	1.000	0.000	0.000	0.000	0.000	0.000	0.000	0.000	0.000
1	0.200	0.450	0.200	0.100	0.050	0.000	0.000	0.000	0.000
2	0.207	0.100	0.556	0.101	0.086	0.040	0.000	0.000	0.000
3	0.115	0.000	0.033	0.713	0.102	0.020	0.012	0.000	0.004
4	0.145	0.000	0.005	0.023	0.626	0.150	0.028	0.023	0.000
5	0.140	0.000	0.014	0.000	0.021	0.650	0.091	0.049	0.035
6	0.185	0.000	0.015	0.000	0.000	0.031	0.662	0.092	0.015
7	0.147	0.000	0.000	0.000	0.000	0.007	0.042	0.748	0.056
8	0.131	0.000	0.000	0.000	0.000	0.000	0.000	0.024	0.845

Source: Neil C. Churchill and John K. Shank, "Accounting for Affirmative Action Programs: A Stochastic Flow Approach," *Accounting Review* (October 1975): 649. © 1975 by the American Accounting Association. Reprinted by permission.

Exhibit 7.5
Transition Probabilities Matrix for Promotion of Female Employees for a Selected Multilocation Retail Enterprise

JOB CATEGORY AT BEGINNING OF YEAR	JOB CATEGORY AT THE END OF THE YEAR								
	0	1	2	3	4	5	6	7	8
0	1.000	0.000	0.000	0.000	0.000	0.000	0.000	0.000	0.000
1	0.215	0.595	0.139	0.044	0.004	0.000	0.000	0.000	0.000
2	0.152	0.004	0.750	0.053	0.024	0.015	0.000	0.000	0.000
3	0.137	0.000	0.024	0.742	0.045	0.048	0.000	0.000	0.000
4	0.113	0.000	0.025	0.014	0.675	0.155	0.014	0.000	0.000
5	0.141	0.000	0.026	0.000	0.038	0.693	0.026	0.051	0.026
6	0.000	0.000	0.000	0.000	0.000	0.000	0.786	0.214	0.000
7	0.152	0.000	0.030	0.000	0.030	0.000	0.091	0.667	0.030
8	9.000	0.000	0.000	0.000	0.000	0.000	0.000	0.000	0.091

Source: Neil C. Churchill and John K. Shank, "Accounting for Affirmative Action Programs: A Stochastic Flow Approach," *Accounting Review* (October 1975): 649. © 1975 by the American Accounting Association. Reprinted by permission.

Opportunity (EEO)-1 report that exemplifies this approach. Objecting to this "stock" approach, Neil Churchill and John Shank propose a "flow" measurement to monitor the rate of progression of employees within the management ranks.[75] Using information available in current personnel files from an actual corporation, they developed the matrices of employee transition probabilities shown in Exhibits 7.4 and 7.5. These matrices show the probability of being separated or promoted from any of the eight categories to any of the other categories and may be used to observe and assess management succession processes for men and women.

Possible generalizations concerning the type of analysis to which such data can be subjected are (1) the diagonal drag—the diagonal in each matrix exhibit represents employees who stayed in the same category from one year to the next; (2) separations—column 1 of both exhibits (when zero stands for separation) represents employees who left the firm from all categories; (3) backsliding—entries below the main diagonal represent employees who were demoted; (4) leapfrogging—entries above the main diagonal represent employees who were promoted; and (5) promotions—entries one level above the main diagonal represent normal, one-step promotions. Once these generalizations are made, a suggested follow-up would be a statistical test X^2 to determine if there are any significant overall differences among the various matrices.

This approach is intended to provide more relevant information to users for evaluating the efficiency of affirmative action programs by providing insights concerning comparative retention rates and promotion rates at various levels of management.

CONCLUSIONS

This chapter reviewed the nature, rationale, and forms of measurement of social performance as presented in the professional and academic accounting, management, and sociological literature. The literature on social performance shows a great degree of maturity and development. Various forms of measurement have been proposed, and a great deal of experimentation has already taken place.

NOTES

1. See A. Belkaoui, *Socio-Economic Accounting* (Westport, CT: Quorum Books, 1984).

2. M. R. Mathews, "A Suggested Classification for Social Accounting Research," *Journal of Accounting and Public Policy*, Fall 1984, pp. 199–222.

3. K. V. Ramanathan, "Toward a Theory of Corporate Social Accounting," *Accounting Review*, July 1976, p. 518.

4. R. Gray, D. Owen, and K. Maunders, "Corporate Social Reporting: Emerging Trends in Accountability and the Social Contract," *Accounting, Auditing, and Accountability*, no. 1 (Jan. 1998): 8.

5. Ibid., p. 5.

6. Ibid., p. 13.

7. See D. B. Henriques, "Tracking Environmental Risk," *New York Times*, 28 Apr. 1991, p. 13.

8. J. A. Rawls, *A Theory of Justice* (Cambridge: Harvard University Press, 1971).

9. A. M. Nozick, *Anarchy, State, and Utopia* (New York: Basic Books, 1974).

10. A. Gerwith, *Reason and Morality* (Chicago IL: Chicago University Press, 1978).

11. Paul F. Williams, "The Legitimate Concern with Fairness," *Accounting, Organizations and Society*, March 1987, p. 184.

12. Ibid.

13. A. Belkaoui, "Fairness and Social Justice in Accounting" (Working paper, University of Illinois at Chicago, 1991).

14. Gerwith, *Reason and Morality*, p. 147–48.

15. Ibid., p. 150.

16. Marc J. Epstein, "What Shareholders Really Want," *New York Times*, 28 Apr. 1991, p. 11.

17. Ibid.

18. See "Pollution Price Tag: 71 Billion Dollars," *U.S. News & World Report*, 17 Aug. 1970, p. 41.

19. American Accounting Association, Report of the Committee on External Reporting. *Accounting Review* 44 (1969 Supplement): 11.

20. American Accounting Association, Report of the Committee on Environmental Effects of Organizational Behavior, *Accounting Review* 48 (1973 Supplement): 75–119.

21. J. Rockness and P. F. Williams, "A Descriptive Study of Social Responsibility Mutual Funds," *Accounting, Organizations and Society* 13 (1988): 397–411.

22. S. T. Bruyn *The Field of Social Investment* (Cambridge: Cambridge University Press, 1987), p. 12.

23. W. Keller, "Accounting for Corporate Social Performance," *Management Accounting*, Feb. 1974, pp. 39–41.

24. M. Epstein, E. Flamholtz, and J. McDonough, *Corporate Social Performance: The Measurement of Product and Service Contributions* (New York: National Association of Accountants, 1976), p. 14.

25. Ibid., p. 84.

26. Ibid., p. 15.

27. Ibid., p. 67.

28. L. A. Nikolai, J. D. Bazley, and R. L. Brummet, *The Measurement of Corporate Environmental Activity* (New York: National Association of Accountants, 1976).

29. Ibid., p. 25.

30. Ibid., p. 2.

31. Ibid., p. 3.

32. Ibid., p. 32.

33. Ibid., p. 59.

34. American Accounting Association, "Report of the Committee on Measures of Effectiveness for Social Programs," *Accounting Review* 47 (1972 Supplement): 337–96.

35. M. Francis, "Thoughts on Some Measure of Effectiveness of Social Programs" (Paper prepared for Robert E. Jensen, College of Business Administration, University of Maine, Orono, March 1971), p. 3.

36. American Accounting Association, "Report of the Committee on Measures of Effectiveness for Social Programs," p. 348.

37. Ibid., p. 349.

38. Ibid.

39. American Accounting Association, "Report of the Committee on Environmental Effects of Organizational Behavior," *Accounting Review* 48 (1973 Supplement): 75–119.

40. Ibid., p. 80.

41. Ibid., pp. 116–17.

42. American Accounting Association, "Report of the Committee on the Measurement of Social Costs," *Accounting Review* 49 (1974 Supplement): 98–113.

43. Ibid., pp. 100–1.

44. Ibid., pp. 101–2.

45. Ibid., p. 102.

46. Ibid.

47. American Accounting Association, "Report of the Committee on Social Costs," *Accounting Review* 50 (1975 Supplement): 53.

48. Ibid., p. 55.

49. Ibid., p. 71.

50. Ibid.

51. American Accounting Association, "Report of the Committee on Accounting for Social Performance," *Accounting Review* 51 (1976 Supplement): 36–69.

52. Ibid., p. 41.

53. Ibid., pp. 66–67.

54. American Accounting Association, "Report of the Committee on Measures of Effectiveness for Social Programs."

55. American Institute of Certified Public Accountants, *The Measurement of Corporate Social Performance* (New York: AICPA, 1977).

56. Ibid., p. 23.

57. American Accounting Association, "Report of the Committee on Environmental Effects of Organizational Behavior," p. 110.

58. Floyd A. Beams and Paul E. Fertig, "Pollution Control Through Social Cost Conversion," *Journal of Accountancy*, Nov. 1971, pp. 37–42.

59. Ibid., p. 42.

60. These examples were provided by the editors of the *Journal of Accountancy*, Mar. 1977, p. 76.

61. Floyd A. Beams, "Accounting for Environmental Pollution," *New York Certified Public Accountant*, Aug. 1970, pp. 657–61.

62. American Accounting Association, "Report of the Committee on Environmental Effects of Organizational Behavior," p. 80.

63. Ralph Estes, *Corporate Social Accounting* (New York: Wiley, 1976).

64. John Tepper Marlin, "Accounting for Pollution," *Journal of Accountancy*, Feb. 1973, pp. 41–46.

65. Ibid., p. 44.

66. Ibid., p. 45.

67. Steven C. Dilley and Jerry J. Weygandt, "Measuring Social Responsibility: An Empirical Test." *Journal of Accountancy*, Sept. 1973, p. 64.

68. Wayne Corcoran and Wayne E. Leininger, Jr., "Financial Statements—Who Needs Them?" *Financial Executive*, Aug. 1970, pp. 34–38, 45–47.

69. Ibid., p. 45.

70. Lee J. Seidler, "Dollar Values in the Social Income Statement," *World* (KPMG Peat Marwick) 14 (1973): 16–23.

71. Estes, *Corporate Social Accounting*, p. 91.

72. Ibid., p. 94.

73. Ibid.

74. Claude S. Colantoni, W. W. Cooper, and H. J. Dietzer, "Budgeting Disclosure and Social Accounting," in *Corporate Social Accounting*, edited by Meinhold Dierkes and Raymond Bauer (New York: Praeger, 1973), pp. 376–77.

75. Neill C. Churchill and John C. Shank, "Accounting for Affirmative Action Programs: A Stochastic Flow Approach," *Accounting Review*, Oct. 1975, pp. 643–56.

REFERENCES

American Accounting Association. Report of the Committee on External Reporting. *Accounting Review* 44 (1969 Supplement): 11.

———. Report of the Committee on Environmental Effects of Organizational Behavior. *Accounting Review* 44 (1969 Supplement): 88.

———. Report of the Committee on Measures of Effectiveness for Social Programs. *Accounting Review* 47 (1972 Supplement): 337–96.

———. Report of the Committee on Environmental Effects of Organizational Behavior. *Accounting Review* 48 (1973 Supplement): 75–119.

———. Report of the Committee on the Measurement of Social Costs. *Accounting Review* 49 (1974 Supplement): 98–113.

———. Report of the Committee on Social Costs. *Accounting Review* 50 (1975 Supplement): 53.

———. Report of the Committee on Accounting for Social Performance. *Accounting Review* 51 (1976 Supplement): 36–69.

American Institute of Certified Public Accountants. *Social Measurement*. New York: AICPA, 1972.

———. *The Measurement of Corporate Social Performance*. New York: AICPA, 1977.

Beams, Floyd A. "Accounting for Environmental Pollution." *New York: Certified Public Accountant*, August 1970, 657–61.

Beams, Floyd A., and Paul E. Fertig. "Pollution Control Through Social Cost Conversion." *Journal of Accountancy*, Nov. 1971, 37–42.

Belkaoui, A. "Fairness and Social Justice in Accounting." Working paper. University of Illinois at Chicago, 1991.

———. *Socio-Economic Accounting*. Westport, CT: Quorum Books, 1984.

Bruyn, S. T. *The Field of Social Investment*. Cambridge: Cambridge University Press, 1987.

Churchill, Neill C., and John C. Shank. "Accounting for Affirmative action Programs: A Stochastic Flow Approach." *Accounting Review*, Oct. 1975, 643–56.

Colantoni, Claude S., W. W. Cooper, and H. J. Dietzer. "Budgeting Disclosure and Social Accounting." In *Corporate Social Accounting*, edited by Meinholf Dierkes and Raymond Bauer, 376–77. New York: Praeger, 1973.

Dilley, Steven C., and Jerry J. Weygandt. "Measuring Social Responsibility: An Empirical Test." *Journal of Accountancy*, Sept. 1973, 64.

Epstein, Marc J. "What Shareholders Really Want." *New York Times*, 28 Apr. 1991, 11.

Epstein M., E. Flamholtz, and J. McDonough. *Corporate Social Performance: The Measurement of Product and Service Contributions*. New York: National Association of Accountants, 1976.

Estes, Ralph. *Corporate Social Accounting*. New York: Wiley, 1976.

Gerwith, A. *Reason and Morality*. Chicago, IL: Chicago University Press, 1978.

Gray, R., D. Owen, and K. Maunders. "Corporate Social Reporting: Emerging Trends in Accountability and the Social Contract. *Accounting, Auditing, and Accountability* 1, no. 1 (Jan. 1998): 8.

Henriques, D. B. "Tracking Environmental Risk." *New York Times*, 28 Apr. 1991, 13.

Keller, W. "Accounting for Corporate Social Performance." *Management Accounting*, Feb. 1974, 39–41.

Mathews, M. R. "A Suggested Classification for Social Accounting Research." *Journal of Accounting and Public Policy*, Fall 1984, 199–222.

Nozick, A. M. *Anarchy, State, and Utopia*. New York: Basic Books, 1974.

Ramanathan, K. V. "Toward a Theory of Corporate Social Accounting." *Accounting Review*, July 1976, 518.

Rawls, J. A. *A Theory of Justice*. Cambridge: Harvard University Press, 1971.

Roclenen, J., and P. F. Williams. "A Descriptive Study of Social Responsibility Mutual Funds." *Accounting, Organizations and Society* 13 (1988): 397–411.

Seidler, Lee J. "Dollar Values in the Social Income Statement." *World* (KPMG Peat Marwick) 14 (1973): 16–23.

Taylor, J. C., and D. C. Bowers. *The Survey of Organizations*. Ann Arbor, MI: Institute for Social Research, 1972.

Williams, Paul F. "The Legitimate Concern with Fairness." *Accounting, Organizations and Society*, Mar. 1987, 184.

Chapter 8

The Human Asset Report

INTRODUCTION

Most annual reports claim in their narrative part that their human resources are the best assets of the firm; and yet, a reading of the financial statements indicates no data for the values and changes in the values of human assets. It is the purpose of the human asset report and human asset valuation to produce and disclose vital information about the value of the human assets of the firm. Accordingly, this chapter examines the rationale for human resource accounting and the methods proposed both in the literature and practice for human resource valuation and the production of human asset reports.

REPORTING HUMAN ASSETS

Models for conceptualizing and measuring the economic effects of human resource activities can be drawn from the fields of labor economics, accounting, and industrial psychology. Basically, firm-specific human capital theory is drawn from labor economics, human resource accounting from accounting, and utility analysis from industrial psychology.

Human resource accounting (HRA) focuses on the provision of information about human assets. Why is there a need for human resource accounting? The answer lies in the usefulness of the information about human resources. The objective of financial accounting is to provide information relevant to the decisions of users. Investors should be provided with all the information necessary to make their decisions. Thus, users may need to have adequate information about one "neglected" asset of the firm, the human asset. More specifically, investors may greatly benefit from a knowledge of the extent to which the human assets of an organization have been increased or decreased during a given period. The conventional accounting treatment of human resource outlays consists of *expensing* all human capital formation expenditures, whereas similar outlays on physical capital are capitalized. More valid treatments of human assets are needed rather than the mere expensing approach. This concern for the adequate measurement of the value of human resources to an organization led to the development of the field of inquiry in accounting known as human resource accounting. A broad definition of human resource accounting is "the process of identifying and measuring data about human resources and communicating this information to interested users."[1] This definition implies three major academic objectives of human resource accounting, namely, (1) identification of human resource value, (2) measurement of the cost and value of people to organizations, and (3) investigation of the cognitive and behavioral impact of such information. The functional objectives of HRA are

1. To furnish cost value information for making management decisions about acquiring, allocating, developing, and maintaining human resources in order to attain cost effective organizational objectives;
2. To allow managerial personnel to effectively monitor the use of human resources;
3. To provide for a determination of asset control, i.e., whether assets are conserved, depleted, or appreciated;
4. To aid in the development of management principles by clarifying the financial consequences of various practices.[2]

Since appearing in the literature, HRA has gone through three specific stages: phase 1 of development and validation, phase 2 of organizational applications, and phase 3 of empirical research investigation. The three phases, outlined in Exhibit 8.1, are examined in the remainder of this chapter.

ARGUMENTS IN SUPPORT OF REPORTING HUMAN ASSETS

Competitive Strategy, Human Resource Strategy, and Human Resource Accounting

The advantage of a competitive strategy is relatively well established. What is needed is an efficient use of capabilities, resources, relationships, and decisions to allow a firm to benefit from all opportunities and fend off all threats.[3] The human resource, when well managed, can be used to guarantee the success of any competitive strategy.[4] The management of human resources toward achieving the strategic objectives of a firm has taken one of three routes:

Exhibit 8.1
An Overview of Research in Human Resource Accounting (HRA)

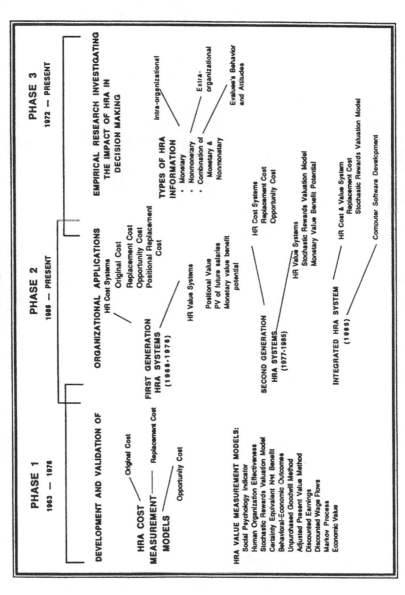

Source: Sonja A. Sackman, Eric G. Flamholtz, and Maria Lombardi Bullen, "Human Resource Accounting: A State-cf-the-Art Review," *Journal of Accounting Literature* 8 (1989): 238. Reprinted with the permission of the *Journal of Accounting Literature.*

(a) matching managerial style or personnel activities with strategies, (b) forecasting manpower requirements given certain strategic objectives or environmental conditions, or (c) presenting means for integrating human resource management into the overall effort to match strategy and structures.[5]

It is the third route that is proving the most beneficial to firms. I. C. MacMillan and R. S. Schuler note that it is becoming very desirable to integrate human resources management and strategic choice.[6] Cynthia and Mark Lengnick-Hall offer the following reasons:

First, integration provides a broader range of solutions for solving complex organizational problems. Second, integration ensures that human, financial, and technological resources are given consideration in setting goals and assessing implementation capabilities. Third, through integration organizations must explicitly consider the individuals who comprise them and must implement policies. Finally, reciprocity in integrating human resource and strategic concerns limits the subordination of strategic considerations to human resource preferences and the neglect of human resources as a vital source of organizational competence and competitive advantage.[7]

The consequence of this integration is still an empirical question. It is, however, evident that competitive strategy in terms of competitive advantage and distinct competence rests on talented, efficient, and valuable human resources. Because the value of human resources enters into the formulation of the competitive strategy, the human resource strategy needs to include a measurement of the value of these human resources. In other words, efficient integration of competitive strategy and human resource strategy requires the implementation of a human resource accounting system. Selection of appropriate human resource accounting practices is appropriate to the competitive strategy and will lead to behaviors that are supportive of the corporate competitive strategy.

Third Wave and Human Resource Accounting

The shape of the global system is constantly changing. Dividing countries into developed and developing countries does not capture the profound economic and social changes taking place. A very useful classification is provided by Alvin Toffler's image of the new global system.[8] A distinction is made between three types of societies: first wave, second wave, and third wave societies.

First wave societies are essentially agrarian states that rely on cheap and abundant peasant labor to sustain a large and dominant agricultural sector. For first wave, or agricultural, economies the essentials for survival are land, energy, water for irrigation, cooking oil, food, minimal literacy, and markets for cash crops or raw materials. Their natural resources and farm products are their chief salable assets.[9]

Second wave societies are industrial societies that still rely on cheap, manual labor and mass production with concentrated, integrated national economies.[10] "They need high inputs of energy per unit of production. They need bulk raw materials to keep their factories going iron, steel, cement, timber, petrochemicals and the like."[11]

Third wave societies specialize in the world's economically relevant "knowledge work," based on sophisticated knowledge and high technology. They need knowledge that can be connected to wealth. "They need access to, or control of, world data banks and telecommunications networks. They need markets for products and services that depend on knowledge."[12]

Third wave societies with their heavy reliance on information technology call for fundamental changes in accounting practice, accounting information and management.[13] Notice the change in the new accountability technology from single entry in the first wave to triple or multiple entries in the third wave, that is, an expansion of the accounting information and disclosure. Noticeable changes are (a) worker focus from blue collar/white collar to knowledge worker, (b) communications from paper to electronics, and (c) value from tangibles to intangibles.

These changes call for a new third wave accounting system. As stated by Robert Elliott:

The resources and obligations measured in a third wave accounting system must also change. The resources that drive the third wave company are information based assets, such as R&D, human assets, knowledge, data, and capacity for innovation. These assets don't even appear on second wave balance sheets. We cannot leave them out of the accountability set and expect managers and investors to reach sound decisions.[14]

Therefore, a third wave accounting system calls for a human resource accounting that provides more relevant information on the knowledge worker, the human asset that is crucial to the organizations in third wave societies.

Adversary Accounting and Human Resource Accounting

Empirical evidence on income smoothing and earnings management suggests that accounting information is used strategically to create the desired image of the firm and/or a position from which to fend off any potential adversary. Accounting techniques in these situations are no more than techniques of adversary accounting used to support any desired position. As stated by Doreen McBarnet et al.:

Accordingly, a strategy of adversary accounting may follow a genuine concern that the accounting picture presented by an adversary has obscured economic reality, perhaps as a result of an emphasis on legal "form" over economic "substance." It may also reflect the view that accounting is intrinsically an exercise in subjective calculation. In this version of adversary accounting, the subjectivity and creativity involved in accounting are treated in an adversarial situation as opportunities for challenge. In both cases, though, accounting information is used to support one's own position. In a way, similar to the lawyer advocate in the adversary legal system where evidence is presented, examined and cross examined and arguments are used in a partisan way in the interests of the clients, accounting figures are constructed, deconstructed and used by conflicting interests in the struggle for economic ascendancy.[15]

What appears from the McBarnet et al. analysis is that accounting is used as "partisan" or "adversary" accounting by the owners of both capital and labor. As a result, in capital/labor conflicts, accounting may be used by both sides to advance their respective positions. What can happen is a total unacceptance of the accounting information presented by each side; threatening in the process the neutrality, the credibility, and the potential usefulness of accounting information. To reduce and/or eliminate the suspicion of management figures, and the union's rejection of the accounting basis of the information, management may take the lead and provide a human resource accounting that presents a valuation of the present human resources in the firm. The provision of this type of information may create a better atmosphere for collective bargaining and show in good faith that management has elected not to rely exclusively on adversary or partisan accounting. The tools of accounting are then used to help reduce the conflicts between labor and capital and to facilitate decisions based on financial information made by both parties. Human resource accounting is in this outset a reconstruction of financial information to provide human resource information that can be used by both labor and capital to resolve conflicts.

The Empowerment Process and Human Resource Accounting

The beneficial role of empowerment in management theory and practice is largely recognized. The construct of empowerment is best defined as "a process of enhancing feelings of self-efficacy among organizational members through the identification of conditions that foster powerlessness and through their removal by both formal organizational practices and informal techniques of providing efficacy information."[16] A review of the literature reveals that empowerment (a) is a principal component of managerial and organizational effectiveness, (b) results in the growth of the total productive forms of organizational power and effectiveness, and (c) plays a crucial role in group development and maintenance.[17] The process of empowerment has included five stages: (1) psychological state of empowering experience, (2) the use of managerial strategies and techniques, (3) the provision of self-efficacy information to subordinates, (4) the empowering experience of subordinates, and (5) the behavioral consequences.[18] Of particular interest are the managerial strategies and techniques used in the empowerment process. They include participative management, goal setting, feedback system, modeling, contingent/competence based reward, and job enrichment. Although this list includes legitimate and tried techniques of empowerment, another effective technique would be to engage in a human resource accounting that provides employees with their values and changes in values. Basically human resource accounting would be perceived by subordinates as a technique of empowerment that will enhance feelings of self-efficacy as well as providing efficacy information.

Usefulness of Human Resource Information

The conventional treatment of expensing investment in human resources presents a clear distortment of the financial statements and reduces the usefulness of accounting information. If people were perceived as assets, other accounting treatments than expensing might be required that would highlight the cost or value of human resources as capital investments. The question remains whether or not people can be considered as assets of the firm. W. A. Paton, in his classic book *Accounting Theory* referred to people as assets:

In the business enterprise, a well organized and loyal personnel may be a more important "asset" than a stock of merchandise. . . . At least there seems to be no way of measuring such factor in terms of the dollar. . . . [T]hey cannot be recognized as specific economic assets. But let's not, accordingly admit the serious limitation of the conventional balance sheet as a statement of financial condition.[19]

To define an asset, E. Flamholtz suggests three criteria: (a) the asset must possess future service potential, (b) it is measurable in monetary terms, and (c) it is subject to the ownership and control of the firm.[20] The first criterion is the most important. Therefore, given the existence of future service potential from their activities, human resources can be considered as assets of the firm. As stated by R. L. Brummet et al.,

The essential criterion for determining whether a cost is an "asset" or an "expense" relates to the notion of future service potential. Thus human resource costs, which are sacrifices incurred by the firm in obtaining services with the objective of deriving future benefits, can be classified as either assets or expenses. They should be treated as expenses in the periods in which benefits result. If these benefits relate to a future time period they should be treated as assets.[21]

The second criterion is necessary only if the measurement of human resources can only be measured in monetary terms. The fact is that human resources can be measured in both monetary and nonmonetary terms. Therefore, the second criterion is unnecessarily restrictive.

The third criterion of ownership and control presents an ethical dilemma given that humans cannot be bought, sold, or bartered for in a transaction. Eric Flamholtz confronted this ethical dilemma by suggesting that "people are not assets;

the services people are expected to provide to an organization confuse the assets."[22]

Similarly, J. J. Tsay suggests that the capitalization of lease payments treatment is also notable for investment in human resources:

A leasehold payment in advance gives the lessor the right to use the property for a period of time, not the ownership of the property, and it is considered an asset. The recruiting and training expenditure represents the service potential of the employee to the company, not the right to own the employee. If the expenditure is beneficial to the future operations, it should be regarded as an asset. Whether the company can legally own its employees should not be a concern.[23]

HUMAN RESOURCE VALUE THEORY

The concept of human value can be derived from the general economic value theory. Like physical assets, individual or groups can be attributed a value because of their ability to render future economic services. In line with the economic thinking that associates the value of an object with its ability to render benefits, the individual or group value is usually defined as the present worth of the services rendered to the organization throughout the individual's or the group's expected service life.

How do we determine the value of a human asset? To measure and disclose "human resource value," we used a theoretical framework, or "human resource value theory" to explicate the nature and determinants of the value of people to an organization. Basically, two models examine the nature and determinants of human resource value, one advanced by Flamholtz[24] and one by Rensis Liken and David Bowers.[25] We shall discuss each of the models in the following sections.

Determinants of Individual Value

In Flamholtz's model, the measure of a person's worth is his or her expected realizable value to a formal organization. Flamholtz's model suggests that such a measure of individual value results from the interaction of two variables: (1) the individual's conditional value and (2) the probability that the individual will maintain membership in the organization.

Conditional value is the amount the organization would potentially realize from a person's services. It is a multidimensional variable comprising three factors: *productivity, transferability*, and *promotability*. They are defined as follows:

"Productivity" refers to a set of services an individual is expected to provide while occupying his present position. A synonym for productivity is performance. "Transferability" is the set of services an individual is expected to provide if and when he transfers to offer positions at the same position level in a different promotion channel. "Promotability" represents the set of services the individual is expected to provide if and when he occupies higher level positions in his present or different promotion channels.[26]

These three elements of conditional value are perceived to be the product of certain attitudes of the person and certain dimensions of the organization. Two individual determinants are identified as important, namely, the person's skills and activation level. Similarly, the organizational determinants that interact with the individual values are identified as the organizational role of the individual and the rewards that people expect from the different aspects of their membership in a firm. In addition, the probability of maintaining organizational membership is considered to be related to a person's degree of job satisfaction.

The model was tested empirically in a field study both to test the hypothesized determinants and to identify any missing variables.[27] The results show that personnel managers, when asked to assess the value to an organization of auditing staff individuals, considered all the variables hypothesized to influence the individual's value to an organization, except organizational rewards. The strongest variables were productivity and probability of maintaining organizational membership, whereas the weakest were activation level, transferability, and satisfaction. In addition, individual attributes, including cognitive abilities and personality traits, and organizational attributes, including organizational structure and management style, were included as additional variables. A revised model was proposed as shown in Exhibit 8.2.

A brief and excellent description of the model is as follows:

The individual brings certain attributes to the organization: cognitive abilities such as intelligence; and personality traits such as needed for achievement. These individual attributes are the source of work related value determinants: The person's skills, activation level (motivation) and attitudes. However, the individual is not valuable to the firm in the abstract; he is valuable in relation to the roles (position) he can or will potentially occupy. Organizational attributes of structure and management style determine the roles and rewards available within the organization: and these organizational determinants interact with the individual determinants to produce the elements of conditional value (productivity, promotability, and transferability) and the person's satisfaction with the organization. Satisfaction and the latter variable (conditional value) produce the ultimate construct the person's expected realizable value.[28]

Determinants of Group Value

While Flamholtz's model examined the determinants of an individual's value to an organization, Liken and Bower's model examined the determinants of group value. Intended to represent the "productive capability of the human organization of any enterprise or unit within it,"[29] the model consists of the interrelationships among three variables—causal, intervening, and end result—that influence the effectiveness of a firm's human organization:

Exhibit 8.2
Revised Model of the Determinants of an Individual's Value to a Formal
Organization

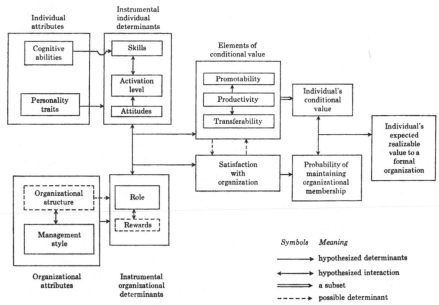

Source: Eric G. Flamholtz, "Assessing the Validity of a Theory of Human Resource Value: A Field
Study," *Journal of Accounting Research* (Empirical Research in Accounting: Selected Studies,
1972): figure 3, p. 257. Reprinted with permission.

1. The *causal* variables are independent variables which can be directly or purposely
   altered or changed by the organization and its management and which, in turn, determine the course of developments within an organization. These causal variables
   include only those which are controllable by the organization and its management.
   General business conditions, for example, although an independent variable, are *not*
   viewed as causal since they are not controllable by the management of a particular
   enterprise. Causal variables include the structure of the organization and management's policies, divisions, business and leadership strategies, skills, and behavior.

2. The *intervening* variables reflect the internal state, health, and performance capabilities
   of the organization, that is, the loyalties, attitudes, motivations, performance goals,
   and perceptions of all members and their collective capability for effective action.

3. The *end result* variables are the dependent variables that reflect the results achieved
   by the organization, such as productivity, costs, scrap loss, growth, share of the market, and earnings.[30]

The model simply states that certain causal variables induce certain levels of
intervening variables, which yield certain levels of end result variables. The

causal variables are managerial behavior, organizational structure, and subordinate peer behavior. The intervening variables are such organization processes as perception, communication, motivation, decision making, control, and coordination. The end result variables are health, satisfaction, productivity, and financial performance. Partial support exists for the model. First, Liken and Bowers showed that participative management, where managers support their subordinates rather than dictate to them, yields more favorable attitudes as expressed by such intervening variables as confidence and trust in superiors, ease and accuracy of communication, and group loyalties.[31] The correlations between performance costs and managerial behavior ranged from −.48 to −.58, showing the better managerial behavior is perceived to be, the lower the performance costs. In another experiment, Liken and William Pyle showed some association between cost performance and managerial behavior where managerial behavior was assured by three indices: managerial support, managerial team building, and managerial work facilitation.[32]

These findings prompted B. A. Robinson to propose the constructive participative involvement (CPI) approach, which relies on the constructive ideas of moderates; participative goals settings by departments; and involvement of all levels of the organization in the decision making, performance appraisal, and goal achievement.[33] The development of the human resource assets is evidenced by

- continued concern by everyone for the attainment of profitable objectives
- increased confidence and trust in their own and their superior's attitude to perform effectively
- reduced turnover and grievance among rank and file
- the self-imposition of higher quality and performance standards by subordinate departments, groups, and individuals
- increased pride of accomplishment in maintaining a competitive position in the industry over the long term (results in containing for security and increased earnings)
- reduced need for permission, inspections, and imposition of work standards with a corresponding reduction of overhead expenses.[34]

Another similar model, proposed by M. Scott Myers and V. S. Flowers, measures the conversion of human resources into job behavior.[35] The dimension of human assets, following a flow process leading to job performance is as follows: "knowledge, skills, health, availability, attitudes, job performance."[36]

HUMAN RESOURCE COST MODELS

Various resources models have been proposed in the literature for accounting for the cost and value of human resources. These models include human resources cost models and human resource value models.[37] They are explained next.

Historical Cost Method

The historical, or acquisition, cost method consists of capitalizing all the costs associated with recruiting, selecting, hiring, and training, and then amortizing these costs over the projected useful life of the asset, recognizing losses by the class of the assets, or increasing the value of the assets for any additional cost intended to increase the benefit potential of the asset. Similar to any of the conventional accounting treatments for other assets, this treatment is practical and objective in the sense that the data are verifiable.[38] In addition, it seems that "the development of an outlay cost system for human resource accounting should be viewed as a first step for the providing of an important first installment of a useful set of human resource information."[39] These advantages of the historical cost method are also recognized by Bilski L. Jaggi[40] and George M. N. Baker.[41]

Several limitations exist, however, with the use of these measurements. First, the economic value of a human asset does not necessarily correspond to its historical cost. Second, any appreciation or amortization may be subjective, with no relation to any increase or decrease in the productivity of human assets. Third, because the costs associated with recruiting, selecting, hiring, training, placing, and developing employees may differ from one individual to another within a firm, historical cost does not result in comparable human resource values.

Replacement Cost Method

The replacement cost consists of estimating the cost of replacing a firm's existing human resources. Such costs may include all the costs of recruiting, selecting, hiring, training, placing, and developing new employees to reach the level of competence of existing employees. Flamholtz developed a model for measuring human resource replacement costs that add separation costs to acquisition and learning costs.[42] The model is shown in Exhibit 8.3. The principal advantage of the replacement cost method is that it is a good surrogate for the economic value of the asset in the sense that market considerations are essential in reaching a final figure. Such a final figure is also generally intended to be conceptually equivalent to a notion of a person's economic value.[43] Several limitations exist, however, in the use of replacement cost. The replacement cost method has been considered subjective. As noted by Liken and Bowers, managers asked to estimate the cost of completely replacing their human organization may have difficulty doing so, and different managers may arrive at quite

Exhibit 8.3
Model for Measurement of Human Replacement Costs

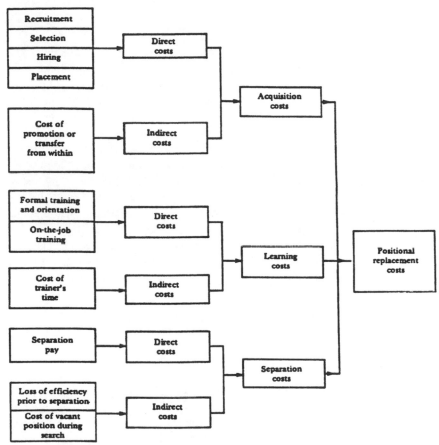

Source: Eric G. Flamholtz, "Human Resource Accounting: Measuring Potential Replacement Cost," *Human Resource Management* (Spring 1973): 11. Copyright © 1973 by John Wiley & Sons, Inc. Reprinted by permission of John Wiley & Sons, Inc.

different estimates.[44] The estimates ranged from two to ten times the annual payroll. Two limitations are noted by J. S. Hekimian and J. G. Jones as follows:

1. Management may have some particular asset which it is unwilling to replace at current cost, but which it wants to keep using because the asset has a value greater than its scrap value. There must be some method of valuing such an asset.

2. There may be no similar replacement for a certain existing asset. This situation is caused either by a changing technology, where an asset has to be replaced by a "new model," or by the simple fact that the asset is custom-made. We feel that a proper

system of asset valuation must include a methodology for valuing assets in these circumstances.[45]

Opportunity Cost Method

Hekimian and Jones proposed the opportunity cost method to overcome the limitations of the replacement cost method.[46] They suggested that human resource value be established through a competitive bidding process within the firm, based on the concept of "opportunity" cost. More specifically, under this method, investment center managers will bid for the scarce employees they need to recruit. These "scarce" employees all come from within the firm and only include those who are the subject of a recruitment request by an investment center manager. In other words, employees not considered "scarce" are not included in the human asset base of the organization. The method is suggested to provide for a more optimal allocation of personnel[47] and greater feasibility.[48]

Obviously, several limitations exist in the use of the opportunity cost method. First, the inclusion of only "scarce" employees in the asset base may be interpreted as "discriminatory" by other employees. Second, the less profitable divisions may be penalized by their inability to outbid for the recruitment of better employees. Third, the method may be perceived as artificial and even immoral.[49]

HUMAN RESOURCE MODELS: STRICTLY MONETARY METHODS

Discounted Wage Flows Method

Given the uncertainty and the difficulty associated with determining the value of human capital, B. Lev and A. Schwartz suggest the use of a person's future compensation as a surrogate of his or her value.[50] Accordingly, the * value of human capital embodied in a person of age τ is the present value of his or her remaining future earnings from employment. This valuation model is expressed as

$$V_\tau = \sum_{t-\tau}^{T} \frac{I(r)}{(1+r)^{t-\tau}}$$

Where

$V\tau$ = the human capital value of a person τ years old

$I(r)$ = the person's annual earnings up to retirement

r = a discount rate specific to the person

T = retirement age

t = current time.

Because $V\tau$ is an ex post value, given that $I(r)$ is obtained only after retirement and because $V\tau$ ignores the possibility of death before retirement age, B. Lev and A. Schwartz refined the valuation model as follows:

$$E(V_\tau^*) = \sum_{t=\tau}^{T} P_\tau(t+1) \sum_{i=\tau}^{t} \frac{I_i^*}{(1+r)^{t-\tau}}$$

where

I_i^* = future annual earnings

$E(V_\tau^*)$ = expected value of a person's human capital

$P\tau(t)$ = probability of a person dying at age t

The principal limitation of the compensation model is the subjectivity associated with the determination of the level of future salary, the level of expected employment within the firm, and the discount rate.

Abraham Friedman and Lev suggested the use of a surrogate measure for a firm's investment in human resources that relies on the compensation model, and is based on firm-versus-market wage relationships.[51] Basically, the differences between a firm's wage structure and the average industry wage is assured to be caused mainly by the firm's personnel policies, extent of training, and indirect compensation systems. The firm's investment in human resources is measured by an "internal human resource value" (or the discounted value of actual wages to be paid to current employees over their expected service life) and "external human resource value" (or discounted value of hypothetical wages based on the average industry wages).[52] The following result is envisioned:

A positive difference will indicate the discounted value of the stream of wage savings (relative to the market) resulting from the firm's personnel policies (investment in human resources), while a negative difference will indicate the discounted value of the stream of wage dissavings resulting from below-average compensation, training, etc. Thus management's specific policies in hiring, developing, and maintaining the workforce affecting its wage scale would be reflected by the proposed surrogate measure.[53]

Adjusted Discounted Future Wages Method

R. H. Hermanson proposed using an adjusted compensation value as a proxy for the value of an individual to a firm.[54] The discounted future wages are adjusted by an "efficiency factor" intended to measure the relative effectiveness of the human capital of a given firm. This efficiency factor is measured by a ratio of the return on investment of the given firm to all other firms in the economy for a given period. It is computed by the following expression:

$$\text{Efficiency ratio} = \frac{5\dfrac{RF_0}{RE_0} + 4\dfrac{RF_1}{RE_1} + 3\dfrac{RF_2}{RE_2} + 2\dfrac{RF_3}{RE_3} + 1\dfrac{RF_4}{RE_4}}{15}$$

where

RF_i = the rate of accounting income on owned assets for the firm for the year i

RE_i = the rate of accounting income on owned assets for all forms in the economy for the year i

$_i$ = years (0 to 4).

The justification of this ratio rests on the thesis that difference in profitability is due to differences in human assets performance. Thus, it is necessary to adjust the compensation value by the efficiency factor.

Present Monetary Value Method

Wayne J. Morse equated the value of human assets to a formal organization to the net present value of the services rendered the organization by its employees.[55] It is expressed as

$$A = \sum_{i=1}^{N} \int_{\tau}^{T} \frac{G_i(t)}{(1 + r)^{t-\tau}} dt + \int_{\tau}^{T} \frac{X(t)}{(1 + r)^{t-\tau}} dt - \sum_{i=1}^{N} \int_{\tau}^{T} \frac{E_i(t)}{(1 + r)^{t-\tau}} dt$$

where

A = value of human assets to a formal organization

N = number of individuals currently employed by the organization

t = current time

T = highest time at which an individual currently employed leaves the organization

$G_i(t)$ = gross value of services rendered by individual I at time t to the organization

$E_i(t)$ = all direct and indirect compensation given individual I at time t by the organization

X(t) = value of the services of all individuals currently employed working together in excess of the value of their individual services at time t; and

r = time value of time

Pekin Ogan proposed a human resource value model that builds on the previous model.[56] The model rests in a concept of certainty-equivalent net benefits as follows:

$$K_{kj}^{\Omega} = \sum_{j=1}^{N} \sum_{k=t}^{L=t} \frac{1}{(1+r)^k} \overline{V}_{aj}$$

where

K_{kj}^{Ω} = total adjusted net present values of human resources in a professional service organization

$\overline{V}_{aj}$ = certainty-equivalent net benefits

L = end of estimated useful life of the employee of the organization

j = jth individual; j = 1, 2, . . . , n

r = a discount rate external to the organization;

and

$$\overline{V}_{aj} = f \{[\overset{\lambda}{V}_{aj} = h(V_{aj}, TC_{aj})], [CF_{aj} = g(P_{aj}^c = g(P_{aj}^c, P_{aj}^s)]\}$$

where

$\overset{\lambda}{V}_{aj}$ = net benefits

V_{aj} = expected benefits

TC_{aj} = total costs

CF_{aj} = certainty factor

P_{aj}^c = probability of continued employment

P_{aj}^s = probability of survival.

The certainty-equivalent net benefits include two elements: "(1) his or her *net benefits* which are a function of the employee's expected benefits and total costs; and (2) a *certainty factor* which is comprised of the employee's probability of continued employment and probability of survival."[57]

Discounted Future Value and Goodwill Methods

The discounted future value method was advanced by Brummet, Flamholtz, and Pyle.[58] They suggest forecasting a firm's present value of earnings at a normal rate of return and allocate a portion of this economic value of the firm to human resources based on their relative contribution.

The unpurchased goodwill method was advanced by Hermanson.[59] He suggests the discounting of the excess above normal expected earnings, based on a comparison of firms within an industry, and allocating this value to unidentified assets including human resources. A similar method is suggested by M. H.

Gilbert[60] where the value of the goodwill is allocated to human and nonhuman assets on their ratio to total assets.

Economic Value Approach

An economic value model proposed by Flamholtz[61] uses a monetary representation of expected future services as they move through services levels and service groups of a firm. Position and salary grade levels constitute the service levels, whereas different degrees of performance constitute the service group. Given the probability $P(Si)$ that an individual will occupy each state in the set of service states, the expected service output value is expressed as "the sum of products of service quantity expected to be derived in each possible service state multiplied by their expected probabilities of occurrences."[62] The probabilities are either historical probabilities derived by actuarial prediction or judgmental probabilities. Jaggi and S. Lau[63] and S. Sadan and R. Auerback[64] expanded this economic value model by (a) changing the probability estimate from an individual to a group basis and (b) using a Markovian chain technique to consider the multiple probabilities of potential changes in service states experienced by the employees.

Nonmonetary Measures

Many nortmonetary measures of human assets can be used, such as a simple inventory of skills and capabilities of people, the assignment of ratings or rankings to individual performance, and measurement of attitudes. The most frequently used nonmonetary measure of human value is derived from Liken and Bowers' model of the variables that determine the effectiveness of a firm's human organization. A questionnaire based on the theoretical model called "survey of organizations" was designed to measure the "organizational climate."[65] The results of such a questionnaire can serve as a nonmonetary measure of human assets by portraying employees' perceptions of the working atmosphere in the firm. Combined behavioral and economic approaches were proposed. A first example is provided by the "dollarized attitudes" of Myers and Flowers.[66] They presented a formula for converting attitude scores into financial returns on payroll investment expressed in terms of gain, break-even, or deficit. A second example is provided by the "behavioral-economic outcomes" approach of B. A. Macy and P. H. Mirvis[67] and Mirvis and Macy.[68] Three criteria are offered for the inclusion of a behavior in organizational assessment:

1. The behavior must be defined so that it is significantly affected by the work structure.
2. The behavior must be measurable and convertible to significant costs to the organization.
3. The measures and costs for each behavior must be mutually exclusive.[69]

These behaviors are then expected to produce performance outcomes measureable and costable in economic terms. Two sets of behaviors are identified: (a) those reflecting member participation in terms of membership and attendance at work and (b) those reflecting performance on the job. The behaviors reflecting participation include (a) absenteeism, (b) turnover, (c) strikes, and (d) tardiness. The behaviors reflecting performance on the job include (a) production under standard, (b) quality under standard, (c) grievances, (d) accidents, (e) unscheduled downtime and machine repair, and (f) material utilization and inventory shrinkage.[70]

CONCLUSIONS

This chapter elaborated on the value of the arguments for and the techniques of human resource accounting. It appears that the literature has provided a sufficient number of options that can be used for experimentation by innovative firms interested in implementing human resource accounting. More needs to be done on both the theoretical and technical options offered by human resource accounting.

NOTES

1. Committee on Human Resource Accounting, "Report of the Committee on Human Resource Accounting," *Accounting Review* 48 (1973 Supplement): 169.

2. Sonja A. Sackmann, Eric G. Flamholtz, and Maria Lombardi Bullen, "Human Resource Accounting: A State-of-the-Art Review," *Journal of Accounting Literature* 8 (1989): 235–264.

3. C. W. Hofer and D. Schendel, *Strategy Formulation: Analytical Concepts* (St. Paul: West, 1978).

4. M. E. Porter, *Competitive Advantage* (New York: Free Press, 1980).

5. Cynthia A. Lengnick-Hall and Mark L. Lengnick-Hall, "Strategic Human Resource Management: A Review of the Literature and a Proposed Typology," *Academy of Management Review* 13 (1988): 454.

6. I. C. MacMillan and R. S. Schuler, "Gaining a Competitive Edge through Human Resources," *Personnel* 62 (1985): 24–29.

7. Lengnick-Hall and Lengnick-Hall, "Strategic Human Resources Management: A Review of the Literature and a Proposed Typology," pp. 455–56.

8. Alvin Toffler, *The Third Wave* (New York: Morrow, 1980).

9. Alvin Toffler and Heidi Toffler, "Societies at Hyper-Speed," *New York Times*, 31 October 1992, E17.

10. Ibid.

11. Ibid.

12. Ibid.

13. Robert Elliott, "The Third Wave Breaks on the Shores of Accounting," *Accounting Horizons*, Dec. 1991 pp. 61–85.

14. Ibid., p. 70

15. Doreen McBarnet, Syd Weston, and Christopher J. Whelan, "Adversary Account-

ing: Strategic Uses of Financial Information by Capital and Labor," *Accounting, Organizations and Society* 18 (1993): 81–100.

16. Jay A. Conger and Rabindra N. Kanungo, "The Empowerment Process: Integrating Theory and Practice," *Academy of Management Review* 13 (1988): 474.

17. Ibid., p. 471.

18. Ibid., p. 421.

19. W. A. Paton, *Accounting Theory* (New York: Ronald Press, 1922), pp. 486–87.

20. E. Flamholtz, *Human Resource Accounting: Advances in Concepts, Methods and Applications* (San Francisco: Jossey-Bass Inc., 1985), p. 35.

21. R. L. Brummet, E. G. Flamholtz, W. C. Pyle, "Human Resource Measurement: A Challenge for Accountants," *Accounting Review*, Apr. 1968, p. 218.

22. E. Flamholtz, *Human Resource Accounting* (Encino CA: Dickenson, 1974), p. 292.

23. J. J. Tsay, "Human Resource Accounting," *Management Accounting*, Mar. 1977, p. 35.

24. Eric G. Flamholtz, "Toward a Theory of Human Resource Value in Formal Organizations," *Accounting Review*, October 1972, pp. 666–78.

25. R. Liken and D. G. Bowers, "Improving the Accuracy of P/L Reports by Estimating the Change in Dollar Value of the Human Organization," *Michigan Business Review*, Mar. 1973, pp. 15–24.

26. Flamholtz, "Toward a Theory of Human Resource Value in Formal Organizations," p. 669.

27. E. Flamholtz, "Assessing the Validity of a Theory of Human Resource Value: A Field Study," *Empirical Research in Accounting: Selected Studies*, 1972, pp. 241–66.

28. Committee on Human Resource Accounting, "Report of the Committee on Human Resource Accounting," Accounting Review 48 (1973 Supplement): 177.

29. Liken and Bowers, "Improving the Accuracy of P/L Reports," p. 15.

30. Rensis Liken and David G. Bowers, "Organizational Theory and Human Resource Accounting," *American Psychologies*, June 1969, p. 586.

31. Ibid.

32. Rensis Liken and William C. Pyle, "Human Resource Accounting: A Human Organizational Measurement Approach," *Financial Analysts Journal*, Jan./Feb. 1971, pp. 75–84.

33. B. A. Robinson, "An Approach to Human Resource Accounting," *Cost and Management*, May-June 1974, pp. 26–32.

34. Ibid., p. 27.

35. M. Scott Myers and V. S. Flowers, "A Framework for Measuring Human Assets," *California Management Review*, Summer 1974, pp. 5–16.

36. Ibid.

37. Sackmann, Flamholtz, and Bullen, "Human Resource Accounting: A State-of-the-Art Review," pp. 235–64.

38. N. W. E. Glautier and B. Underdown, "Problems and Prospects of Accounting for Human Assets," *Management Accounting*, Mar. 1973, p. 99.

39. R. L. Brummet, "Accounting for Human Resources," speech given at the annual convention of the American Accounting Association, South Bend, IN, August 26, 1969, quoted in the *New York Certified Public Accountant*, July 1970, pp. 16–25.

40. Bilski L. Jaggi, "The Valuation of Human Resources in a Firm," *Chartered Accountant* (India), March 1974, pp. 467–70.

41. George M. N. Baker, "The Feasibility and Utility of Human Resource Accounting," *California Management Review*, Summer 1974, pp. 17–23.

42. Eric G. Flamholtz, "Human Resource Accounting: Measuring Potential Replacement Costs," *Human Resource Management*, Spring 1973, pp. 8–16.

43. Flamholtz, *Human Resource Accounting*, p. 190.

44. Liken and Bowers, "Organizational Theory and Human Resource Accounting," p. 588.

45. J. S. Hekimian and J. G. Jones, "Put People on Your Balance Sheet," *Harvard Business Review*, Jan.-Feb. 1967, p. 108.

46. Ibid., pp. 108–9.

47. Ibid.

48. Jaggi, "The Valuation of Human Resources in a Firm."

49. D. Elovitz, "From the Thoughtful Businessman," *Harvard Business Review*, May-June 1967, p. 59.

50. B. Lev and A. Schwartz, "On the Use of the Economic Concept of Human Capital in Financial Statements," *Accounting Review*, Jan. 1971, p. 105.

51. Abraham Friedman and Banich Lev, "A Surrogate Measure for the Firm's Investment in Human Resources," *Journal of Accounting Research*, Fall 1974, pp. 235–50.

52. Ibid., p. 239.

53. Ibid.

54. R. H. Hermanson, "Accounting for Human Assets," *Occasional Paper No. 14* (East Lansing, MI: Bureau of Business and Economic Research, Graduate School of Business Administration, Michigan State University, 1964).

55. Wayne J. Morse, "A Note on the Relationship Between Human Assets and Human Capital," *Accounting Review* July 1973, p. 589.

56. Pekin Ogan, "A Human Resource Value Model for Professional Service Organization," *Accounting Review*, April 1976, pp. 306–10.

57. Ibid., p. 310.

58. R. L. Brummet, E. G. Flamholtz, and W. C. Pyle, "Human Resource Measurement: A Challenge for Accountants," *Accounting Review* 2 (1968): 217–24.

59. Hermanson, "Accounting for Human Assets."

60. M. H. Gilbert, "The Asset Value of the Human Organization," *Management Accounting*, July 1970, pp. 25–28.

61. E. Flamholtz, "A Model for Human Resource Valuation: A Scholastic Process with Service Rewards," *Accounting Review*, Apr. 1971, pp. 253–67.

62. Ibid., p. 257.

63. B. Jaggi and S. Lau, "Toward a Model for Human Resource Valuation," *Accounting Review*, Apr. 1974, pp. 321–29.

64. S. Sadan and R. Auerback, "A Stochastic Model for Human Resources," *California Management Review*, Summer 1974, pp. 24–31.

65. J. C. Taylor and D. G. Bowers, *The Survey of Organizations* (Ann Arbor, MI: Institute of Social Research, 1972).

66. Myers and Flowers, "A Framework for Measuring Human Assets," pp. 5–16.

67. B. A. Macy and P. H. Mirvis, "A Methodology for the Assessment of Quality of Work Life and Organizational Effectiveness in Behavioral-Economic Terms," *Administrative Science Quarterly* 21, no. 6 (1976): 212–26.

68. P. H. Mirvis and B. A. Macy, "Human Resource Accounting: A Measurement Perspective," *Academy of Management Review*, Apr. 1976, pp. 74–83.

69. Ibid., p. 77.

70. Ibid., p. 78.

REFERENCES

Acland, D. "The Effects of Behavioral Indicators on Investor Decision: An Exploratory Study." *Accounting, Organizations and Society* 1, no. 8 (1976): 133–42.

Alexander, M. O. "An Accountant's View of the Human Resource." *The Personnel Administrator*, Nov./Dec. 1971, 9–13.

American Accounting Association. "Report of the Committee on Accounting for Human Resources." Committee Reports. *Accounting Review* 48 (1973 Supplement): 169–85.

———. "Report of the Committee on Accounting for Human Resources." Committee Reports. *Accounting Review* 49 (1974 Supplement): 115–26.

Ansari, S. L., and D. T. Flamholtz. "Management Science and the Development of Human Resource Accounting." *The Accounting Historians Journal*, Fall 1978, 11–35.

Becker, S. *Human Capital*. New York: National Bureau of Economic Research, 1962.

Biagioni, L. F., and P. Ogan. "Human Resource Accounting for Professional Sports Teams." *Management Accounting*, November 1977, 25–29.

Brummet, R. L., E. G. Flamholtz, and W. C. Pyle. "Human Resource Measurement: A Challenge for Accountants." *Accounting Review* April 1968, 217–24.

Cannon, J. A. "Applying the Human Resource Accounting Framework to an International Airline." *Accounting, Organizations and Society* 1, no. 8 (1976): 253–63.

Caplan, E. H., and S. Landekich. *Human Resource Accounting: Past, Present, and Future*. New York: National Association of Accountants, 1974.

Career, W. B., and J. M. Posey. "The Validity of Selected Surrogate Measures of Human Resource Value: A Field Study." *Accounting, Organizations and Society* 1, no. 8 (1976): 143–52.

Conger, Jay A., and Rabindra N. Kanungo. "The Empowerment Process: Integrating Theory and Practice." *Academy of Management Review* 13 (1988): 471–82.

Denver, J., and J. P. Siegel. "The Role of Behavioral Measures in Accounting for Human Resources." *Accounting Review*, Jan. 1974, 88–97.

Dittman, D. A., H. A. Juris, and L. Revsine. "On the Existence of Unrecorded Human Assets: An Economic Perspective." *Journal of Accounting Research*, Spring 1976, 49–65.

———. "Unrecorded Human Assets: A Survey of Accounting Films' Training Programs." *Accounting Review*, April 1980, 640–48.

Elias, N. "The Effects of Human Assets Statements on the Investment Decision: An Experiment." *Empirical Research in Accounting: Selected Studies*, 1972, 215–33.

Elliott, Robert K. "The Third Wave Breaks on the Shores of Accounting." *Accounting Horizons*, December 1991, 61–81.

Flamholtz, E. "Assessing the Validity of a Theory of Human Resource Value: A Field Study." *Empirical Research in Accounting: Selected Studies*, 1972, 241–66.

———. *Human Resource Accounting*. Encino, CA: Dickenson, 1974.

————. *Human Resource Accounting: Advances in Concepts, Methods and Applications.* San Francisco: Jossey-Bass Publishers, 1985.

————. "Human Resource Accounting: Measuring Positional Replacement Cost." *Human Resource Measurement*, Spring 1973, 8–16.

————. "The Impact of Human Resource Valuation on Management Decisions: A Laboratory Experiment." *Accounting, Organizations and Society* 1, no. 8 (1976): 153–65.

————. "A Model for Human Resource Valuation: A Stochastic Process with Service Rewards." *Accounting Review*, April 1971, 253–67.

————. "The Process of Measurement in Managerial Accounting: A Psycho-technical Systems Perspective." *Accounting, Organizations and Society* 5, no. 8 (1980): 31–42.

————. "The Theory and Measurement of an Individual's Value to an Organization." Ph.D. dissertation, University of Michigan, 1969.

————. "Towards a Psycho-technical Systems Paradigm of Organizational Measurement." *Decision Sciences*, Jan. 1979, 71–84.

————. "Valuation of Human Assets in a Securities Brokerage Firm: An Empirical Study." *Accounting, Organizations and Society* 12, no. 7 (1987): 309–18.

Flamholtz, E., and R. Coff. "Valuing Human Resources in Buying Service Companies." *Mergers and Acquisitions*, Jan./Feb. 1989, 40–44.

Flamholtz, E., and G. Geis. "The Development and Implementation of a Replacement Cost Model for Measuring Human Capital: A Field Study." *Personnel Review* (U.K.) 13, no. 2 (1984): 25–35.

Flamholtz, E., G. Geis, and R. J. Perle. "A Markovian Model for the Valuation of Human Assets, Acquired by an Organizational Purchase." *Interfaces*, Nov./Dec. 1984, 11–15.

Flamholtz, E., and R. A. Kaumeyer, Jr. "Human Resource Replacement Cost Information and Personnel Decisions: A Field Study." *Human Resource Planning*, Fall 1980, 111–38.

Flamholtz, E., and T. Lundy. "Human Resource Accounting for CPA Firms." *CPA Journal* 45 (October 1975): 45–51.

Flamholtz, E., J. Bell Oliver, and R. Teague. "Subjective Information Valuation and Decision-Making." Paper presented at the American Accounting Association Annual Meeting, Atlanta, Georgia, 1976.

Flamholtz, E., and D. G. Searfoss. "Developing an Integrated System." In *Human Resource Accounting*, 336–55. San Francisco: Jossey-Bass Publishers, 1985.

Flamholtz, E., and J. B. Wollman. "The Development and Implementation of the Stochastic Rewards Model for Human Resource Valuation in a Human Capital Intensive Firm." Paper presented at the Thirteenth International Meeting of the Institute of Management Sciences, Athens, Greece, 1977.

Frantzreb, R. B., L.L.T. Landau, and D. P. Lundberg. "The Valuation of Human Resources." *Business Horizons*, June 1974, 73–80.

Friedman, A., and B. Lev. "A Surrogate Measure for the Firm's Investment in Human Resources." *Journal of Accounting Research*, Autumn 1974, 235–50.

Gambling, T. E. "A System Dynamic Approach to HRA." *Accounting Review*, July 1974, 538–46.

Gordon, F. E., J. G. Rhode, and K. A. Merchant. "The Effects of Salary and Human

Resource Accounting Disclosures on Small Group Relations and Performance."
Accounting, Organizations and Society 2, no. 12 (1977): 295–305.

Grove, H. T., J. Mock, and K. Ehrenteich. "A Review of HRA Measurement Systems
From a Measurement Theory Perspective." *Accounting, Organizations and Society* 2, no. 12 (1977): 233–39.

Gul, F. A. "An Empirical Study of the Usefulness of Human Resources Turnover Costs
in Australian Accounting Firms." *Accounting, Organizations and Society* 9, no. 6 (1984): 233–39.

Harrell, A. M., and H. D. Klick. "Comparing the Impact of Monetary and Nonmonetary
Human Asset Measures on Executive Decision-Making." *Accounting, Organizations and Society* 5, no. 12 (1980): 393–400.

Hekimian, J. S., and C. Jones. "Put People on Your Balance Sheet." *Harvard Business Review*, Jan./Feb. 1967, 105–113.

Hendricks, J. "The Impact of Human Resource Accounting Information on Stock Investment Decisions: An Empirical Study." *Accounting Review*, Apr. 1976, 292–305.

Hermanson, R. H. "Accounting for Human Assets." *Occasional Paper No. 14*. East Lansing, Michigan: Bureau of Business and Economic Research, Michigan State University, East Lansing, 1964. Reprint. 1986.

———. "Accounting for Human Resource." *Research Monograph No. 99*. Michigan State University, 1964. Reprint. Atlanta, G. Business Publishing Division, College of Business Administration, Georgia State University, 1986.

———. "A Method for Recording all Assets and the Resulting Accounting and Economic Implications." Ph.D. dissertation, Michigan State University, 1963.

Hermanson, R. H., F. A. Massey, and M. E. Schaefer. "An Extension of the Human Asset
Model: A Conceptual Foundation for Management Strategy." Working paper, College of Business Administration, Georgia State University, 1989.

Jaggi, B., and S. Lau. "Toward a Model for Human Resource Valuation." *Accounting Review*, Apr. 1974, 321–29.

Lau, A. H., and H. Lau. "Some Proposed Approaches for Writing Off Capitalized Human
Resource Assets." *Journal of Accounting Research*, Spring 1978, 80–102.

Lengnick-Hall, Cynthia A., and Mark L. Lengnick-Hall. "Strategic Human Resources
Management: A Review of the Literature and a Proposed Typology." *Academy of Management Review* 13 (1988): 454–70.

Lev, B., and A. Schwartz. "On the Use of the Economic Concept of Human Capital in
Financial Statements." *Accounting Review*, January 1971, 103–12.

Liken, R. M. *New Patterns of Management*. New York: McGraw Hill Book Co., 1967.

Liken, R. M., and D. G. Bowers. "Improving the Accuracy of PAL-Reports by Estimating
the Changes in Dollar Value of the Human Organization." *Michigan Business Review* 25, no. 3 (1973): 15–24.

Lombardi, M., and E. Flamholtz. "The Impact of Human Resource Accounting Measurement on Personnel Budgeting Decisions: A Psycho-Technical Systems Approach." Proceedings of the American Accounting Association Annual Meeting, 295–334, Honolulu, Hawaii, 1979.

Macy, B. A., and P. H. Mirvis. "A Methodology for Assessment of Quality of Work Life
and Organizational Effectiveness in Behavioral-Economic Terms." *Administrative Science Quarterly* 21, no. 6 (1976): 212–26.

McBarnet, Doreen, Syd Weston, and Christopher J. Whelan. "Adversary Accounting:

Strategic Uses of Financial Information by Capital and Labor." *Accounting, Organizations and Society* 18, no. 1 (1993): 81–100.

Mirvis, P. H., and B. A. Macy. "Accounting for the Costs and Benefits of Human Resource Development Programs: An Interdisciplinary Approach." *Accounting, Organizations and Society* 1, no. 8 (1993): 181.

Morse, W. J. "A Note on the Relationship Between Human Assets and Human Capital." *Accounting Review*, July 1973, 589–93.

Myers, M. S., and V. S. Flowers. "A Framework for Measuring Human Assets." *California Management Review* 16, Summer 1974, 5–16.

Odiome, G. S. *Personnel Policy: Issues and Practices*. Columbus, Ohio: Charles E. Merrill Books, Inc., 1963.

Ogan, Pekin. "A Human Resource Value Model for Professional Service Organizations." *Accounting Review*, Apr. 1976, 306–20.

———. "Application of a Human Resource Value Model: A Field Study." *Accounting, Organizations and Society* 1, no. 8 (1976): 195–218.

Oliver, J. Bell, and E. Flamholtz. "Human Resource Replacement Cost Numbers, Cognitive Information Processing and Personnel Decisions: A Laboratory Experiment." *Journal of Business Finance and Accounting*, Summer 1978, 137–53.

Paperman, J. B. "The Attitude of CPAs Toward Human Resource Accounting." *The Ohio CPA*, Autumn 1974, 95–99.

Paton, W. A. *Accounting Theory*. Chicago: Accounting Studies Press, 1962.

Pyle, W. C. "Monitoring Human Resources—On Line." *Michigan Business Review*, July 1970, 19–32.

Sadan, S., and R. Auerback. "A Stochastic Model for Human Resources." *California Management Review*, Summer 1974, 24–31.

Schwan, E. S. "The Effects of Human Resource Accounting Data on Financial Decisions: An Empirical Test." *Accounting, Organizations and Society* 1, no. 8 (1976): 219–37.

Scott, D. R. *Theory of Accounts*. New York: Henry Holt Co., 1925.

Spiceland, J. D., and H. C. Zaunbrecher. "The Usefulness of Human Resource Accounting in Personnel Selection." *Management Accounting*, Feb. 1977, 29, 30, 40.

Stephen, P. B., III, "Federal Income Taxation and Human Capital." *Virginia Law Review*, Oct. 1984, 1357–1423.

Toffler, Alvin. *The Third Wave*. New York: Morrow, 1980.

Toffler, Alvin, and Heidi Toffler. "Societies at Hyper-Speed." *New York Times*, 31 Oct. 1993, E17.

Tomassini, L. A. "Human Resource Accounting and Managerial Decision Behavior: An Experimental Study." Ph.D. dissertation, University of California, Los Angeles, 1974.

———. "Assessing the Impact of Human Resource Accounting: An Experimental Study of Managerial Decision Preferences." *Accounting Review*, Mar. 1977, 1–17.

Tsaklanganos, A. A. "Human Resource Accounting: The Measure of a Person." *CA Magazine*, May 1980, 44–48.

Woodruff, R. L., Jr. "Human Resource Accounting." *Canadian Chartered Accountant*, Sept. 1970, 2–7.

Zaunbrecher, H. C. "The Impact of Human Resource Accounting on the Personnel Selection Process." Ph.D. dissertation, Louisiana State University, 1974.

Index

About the Author

AHMED RIAHI-BELKAOUI is CBA Distinguished Professor of Accounting in the College of Business Administration, University of Illinois at Chicago. Author of numerous Quorum Books, published or forthcoming, and coauthor of several more, he is also a prolific contributor to the scholarly and professional journals of his field, and has served on various editorial boards that oversee them.